There are things in this life that we must endure which are all but unendurable, and yet I feel that there is a great goodness. Why, when there could have been nothing, is there something? This is a great mystery. How, when there could have been nothing, does it happen that there is love, kindness, beauty?

JANE KENYON

JANE KENYON

A Literary Life

JOHN H. TIMMERMAN

William B. Eerdmans Publishing Company

Grand Rapids, Michigan / Cambridge, U.K.

Wm. B. Eerdmans Publishing Co.

255 Jefferson Ave. S.E., Grand Rapids, Michigan 49503 /
P.O. Box 163, Cambridge CB3 9PU U.K.

Printed in the United States of America

07 06 05 04 03 02   7 6 5 4 3 2 1

Library of Congress Cataloging-in-Publication Data

Timmerman, John H.

Jane Kenyon: a literary life / John H. Timmerman.

p.   cm.

ISBN 0-8028-3943-6 (hardcover)

1. Kenyon, Jane.

2. Women and literature — United States — History — 20th century.

3. Poets, American — 20th century — Biography.

I. Title.

PS3561.E554 Z89   2002

811'.54 — dc21

[B]

2002072677

www.eerdmans.com

For Donald Hall

Who, from the first moment we met, seemed like a longtime friend, then made the seeming a reality. With appreciation for his support, hospitality, insight, and graciousness.

And especially for going that extra mile to make sure that the smallest details in this text are historically accurate. If there are any inaccuracies, it is because I slipped one by him.

With unfailing appreciation for Patricia, who somehow finds it in her to encourage and support me through yet one more book.

With appreciation also to Amy Cloud, fellow Kenyon scholar, for her insightful and careful reading of this work in manuscript.

Contents

Acknowledgments

I am grateful for archival use of the Jane Kenyon Papers at the Milne Special Collections, University of New Hampshire library, Durham, New Hampshire.

I am also grateful to Donald Hall and to the Jane Kenyon Estate for permission to quote from unpublished work and archival materials, including journals, notebooks, drafts of poems, and unpublished manuscripts. Hall also granted permission to use the photographs that appear in this volume.

I am grateful, too, to Graywolf Press for granting permission to quote from two of Kenyon's volumes, and am happy to include the credit line here: All excerpts from *Otherwise: New & Selected Poems,* copyright 1996 by the Estate of Jane Kenyon. All excerpts from *A Hundred White Daffodils,* copyright 1999 by the Estate of Jane Kenyon. Reprinted with the permission of Graywolf Press, Saint Paul, Minnesota.

And I want to express my deep appreciation to the Calvin College Alumni Association for an Alumni Research Grant and to Calvin College for a Calvin Research Fellowship. Their generous financial support continues to make scholarship a pleasure.

ix

Preface

In the works of Jane Kenyon, life and art intertwine like fine cross-stitch. Each is singularly arresting.

Like the blue-gray mountains shouldering around Eagle Pond Farm, Kenyon evinced a calm dignity — a graceful and lovely demeanor backed by granitic resolve. Unobtrusive by nature, she opened her most private self in public readings. She brought variant audiences together in laughter and in tears. Reclusive in many ways, profoundly attuned to daily life at Eagle Pond Farm, she nonetheless traveled the world as an ambassador of the arts. She returned with images and memories that tormented her and challenged all she believed to be true and just. As a child, she denounced all religion as an intellectual sham. As an adult, she came to her unrelenting faith during a sermon in a small country church. An allusion to Rilke first got her attention — not any particular scriptural text. Those texts, however, powerfully shaped the course of her later life. She was a woman of profound and uncompromising vitality, cut down like one of her beloved peonies by the storm of leukemia. Above all, however, she was the consummate artist of such exquisitely intense lyric verses that, like faceted diamonds casting prismatic light, they throw off soundings of the human soul.

My first aim in this study is in fact to provide a clear and accurate biographical account of the life of Jane Kenyon. In this area I was aided by the use of previously unpublished journals, personal papers, and the recollections of Donald Hall. I have examined that life contextually, considering the historical, social, cultural, psychological, and religious contexts that shaped the story of Jane Kenyon's life. My second aim is to examine how her art grew out of that story. One discovers that Kenyon held clear and fundamental beliefs that guided her art-making. Furthermore, one may observe these beliefs emerging in drafts of her poetry. The close examination of those multiple drafts (in the case of "Having it Out with Melancholy," a stack nearly two inches thick) illuminates her artistic process toward the "intense lyric" and the "luminous particular" she sought.

Unless otherwise noted, all references to Kenyon's poems are taken from *Otherwise: New and Selected Poems* (Saint Paul, Minn.: Graywolf Press, 1996), *Twenty Poems of Anna Akhmatova* (Saint Paul, Minn.: The Nineties Press/Ally Press, 1985), and *A Hundred White Daffodils* (Saint Paul, Minn.: Graywolf Press, 1999). To replicate the extensive changes Kenyon made in her manuscript drafts, I have used several standard procedures. She typically crossed out words or lines with heavily inked lines or hatch marks. These I indicate by a strikeover. In a very few instances a word is so heavily inked over that it is rendered indecipherable. Kenyon's insertion of new words or lines into the text is indicated by brackets at the point of insertion. Working this closely with Kenyon's writing has increased my appreciation of her great gift, and how she used it to speak not only for herself but also for others.

CHAPTER ONE

The Michigan Years

Discovery of the Poetic Self

Jane Kenyon's life is, in many ways, a story of two houses — the first, a two-story house on a gravel road on the outskirts of Ann Arbor where she grew up; the second, the ancestral farmhouse of Donald Hall in New Hampshire, where the couple lived from 1975, three years after their marriage, until Kenyon's death in 1995. Other notable places figure into her life story, of course. Her grandmother's house in Ann Arbor was one. And there were the various apartments she lived in when she was a student at the University of Michigan. But her childhood home and the farmhouse — these two houses and their immediate surroundings — essentially shaped the woman Kenyon became.

Rural Ann Arbor

For the most part, Kenyon remembered her childhood with great fondness, and it served often as a subject for her poetry. It was from the start a fascinating, frolicking household of creative people that she was born into on 23 May 1947. Her father, Reuel Kenyon, had been a piano player in high school, and upon graduation had traveled to Europe, where he spent ten years working as a jazz musician. He returned to the United States at the height of the Great Depression, earning a living by touring with American dance bands.

On one such tour, he met a Chicago girl, Polly (Pauline), who, by the age of eighteen, was a regular singing in nightclubs. Polly's first brief marriage to a professional gambler had ended in divorce. Although it was the second marriage for both, Reuel and Polly's kinship in music made it a close one. When their son, Reuel, was born in 1944, the elder Reuel continued to perform but also settled into giving lessons. In order to be home with her children, Polly became a seamstress and gave sewing lessons. The peacefulness of rusticity is often a myth in our age, when suburbs chew up rural areas in huge gulps. But not in the case of rural Ann Arbor during the 1950s. Donald Hall recalls what the Kenyon household was like:

> Jane's family house was in the Township of Ann Arbor, and originally the road was a dirt road, with a working farm across the street. It had a home-made flavor, that house, and they changed it a good bit. Jane's father was a hardworking gardener, and it was one of the ways in which the family enjoyed being together, to garden all together. It was Jane's beginning as a gardener. But they all shared it.
>
> The house was full of pictures and books, and rather small, with I think only a couple of bedrooms upstairs, for Jane and her brother. Her parents slept on the ground floor.[1]

In particular, however, music worked its magic within the rooms of this house.

Although Kenyon freely admitted that she lacked the skill of her parents and brother at the piano, she rejoiced in the music that was a near constant in her home. The house had two uprights in the living room, one for each parent. More important for Kenyon was the record player, which she lovingly described in an unpublished and unfinished essay found among her papers:

1. From a letter dated May 2001 by Donald Hall to the author.

2

The hulking brown console radio and record player fills one whole corner of the living room. The speaker is hidden behind a screen of brown horsehair with a grill of gold metal. Below the turntable there are cupboards for record albums. I run my finger endlessly over their multi-colored spines with gold lettering.

The record player is the body out of which music comes. It is mother-music, and I know every inch of it — the domed red plastic dot and behind it the light which indicates that the power is on; the decal of the RCA Victor dog on the underside of the lid, listening alertly with its head tilted toward the speaker of a gramophone.[2]

Jane and Reuel were often serenaded to sleep at night by the sounds of the record player:

Seven years old, I scamper up the stairs to bed, my hands on the risers two steps ahead of my feet so I sound like two people going up the stairs, a maneuver which cannot be accomplished while wearing a nightgown: I prefer p.j.'s. I flip back the covers to check for spiders, then jump in and pull the covers up to my chin. Immediately, I sit up again to reach for the string with its small bell-shaped aluminum pull, and the ceiling light snaps out in the old tenant farmhouse in the country outside Ann Arbor, Michigan.

2. In this same essay, Kenyon recalls how taken she was by the RCA Victor dog, and how she and Reuel begged for one of their own:

This decal is one of the most beautiful things in my life, with its gold and brown and white colors, the little dog, white with brown spots, delicate nose and legs, just the kind of dog I would want if we were to have a dog, which we will not, because we tried once, and after one night of persistent whimpering, and the next day finding all the clothes in the closet on the floor, and peed on, mother took our one and only puppy back to the neighbor who had given it to us, saying she didn't think we could keep the dog.

This scene reveals the kind of deep attachment she had to her dog Gus, who accompanied her on her daily walks on the farm in New Hampshire.

My brother is already settled in bed in the adjoining room. I begin the nightly chant: *Mama, put on a stack of records.* He joins me, and we sing the major third together: *Ma-ma, put on a stack of records . . .*

Downstairs mother starts the machine with a click. We hear the clap of the first 78 being let down onto the turn table. . . . It is Edvard Grieg's "Peer Gynt Suite." "Morning," the first movement, brightens before my closed eyes, closed the better to listen. Birds sing in the trees and I imagine sunlight streaming into the forest. But soon the idyll is over. Now comes the mournful music when Peer Gynt dies. To this day I'll switch stations or even turn off the radio to avoid hearing it.[3]

There is little question that the influence of growing up in a household filled with music infused the rich lyric nature of her mature poetry. Indeed, in her interview with Marian Blue in April 1993, she compared her work to her husband's and observed, "I am working at one thing — the short lyric. It is all I want, at this point: to write short, intense, musical cries of the spirit."[4]

Another major influence on Kenyon's youth was her paternal grandmother, who, for better or for worse, powerfully influenced Kenyon's religious thinking as a child. It was impossible for her to reflect upon her grandmother — with whom she and her brother frequently stayed when their parents were out of town — without thinking of religion. "What happened to me in my childhood was my grandmother, father's mother," she wrote in "Childhood, When You Are in It," an unfinished essay collected in *A Hundred White Daffodils.* "The central psychic fact of that time was Grandmother's spiritual obsession, and her effort to secure me in her religious fold."[5]

Dora Baldwin was born in 1878 near Owosso, Michigan, a

3. This essay is in the Kenyon Archives, Milne Special Collections, University of New Hampshire, Box 19, Folder 2.

4. Kenyon, *A Hundred White Daffodils* (Saint Paul, Minn.: Graywolf Press, 1999), p. 195.

5. Kenyon, *A Hundred White Daffodils*, p. 61.

small community about fifty miles north of Ann Arbor. The daughter of a Methodist minister and a devout Methodist mother, Dora was well tutored in Scripture and doctrine when she married George Kenyon and moved with him to Ann Arbor to start a grocery store.[6] There their three children — Reuel, Geraldine, and Paul — were born. In an early draft of "Childhood, When You Are in It," Kenyon relates that Dora cried "for days" (exactly why, Kenyon doesn't tell us) when her husband proclaimed that their son would be called Reuel (a family name, the word *reuel* derives from the Hebrew, meaning "friend of God"). Born small and sickly, often so fragile that Dora had to carry him on a pillow in her arms, Reuel nonetheless lived to be seventy-seven.

George Kenyon grew seriously ill long before his son Reuel. Kenyon describes her faint recollection of her grandfather: "I have no memory of him, except of sitting on his bony knees after he had had strokes. The stubble on his face was white, and a cane lay beside his chair, which smelled vaguely of urine. I was afraid of his incapacity, but not of him."[7] After George Kenyon died, Dora let out rooms in the large house on State Street to University of Michigan students.

In many ways, Kenyon remembers her grandmother wistfully and lovingly:

Dora Baldwin Kenyon was tall and slim, with a handsome build, and a mournful expression. I loved to stand behind her when she sat at her dressing table, brushing her long gray hair, then braiding it for the night. She used cold cream on her face, and the smell overpowered me. Her house in general smelled of Ivory soap and gas from the kitchen range — a different smell from our house, which had, it seemed to me, no smell.[8]

6. Details about Dora Baldwin are found in an untitled, uncompleted essay of Kenyon's located in Box 19, Folder 2 of the Kenyon Archives. The essay appears to be an early draft of "Childhood, When You Are in It."

7. Kenyon, *A Hundred White Daffodils*, p. 61.

8. Kenyon, *A Hundred White Daffodils*, p. 61.

What troubled Kenyon was her grandmother's unflagging religious zeal.

Grandmother's religious life was ordered by custom. Each day began with a reading from Scripture, the devotional guide *The Upper Room,* and prayer. Then, after breakfast, she would go upstairs to clean the students' rooms — and if Jane was there, she would tag along to help her. They would make the beds and empty stuffed ashtrays and paper scrap into a large paper bag to burn in the incinerator in the basement. Her grandmother's conversation was predictable: "As we worked, Grandmother talked about hell, a lake of fire, burning endlessly, or about the Second Coming of Christ, which would put an end to the world as I knew it."[9] Grandmother often played the piano her son had given her; her favorite hymn was "Onward Christian Soldiers." Jane noticed the absence of the kind of classical pieces her parents liked to play: the piano bench at Grandmother's house "was groaning with hymnals and religious sheet music."[10] Grandmother's religious life was clearly marked by biblical interjections and a keen expectation of the Apocalypse and the final judgment.

Kenyon recalls that she was about eight the day that Grandmother's eyes widened and she echoed Saint Paul by saying, "The body is the temple of the Holy Ghost" (1 Cor. 6:19). Kenyon reacted with the confusion typical of an eight-year-old. What does it mean that the body is a temple? And what does this "Holy Ghost" thing mean? The scene so powerfully impressed Kenyon that she re-enacted it in "Staying at Grandma's" from *Let Evening Come:*

"You know," she'd say, turning
her straight and handsome back to me,
"that the body is the temple
of the Holy Ghost."

9. Kenyon, *A Hundred White Daffodils,* p. 63.
10. Kenyon, *A Hundred White Daffodils,* p. 62.

The Holy Ghost, the oh, oh . . . the *uh*
oh, I thought, studying the toe of my new shoe,
and glad she wasn't looking at me.

Soon I'd be back in school. No more mornings
at Grandma's side while she swept the walk
or shook the dust mop by the neck.

If she loved me why did she say that
two women would be grinding at the mill,
that God would come out of the clouds
when they were least expecting him,
choose one to be with him in heaven
and leave the other there alone?

Kenyon clearly intuited that it was her *own* body Grandmother referred to. What was this Ghost doing in her?

The prospect of the Apocalypse was even more fearful, however. When they burned the trash from the boarders' rooms,
Grandmother looked at the fire with an exultant eye. "I watched the
fire move inexorably," Kenyon recalls,

and thought about burning forever, not burning and then going
out, but burning eternally — the fate of boys and girls who
sassed their parents, or gave grudgingly to the offering at Sunday school, or played with cards. And of course that would be
the fate of those who gambled or drank. I myself had played
with cards, and my parents had a scotch and soda every night
before dinner. I lived in terror of letting it slip.

Kenyon's personal image of God shifted to "a larger, gray-haired Jesus — Jesus Senior, so to speak."[11] She began to make a youthful
distinction between her sense of a God of love and her grandmother's rigid religion of scriptural rules.

11. Kenyon, *A Hundred White Daffodils*, pp. 63-64.

Nonetheless, Kenyon grew keenly aware of her own lapses into disobedience. She once caught herself swearing heartily at a classmate and then waited expectantly to be struck down on the spot. Another time, she felt her teacher (Miss Sikima, who presided over Foster School like a female deity, establishing and enforcing rules) had treated her unfairly. Angry, she tried to skip school. But after walking just a short way down the gravel road toward home, she turned back, unnerved by the feeling that "I had neither the courage to rebel, nor an obedient heart."[12] Here was the divide: the risk of pursuing personal freedom or the safety of following rules made by others. Although she projected the course of a rebel, she was still bound unwillingly to those rules.

The narrow world of Grandmother's tutoring and the Foster School curriculum broadened considerably when, in the fifth grade, Kenyon began taking the bus to a school in the city. Foster School was a simple, white-clapboard building with a large bell, a flagpole, and swing sets, surrounded by ferns and orchids. Now Kenyon traveled to a new and unnerving world of maze-like halls and rows upon rows of lockers. It seemed she could never locate her own. At Foster School there were four students in her kindergarten class; at the city school there were nine hundred students in her senior class.

She did not remember her days at Forsythe Junior High School favorably. In "Dreams of Math," which first appeared in *The Concord [New Hampshire] Monitor* of 12 September 1992, Kenyon recalls the "nightmares" of her schooling when she now reads the list of school bus routes published in the paper. Her nightmares are typical: over and over she dreams that she has a final physics exam — but she hasn't attended the class all semester. She laments, "Trouble, trouble. Why is there no happy moment in these dreams of school?" As she advanced through the higher grades, what trou-

---

12. Kenyon, *A Hundred White Daffodils*, p. 65. In an earlier partial draft, Kenyon spelled the Frisian name of her teacher more accurately as Sikkima (the customary spelling is Sikkema). In her essay "Dreams of Math," Kenyon identifies her teacher as Miss Irwin.

bled her most was that she "had to obey and perform for teachers whose judgment I didn't respect."[13] Jane the rebellious individualist began to emerge.

This rebelliousness was evident when she liberated herself from the confusing religious conflicts of her youth by simply declaring that she would have nothing more to do with religion. In her forthright essay "A Gardener of the True Vine," which tells the moving story of the late Reverend Jack Jensen's influence upon her life, Kenyon reflects on her youthful denunciation of all religion:

> Except for weddings and funerals, I hadn't been in church since my adolescence, when I'd announced to my parents that I wanted to stop attending Ann Arbor's First Methodist Church because "you can't be an intellectual and a Christian." (Big news, certainly, for Thomas Aquinas, Paul Tillich, Martin Luther, Soren Kierkegaard, and others.)
>
> I had put my gold and blue Methodist Youth Fellowship pin in the bottom of my jewelry box, where I would never see it. Nature and beauty would be my god, and I would be a good person without benefit of the sacraments, just by trying.[14]

Her adult choice was different. When she made this choice in adolescence, however, she made it willingly and with certitude. The temple of the Holy Ghost slowly shifted to the altar of literature and the creative spirit.

---

13. Kenyon, *A Hundred White Daffodils*, pp. 120, 121. Kenyon never lost her suspicion of school systems as bureaucracies rather than nurturers of the human spirit. In "A Proposal for New Hampshire Writers," a brief essay imploring artists to give free readings in schools and libraries, she wrote, "The school boards in our state are weighing the worth of arts programs, and, to most citizens, literature seems more expendable than physics, bookkeeping, computer skills, or even football. Literature, the garden of our inward life, loses its caretaker, and the water fails in the fountain when set against the demands of the outer life — the life of highway construction, stock reports, and medical technology" (*A Hundred White Daffodils*, p. 136).

14. Kenyon, *A Hundred White Daffodils*, p. 94.

This liberation was not as smooth or as simple as the preceding quotation makes it sound. In fact, Kenyon grappled with her grandmother's strictures well into her college years.[15] But the liberation began here, in an emphatic way.

Kenyon's increasing sense of liberation from Grandmother's rules also signaled a fierce, often rebellious spirit of independence. One finds traces of this in the journal Kenyon was required to keep for the 1961-62 school year, which she started when she was fourteen. The entries are important both because they capture her personality on the threshold of adolescence and because they show her forthright candor about herself. One of the earliest entries, dated September 19, has a rather startling lead: "I have always wanted to be a boy. I have always been a tom-boy, I admit without hesitation. I love sports, I love to be outside, I love comfortable clothes. I hate pink, I hate bows, and I hate lace. Boys are allowed to be more independent than girls. They don't have to be so quiet, or sit a certain way, or wear white gloves or cripple themselves for life in a pair of heels."[16]

15. This struggle — which often expressed itself in a kind of tense ambivalence toward her grandmother — was evident in her writing notebook from 1970 (in the Kenyon Archives, Box 26, Folder 11), where an untitled poem appears in four drafts, the final of which reads as follows:

> Wrapped in righteousness
> More shroud than shawl
> Grandmother intones
> Her life as a farm child —
> How she went to sleep weeping
> For want of books and learning.
> Better to have taken
> From the omniscient barnyard
> What teachers fail to give
> And prophets are dumb to.

Approval and disdain slide back and forth with nearly every line here. No one would mistake this poem as expressive of Kenyon's mature sentiments, either poetically or religiously, but it does demonstrate how the conflict endured through her college years.

16. Kenyon Archives, Box 26, Folder 1.

Kenyon goes on to point out her distaste of rules for the sake of rules. "What I really need," she confesses in the closing line, "is an excuse for being me!"

The journal is a mixture of the predictable and the surprisingly significant. It contains many of the kinds of entries one would expect of an adolescent — a paean on her mother's birthday; stories of hi-jinks with her friends Priscilla, Mary, and Sue; even a quotation from "a good friend of mine, Bill Shakespeare." In several entries she raves over the Detroit Tigers, particularly in one entry in which she anticipates going to a game. Occasionally descriptive passages appear. But there is also early and important evidence of Kenyon's beginning to write poetry. At about the same time that she made these early journal entries, she came across a translation of Chinese poetry by Witter Bynner. Perhaps her youthful attention was captured by the compression and concision of such poetry, or by the singularly arresting visual images. While uncertainty remains about the direct influence, Kenyon did begin experimenting with her own verse forms.[17] Notable is a poem on Algebra in her entry for 23 February 1962:

> Algebra, you drive me crazy.
> Thinking of you makes me hazy.
>
> You depress me through and through,
> When all I do is look at you.
>
> X and y and z and π
> I'll understand you by and by.
>
> But until the time I do,
> Don't solve me, I'll solve you.

17. Dozens of pieces of poetic ephemera appear in Kenyon's journals and later notebooks.

One thinks of her essay "Dreams of Math," in which Kenyon confesses, "I had math anxiety, as it's come to be called. Letters, reading, spelling made sense to me, but numbers had such strange proclivities. That zero times four was zero, canceling the existence of the four, seemed dubious at best."[18] Even in college, Kenyon avoided math and science courses as if they carried a virus.

While the anti-academic sentiments that appear in her journals might be stereotypical of an adolescent, Kenyon was also probing some deeply personal feelings in a highly intelligent way. In her entry for 24 September 1960, she reflects on an earlier entry:

> I may be hard, cruel and inconsiderate, but I am not *that* hard, cruel and inconsiderate. I have many vises [sic], but somewhere, deep, deep, down inside of me there must be some good! Sometimes I wonder how deep the goodness in me really is. Oh well, to err is human. I must be just about as human as people come! However it is all in my attitude. I must change my attitude, but I must not try to be something I am not. Some of my teachers even think I am bitter! Maybe I shouldn't ask, but, *bitter about what?* I am not ready to be put away by the men in white just yet!

Increasingly, as Kenyon notes in a later entry, she uses her journal to "let go my anger."

Discordant notes signal the despair that would sometimes so powerfully overwhelm Kenyon in later life. Was it merely teenage anxiety, or was it in fact the early onset of bipolar disorder, not fully diagnosed until years later? Current psychiatric theory has it that bipolar disorder is often masked in juvenile onset, diagnosed instead as attention deficit hyperactivity disorder or some behavioral disorder (oppositional-defiant is one of the most common). While one can only hypothesize here, it is clear that Kenyon's self-image deteriorated steadily through her teenage years.

18. Kenyon, *A Hundred White Daffodils*, p. 121.

During the autumn and early winter of 1961, Kenyon fell prey to several flu-type illnesses that may well have exacerbated her mood. On one occasion, when her mother was called again to pick her up from school, Polly asked her daughter if she got sick just to get out of school. Her first response in her journal: "That made me so damn mad that I couldn't say anything" (27 October 1961). But then she laments, "I don't know what is happening between mother and me, but I know we are drifting farther apart all the time and I am beginning to get worried. We have always been so close!" Despite the rebellious attitudes Kenyon adopted, her insecurity was profound.

Kenyon's entry of 6 December 1961 begins to suggest more keenly the difference she felt between herself and other classmates. While they all seemed to be speeding headlong toward an "adult" life, she longed to hold on to childhood. "I want to have fun," she wrote, "fun in ways most people would consider childish. I like to do silly things — play games, write notes, just be outside doing nothing. . . ." Kenyon derided the "stuffiness" of adulthood, and added, "I can't play games or go for long walks without being laughed at. Phooey." (These long walks became a regular pattern in her adult life.)

The most revealing entries, however, appear after the formal journal ends on December 8. All entries up to this point were read, one presumes, by Mr. Harman, her English teacher. But during Christmas vacation Kenyon returned to the blank pages at the end of the journal and used them for free-flowing reflection. The first entry summarizes her attitude toward the journal as a whole, but also raises once again the fear of adulthood:

> I think I have grown up quite a bit. I'm still a child and I don't mind. I can wait. In fact I'd rather. I am afraid of growing old. I'm afraid of long times (I don't know how else to say it). Being useless — unable to move, think. I'm more worried about being useless to myself — not others.

That last comment triggered the following self-reflective emotions, curiously arranged on the page as follows:

Me in 3 words!
helphelphelp frustrated
helphelphelp unsatisfied
helphelphelp searching

On the lower half of the page doodles in ink and the words *Ho Ho Ho* appear randomly.

The final page of that year's journal, duplicated as nearly as possible here, reveals a turmoil of conflicting emotions:

"Dark lake water
Deep as a nightmare
Stretches for ever
In midnight miles."

This to me suggests detachment fear.
    Why am I such a big, damn phony?
        fear, timidity, inhibitions (damn them)
            lack of true expression (not a means)
            lack of desire to express my real thoughts

"This is not my favorite topic
of conversation, but —
        good-bye."
"Let's not talk about it."

Conformity and   It is terrible to become
Congruity give   extremely attached to
Feelings of security   things. (people) It all
That is pure hell.   has to end so why not
It ruins spontaneity.   spare yourself the agony
                               of saying goodbye and
                               be detached? Be <u>hard</u>.

Phonies	nonphonies
Mary	Judy
Mr. Harman	Lynn
Mr. Peacock	[M.A.C.]?

What good does it do?
Practicality ugh!   Good, good, what good!
damn

One good thing about high school is that it ends, and students can try to make some sense out of these years and then move on. Some don't want to do this, of course. Their lives are forever caught in this time period. But Jane Kenyon couldn't wait to break out, even if it meant riding the tempest of her emotions to some pure hurricane. Yet, Kenyon was, despite all the bravado of her notebooks, a very timid young woman when she graduated. As her future hero John Keats wrote in "Sleep and Poetry,"

Why were ye not awake? But ye were dead
To things ye knew not of — were closely wed
To musty rulers lined out with wretched rule
And compass vile. . . . (ll. 193-96)

She had learned the rules; at the University of Michigan she would learn that the life of the mind, or the energy of imagination, soars far beyond the precinct of mere rules.

The University of Michigan

Perhaps the era of the 1960s was uniquely situated in history to permit a person of Kenyon's temperament the opportunity to explore. The 1950s, to be sure, was an era of deceptive placidity. It began in the bright optimism following the Korean War, when we believed that all our wars were finally behind us. The era ended in the darkening presence of Vietnam during the mid-1960s. But, from the Panmunjon Provisions of 27 July 1953 until the military escalation of Vietnam, the nation enjoyed that rare adventure we simply call "The Fifties."

For millions of postwar baby boomers, it was also the time of coming of age, which is itself an indefinable period. Some never start it; some never end it. But the baby boomers received their driver's licenses right smack in between the Korean and Vietnam wars. It was a rite of passage, as good an event as any to mark coming of age.

During the 1950s, tragedy was often kept personal and private. An ebullient national spirit prevailed and permitted no darkness to besmirch the bright costume of fun and progress that a nation dressed itself in. If you had a problem, you had best keep it to yourself. Yet problems there were, for real people tried to squeeze into that glittering costume. They tripped often over its raveled hem.

During the 1960s, public torment often took precedence over personal joy. As the 1960s deepened into history, the national mood grew more grim and frenetic. We stood on the threshold of war, and then war was upon us once again, and we were stupefied by it all, resorting to bravely chanting slogans into the increasing darkness. This darkness was lit by the fires of burning cities and campuses, and punctuated by the hoarse cough of gunfire.

The 1960s also birthed a raw anger at — and contempt for — the political, economic, and social structures of the day. William Barrett, one of the foremost interpreters of existentialism to an enthusiastic college audience in the 1960s, made this general observation about existentialists: "Common to all these philosophers is that the meaning of religion and religious faith is recast in relation to the individual." He argued that each of us stands alone in the world of humanity.[19]

19. Barrett, *Irrational Man* (Garden City, N.Y.: Doubleday, 1962), p. 17. Barrett's was far from the only voice making such declarations. Francis Crick, who won the Nobel Prize in 1962 for his work on molecular structure, published *Of Molecules and Men* (Seattle: University of Washington Press) in 1966, in which he proclaimed, "[The] ultimate aim of the modern movement in biology is in fact to

Spiritually, socially, and personally, the 1960s thrust students into a rather messy position. As the indecisive but perfectly metrical and rhyming York put it to Bolingbroke in *Richard II,*

> It may be I will go with you; but yet I'll pause,
> For I am loath to break our country's laws.

It was an uncertain age, riddled with insecurities for young people. They became a generation wandering and experimenting, looking for ways to fill the void.

KENYON'S START AT THE University of Michigan in 1965 was less than auspicious. Afflicted with low self-esteem and anxiety, she dropped out during her freshman year and worked instead at Leidy's Gift Shop.[20] The time she took for reflection served her well. Having been raised in a family of musicians, she explored the musical talent that seemed to be her birthright. She discovered that her own musical gift lay in singing, and eventually, after re-enrolling a year later at the university as a French major, she toured Europe with the Michigan Chorale. Kenyon had romantic affairs typical of this age of free love, and they do enter into her unpublished poetry of that time — poetry marked more by emotional excess than skill. (As one studies Kenyon's later poetry, it is hard not to notice the intense sexuality that appears, often side by side with intense spiritu-

---

explain all biology in terms of physics and chemistry" (p. 10). Very deliberately he tossed religion out of the classroom window: "Much of this instruction, from the point of view of most educated men, is utter nonsense," he declared (p. 90). A few pages later he made the same claim about all literary culture.

20. In an informal comment to the author, Donald Hall drew a connection between Jane's psychological, social, and physical states. Her high-school years were socially and psychologically difficult for her, and as a consequence, she weighed 165 pounds at graduation, far above what Hall described as her usual "fighting weight" of 127 pounds. Starting at the university a few months later didn't help; her sense of inferiority at the time left her ill equipped for the competition of university life.

ality. A profoundly sensual woman, she also gloried in the gift of the body.)

Her rejection of organized religion, also typical of many students of that time, was thorough. To satisfy herself, however, Kenyon gave church-going one more try: "I sampled the Unitarian church on Washtenaw Avenue's Fraternity Row, but I rejected even that as too formal, too organized. I'm not a joiner, I thought, with considerable satisfaction. Nature will be my God, and I'll be a good person simply because it is the right thing to do."[21] Even that must be qualified. Kenyon's revolt was against the church as institution — the guardian of Grandmother's rules. In her essay "Childhood, When You Are in It," Kenyon clarified her own *spiritual* position: "Even in the years of my apostasy I never doubted that God exists, and that I exist in relation to God. I doubted everything else that Grandmother ever told me, but never that."[22]

A telling feature of Kenyon's poetry-writing during her college years is her willingness to revise — although her process of revision was different at this early juncture. Unlike drafts of her mature poetry, laden with variations in the margins, with some words or lines quickly stroked out, Kenyon's drafts of these poems bear lines nearly blackened out by intense hatchmark x's. She would rewrite the poem several times, as if to test new variations as they appeared. One of the poems in the unpublished collection of college efforts nicely captures the wit of the emerging poet, but also reveals the inward struggle for acceptance:

Today
I got
no mail.
What is it about the world that it wants
my cubby hole
kept in poverty.

21. Kenyon, *A Hundred White Daffodils*, p. 66.
22. Kenyon, *A Hundred White Daffodils*, p. 68.

My mailbox is bloated with emptiness
its opening —
an orifice
waiting for a word.
Hey.
Occupant.
That's me.

Without question, the further development of her poetry was directly related to her meeting Donald Hall, then a member of the English Department at the university.

In the spring semester of 1969, Kenyon, though still a French major, enrolled in one of Hall's courses — "Introduction to Poetry for Non-English Majors." The course was a favorite of Hall's, as it was of the students who flocked to the class. One year the entire baseball team enrolled. Kenyon's study of poetry in that course thoroughly renewed her love for the genre that she had first begun experimenting with in junior high. No more poetry scribbled recklessly in notebooks. No more excavation of inner turmoil. Kenyon now felt the strong pull of design, of images structured so that the reader might relate to them, and of lyricism that sang through the intensity of the right words and phrasings. (The major transition she made as a mature poet, of course, was to surrender herself as poet to the image and lyric in such a way that the work belongs to the reader.)

Kenyon wanted to pursue her love of poetry by taking Hall's creative writing course in the fall semester. The challenge was getting into the class. Like Kenyon, many students wanted to get in, and admission to the course was competitive: each hopeful applicant had to submit five poems for evaluation. Among the five poems Kenyon submitted was "The Needle," which in revised form appears in her first volume, *From Room to Room*. To her delight, she was accepted.

The deepening of her love of poetry and the validation of her personal worth as a poet powerfully renewed Kenyon. Her work received significant public recognition: in 1969 she received the Avery and Jules Hopwood Award. But, more important, she had also found a *community* of kindred spirits, something she had always longed for. Hall's creative writing classes always extended beyond the classroom. He treated his students with generous respect, as peers. In a letter to the author written in May 2000, Hall remembers that "Jane as a student was outgoing and funny. The whole class argued like crazy, and loved each other. Jane always wore jeans." At first, Jane was just another student in a close-knit community of students exploring their artistic gifts. Hall describes their personal relationship at this stage:

> When Jane was in my class, she was wonderful. It was a great class, and they took over and didn't let me teach. The class went on meeting for two and a half years after the class was over — almost always without my presence. Jane used to come to office hours after the class was over, and I continued to look at her poems. She looked at some of mine. We had many mutual friends among the other poets, and often they would visit and talk to me about Jane. We remained good friends, something more than teacher and student — but not romantic.

It may be difficult to appreciate the closeness of such a community in today's academic setting. In large part it was due to Hall's graciousness as a host. The university then hosted nearly weekly poetry readings in the undergraduate library, after which Hall would often invite the guest poet and a group of students to his home. These gatherings were especially animated when Hall's longtime friend Robert Bly came to visit. In "Kicking the Eggs," a recollection of Bly, Kenyon recalls, "At these parties I observed the host and his guest [Bly] tell stories, joke, squabble, show off, and discuss serious ideas earnestly."[23] And she was a part of it.

In "Remembering Jane Kenyon," Laurence Goldstein recol-

23. Kenyon, *A Hundred White Daffodils*, pp. 133-34.

lects those informal poetry meetings. "Kenyon," he writes, "who seemed the most modest of the aspiring young poets . . . turned out to be the most accomplished of all." He adds,

> In later years I would think back to all the poetry readings by graduate students I had attended in the early 1970s — at the West Park band shell, in classrooms where the audience sat in narrow desks built to take notes upon, in living rooms and gallery space loaned out for the evening, in used bookstores and library reading rooms — and the one writer whose pungent images, witty closures, and joyful declarations came readily to mind was Jane Kenyon. Bespectacled and disarmingly mild-mannered, she would not perform, not orate in the bardic style becoming fashionable again in the 1970s, but speak her poems with a quiet directness that demanded alert respect from her listeners. "While you were away/I matched your socks/and rolled them into balls," she would declare and give a quick peep over the manuscript page at the front row. "Then I filled your drawer with/tight dark fists." An appreciative murmur would rise from the women in the audience, and the men would glance furtively at each other. The poem sounded better each time she read it.[24]

In a roundabout way, Kenyon had rediscovered the freedom of her childhood home — a place where she could be herself. Although reticent and shy by nature, she was homed here in this circle of poets. Just as she had had to free herself from her grandmother's House of Rules, she now was freeing herself from the harder shackles of feelings of worthlessness and self-doubt. Invigorated by her work during her last two years at Michigan, Kenyon completed her B.A. in English in 1970, then went on to complete an M.A. in English in 1972.

Perhaps the most significant event during the years 1969 to 1972, however, was Kenyon's deepening relationship with Hall,

24. Goldstein, "Remembering Jane Kenyon," *Xylem* 12 (Winter 1996): 56.

whom she married in 1972. In a letter to the author written in May 2001, Hall commented at length on the surprising course of their courtship:

> About a year after the class [creative writing] ended, I discovered from mutual friends that Jane had had a reversal in an affair of the heart, and although she prompted the breakup herself, she was miserable. Because I liked her so much I telephoned her and took her out to dinner. Thereafter, I took her out to dinner about once a week, or to a show or something. At first she talked only about her old boyfriend, and I countered with some amorous disasters of my own. We became closer and closer. I found myself gradually separating from other women I was dating at the time. I started seeing Jane a couple of times a week. I had to go out to Los Angeles that summer and I saw Jane the last night in Ann Arbor and the first night that I came back. I became worried. We were getting too close. Obviously we were too far apart in age — nineteen years — to get married. Jane would be a widow for twenty-five years. We brought up the subject of marriage perhaps three times, and dismissed it the first two times and around Christmas time of 1971 we decided we would get married, and we went through with it in April — a time when my son was home from prep school.

Soon after the wedding, Hall had a reading in Connecticut, and Kenyon accompanied him. Since Hall's mother lived in Hamden, he took this opportunity to introduce her to his new wife. The couple had no formal honeymoon in the traditional sense of the word. But that summer they went out to Los Angeles and had a bit of one, and that autumn they went to England together. Both trips were connected with writing projects, but they were also celebrations. Although they traveled to various places, they lived in Ann Arbor for the first three years of their marriage.

Initially the marriage had a confusing effect on Kenyon's work. Not that there was discord between them; there seldom was during the years of their marriage. Rather, there was a confusion of place or relationship between the young poet and the established master twenty years her senior. Hall describes the period this way: "Jane and I were student and teacher and friends for some time before anything romantic happened. When we were first married, we had to cope with that earlier relationship. I couldn't criticize her poems, because then I became the teacher. It was physically confusing; her husband suddenly turns into Professor Hall."[25]

In fact, Kenyon wrote little poetry before she and Hall moved to New Hampshire. For one thing, she was busy continuing her studies for a while, and she had a part-time job with the university, working on the New English Dictionary. Furthermore, she tended to confine her writing largely to periods when Hall was out of town doing readings because she felt inhibited by his presence in the house. A breakthrough of sorts in Kenyon and Hall's common pursuit of writing poetry occurred when they entered a three-way poetry workshop with Gregory Orr in Ann Arbor. Orr recollects the workshops in his essay "Our Lady of Sorrows":

> Somewhere pretty early on [in 1972], Donald and Jane and I began to get together on a regular basis to work on our poems: marathon workshops with a peculiarly affectionate and powerful dynamic, one that I've never found since. I believe my presence there was important for Jane because it was a way for her to listen to Don's comments on her poems without being his student. I existed as a kind of third point on a triangle, a buffer between them. These workshops were wonderful: honest, clear, funny.[26]

The move to New Hampshire was another powerful influence on Kenyon as a poet, as she once explained: "I had twenty-four

---

25. Kenyon, *A Hundred White Daffodils*, p. 190.

26. Orr, "Our Lady of Sorrows," in *Bright, Unequivocal Eye: Poems, Papers, and Remembrances from the First Jane Kenyon Conference*, ed. Bert Hornback (New York: Peter Lang Press, 2000), p. 28.

hours a day to do or not do what I wanted. So I really began to work seriously as a poet when we came here."[27] It was also after the couple moved to New Hampshire that their relationship as fellow poets began to change dramatically. It started with the nickname Kenyon adopted for her husband. In an interview with Dave Barney in *Southern Humanities Review,* Hall tells the story behind the nickname:

> I think one reason why it is not "Don" is that she knew about me before we met each other. I was a teacher and "Don" was the name of some distant, old fellow that was a professor and a published poet, not the fellow that she lives and eats with and goes to bed with each night. We were traveling in Maine once and there was Perkins Cove and Perkins Drug Store and Perkins this and Perkins that, and she said, "This Perkins must have been quite an old boy." Then affectionately and joshingly she started calling me Perkins, and it has gone on and I love it.[28]

So it was that one day she said, "Perkins, there's something on your desk." In turn, Hall might have said something like, "I left some stuff on your footstool." It might have been two poems or five poems. Over time, Kenyon and Hall became each other's closest poetic confidantes and first readers, and the pattern of "leaving something" for each other to read continued for almost twenty years.

27. Kenyon, *A Hundred White Daffodils,* p. 151.
28. Hall, in an interview with Dave Barney, "Happy Men in Desert Places," *Southern Humanities Review* 22, no. 3 (1988): 229.

CHAPTER TWO

The New Hampshire Years

"Amorist of Light"

Kenyon and Hall moved to his ancestral farmhouse on Highway 4 near Wilmot, New Hampshire, in 1975. The decision to move there, initially for a one-year leave and then permanently, was mutual — and enthusiastic. Both Kenyon and Hall were wearying of the university scene. Kenyon felt stifled in the rarefied intellectual community she inhabited in Ann Arbor, a feeling exacerbated by being married to one of the university's luminaries. And her love for pastoral quietude gave Eagle Pond Farm a compelling allure. Although Kenyon never made an overt statement about the strictures of Ann Arbor, her relief at having arrived at Eagle Pond Farm was so powerful that it was startling. During one interview she commented,

> For me the move to New Hampshire was a restoration of something that I love very deeply because Ann Arbor kept creeping outward to the point where the road was paved and the farmer's fields were subdivided and ugly houses were built. The move to New Hampshire was a restoration of a kind of paradise.[1]

---

1. Kenyon, *A Hundred White Daffodils* (Saint Paul, Minn.: Graywolf Press, 1999), pp. 199-200.

Maybe not Eden altogether, but a much-loved corner of it. Here life reduced, as Thoreau said in *Walden,* to the essentials that make life meaningful — friends instead of "acquaintances," time for reflection instead of recovery, a piece of paper on the desk that one can transform from a white blank into a rich tapestry of words that can shape and reveal a whole life.

Hall also welcomed the move to New Hampshire. After fourteen years of teaching, he felt that he wasn't learning as much from it anymore; something of that surprise of classroom discovery had worn off. Then too, the academic environment at the University of Michigan had begun to change. In his interview in *Southern Humanities Review,* Hall observed, "When I left, I left the institution of the university and the compulsory gregariousness of the academic town and its cocktail parties. I was glad to get away from that. The groupishness was hard to avoid. It is difficult to be a recluse in Ann Arbor, Michigan."[2]

The solid sales of his textbook, *Writing Well,* had made the idea of a move possible; the tremendous success of *Kicking the Leaves* seemed affirmation. The decision to move, however, was attended by risk — loss of a substantial and steady income, health benefits, and pension, all for the vagaries of freelance writing. Yet Eagle Pond Farm, with its quintessential New Hampshire farmhouse, acres of pastureland and mixed woods, and miles of hiking trails, had an undeniable pull on both their spirits.

2. Hall, in an interview with Dave Barney, "Happy Men in Desert Places," *Southern Humanities Review* 22, no. 3 (1988): 232. During an interview with David Hamilton published in *The Iowa Review,* Hall expanded considerably on the professional differences between life in Ann Arbor and life at Eagle Pond Farm: "I found displeasure, socially speaking, in the *rôle* of the poet in Ann Arbor. Not unmixed; but much displeasure. But here . . . here it is entirely different. Here there's a convention of eccentricity, and the landscape is full of weird people. If it is weird to be a poet, it is also weird to raise Holstein oxen, or to wear a cowboy outfit to a town meeting, or whatever. People are amused by each other — by 'characters,' as they inevitably call each other. They are not impressed by each other, but amused. Nobody defers to me because I write books. That is just what I do." See "An Interview with Donald Hall," *The Iowa Review* 15, no. 1 (Winter 1985): 11.

The farm, home to Hall's maternal side of the family since 1865, had long been a source for his poetry and stories.[3] "The Oxcart Man" derives from a local legend. And his books of prose are inseparable from Eagle Pond and the farm. Obviously, Kenyon didn't have that kind of history with the farm. She sometimes felt the ghosts of Hall's ancestors peering at her from row upon row of pictures in the various rooms of the farmhouse. But she quickly fell in love with the place even before they decided to make the move there permanently. Anne Farrowe quotes Hall as saying, "We came here for a year, initially, but Jane said she'd chain herself in the root cellar rather than leave." Farrowe adds, "Her tenacity about staying at Eagle Pond Farm was prescient. For both writers, the farm proved a wellspring."[4]

At the farm, they lived closely in tune with the annual cycle of the seasons. It plays through the writing that both of them did — though in very different ways. Indeed, in his Seasons at Eagle Pond, Hall describes how differently they responded to the seasons. While he was comfortable with the attenuated daylight of the winter season, Kenyon reveled in the long days of summer. She was, Hall writes, an "amorist of light."[5] She craved the light that brought her beloved flowers — and, in some ways, herself — to life. And she loved the long, light-filled afternoons that allowed her to spend hours tending her gardens. But Kenyon was also an amorist of light in her poetry, playing like a pointillist with flecks of light across a hazed backdrop.

In fact, it is nearly impossible to understand Jane Kenyon as person or as poet without understanding her passion for nature in general and for gardening in particular. She reveled in life at Eagle Pond Farm, at least in part because it recalled her rural youth and the childhood that she said in her junior-high journal she never

3. For a history of Hall's ancestors and the building of the farm, see *Life Work* (Boston: Beacon Press, 1993), pp. 15-20.

4. Farrowe, "Into Light All Things Must Fall," *The Hartford Courant*, 27 August 1995, p. 9.

5. Hall, *Seasons at Eagle Pond* (New York: Ticknor & Fields, 1987), p. 3.

wanted to leave. Her gardens especially form the starting point for many essays and poems. As was generally the case in her art and her life, gardening was not a reclusive activity. The irises, the peonies, the flora and fauna surrounding Eagle Pond provide images that soar outward. In Robert Frost's words, they "trip us head foremost into the boundless."

Starting in 1990, Kenyon began writing occasional essays for *Yankee* and *The Concord Monitor*. Many of these provide valuable insights into her most private and cherished feelings. For example, her essay "'Good-by and Keep Cold'" (a title borrowed from one of Frost's poems) lyrically commemorates the most mundane of gardening tasks — cutting back the perennials and preparing the beds for winter. The tasks come, she writes, when "The golden days of autumn — when chrysanthemums and asters still bloom, and a cricket or two still chirp in the long, lush grass that needs mowing one more time — those apple-fragrant days are gone." Setting the beds for winter is not merely a mechanical chore: "Let hot life retire, grow still: November's colors are those of the soul." Preparing for winter is also a preparing of one's self. It constitutes a rhythm essential to human well-being, a rhythm of work and rest. Having completed the task, "We wait for winter to pull a chilly sheet over its head."[6]

Reading Kenyon's essays, one imagines her coming to her desk with a picture or an idea fresh from the soil. Many of them mirror the person. In "The Phantom Pruner" we find a snippet of disclosure: "Sensible people grow beans. I grow peonies, campanula, roses, lilies, astilbe, bee balm. No matter how many flowers, there are never enough, and I harbor Napoleonic tendencies toward floral expansion."[7] Sometimes we find such character revelations; at other times Kenyon takes the opportunity to tie natural phenomena to the spiritual reflections they evoke in her. "Season of Change and Loss" begins with a reflection on All Souls' and All

6. Kenyon, *A Hundred White Daffodils*, pp. 43-45.
7. Kenyon, *A Hundred White Daffodils*, p. 48.

Saints' days in the religious calendar. Kenyon was enamored of the church calendar, appreciative of the ordering it gave to the progress of the spirit. But these two days involve both celebration and loss — celebration of the lives of saints and martyrs, but also a remembrance of the souls of "ordinary believers" through all history.

The reflection turns to the present, to Eagle Pond Farm in late October, where nature is also coming into repose and remembrance: "Geese fly over in sweet disorder, controlled chaos, one leader pulling the string for a while, then another emerging to take the leader's place. . . . Leaves come down around us, and the profile of the land emerges again, coming clear as a thought." Acorns fall; flowers fade. "Little deaths," Kenyon writes. "Somewhere in the psyche all these changes and losses register as death. What shall we do against it?" One "defense against reality" is indoor labor — baking and the like. Another, however, "is to confront it — to admit the pervasiveness of change and loss and replacement." Such is Kenyon's way: engagement rather than evasion. Gardening, she adds, "teaches this lesson over and over, but some of us are slow to learn. We can only acknowledge the mystery, and go on planting burgundy lilies."[8]

IF KENYON FELL IN LOVE with Eagle Pond Farm, she fell in love with the farmhouse too. Visiting it, one can see why. As one pulls into the circular dirt-and-gravel drive, heavily shaded by old-growth trees, the white-clapboard house with its many green-shuttered windows suggests sufficient nooks and crannies inside to delight anyone. This is a house whose walls hold comfort. Rimmed by the flowers that Kenyon planted and nurtured, dappled with shade on a sunny morning, it almost seems to emanate a storybook quality — a love story. To the far side the former pasture undulates uphill in green waves; to the southwest lies Eagle Pond and the spot where two lithe birches lean twined together. Hall and Kenyon referred to the spot as their "private beach." The site is also the setting for Ken-

8. Kenyon, *A Hundred White Daffodils*, pp. 85-86.

yon's poem by that name. The side door of the house facing the driveway opens onto the kitchen. In the downstairs living quarters — the living room, Hall's study, a bedroom, and the dining room — the walls are lined with bookshelves. There are thousands of books, even in the hallways. And where the bookshelves stop, galleries of family photos begin.

Kenyon's route to her study was through the back door of the kitchen, then through a door immediately to the left. Perilously steep wooden steps lead to the storage attic, which is crammed from the eaves to the narrow walkway with antiques and memorabilia handed down through generations of Hall's family. One might pause to hold miniature furniture from a pre–Depression era dollhouse, blow dust off china dolls, or roll a handful of old marbles scooped from a tin box. In *Here at Eagle Pond,* Hall refers to the attic as the "Back Chamber" and recalls the discoveries he and Kenyon made there: "We find a sewing machine that my grandmother sewed on for sixty years and a 1903 perambulator she wheeled my mother in. . . . We find fat old wood skis and sleds with bent wood runners. One ancient stove, with cast iron floral reliefs, we cleaned up and use in Jane's study."[9]

To the right is Kenyon's study. On the door hangs a red-and-white DO NOT DISTURB sign; below in parenthesis it reads, "I'm disturbed enough already." Beneath that hangs a poster for The Poetry Center's homage to Anna Akhmatova. It is a different world in here — a separate one. This is a writer's world. When one crosses the threshold, one passes from a mundane world of facts and follies to the fiercely creative world where the imagination invests the mundane with meaning and strips folly of its power.

Next to the door, against the attic wall, is the reclaimed wood-burning stove, the sole source of heat. On those short winter days — days when "the sun will shine no more/than is strictly necessary," as Kenyon put it in "At the Winter Solstice" — she would start a fire in the stove before taking the dog, Gus, for a walk. (In this part of New

9. Hall, *Here at Eagle Pond* (New York: Ticknor & Fields, 1990), p. 9.

Hampshire there are cool days and nights year round, so she sometimes had to use the stove even on summer days.) By the time she returned from walking Gus, the room would be toasty warm.

The room itself is a Cape Cod–style dormer room, papered in a light floral print that seems to fade elegantly into the walls themselves, as if a mere scrim shimmered between inside and outside. The room angles into fascinating corners and cubbyholes. One door off the small study opens on a storage space under the rafters. Prominent at the top of a bookshelf is a collection of well-used tapes. Many of Kenyon's favorites are easily spotted — Mahler, Schumann, Tchaikovsky — but also, in its neon-blue cover, *Anthology* by Marvin Gaye.

Kenyon's desk sits in front of a window facing the barn, which is about fifty yards beyond the circular driveway. Blue irises trim its weathered boards in a triumph of dazzling neatness. A climbing rose clambers up a trellis at one corner. To the north, the granite shoulders of Ragged Mountain (or Mount Ragged, as the locals call it) angle right down to the barn, depositing a terrigenous flow of sparkling sediment all around it. On each side of the window are portraits of her literary saints: Anna Akhmatova on the right, John Keats on the left. At the top of the window is a photograph of an elaborate icon of Christ. Just off center at the head of the desk, a slanting bookshelf, about eighteen inches long, holds dictionaries. To the right, next to the protruding typewriter stand, is a stationery box, but pads with the header "From the Desk of Jane Kenyon" lie scattered over the desk, keeping hectic company with an assortment of staplers, pencils, and pens, a tin of photographs, and other random items.

The study bears out what drafts of Kenyon's poems in her collected papers suggest. Kenyon was not finicky about what she wrote on. First drafts appear on whatever paper was at hand: scrap paper, backs of dittoed church bulletins, thin paper in a variety of colors (yellow, blue, pink-lined notebook paper), torn pieces of paper — even, in one instance, the back of an old postcard. When the ideas came, so did the impulse to write — and whatever paper was at

31

hand would do. Similarly, the early typed drafts appear on a variety of papers, from frangible onion skin to recycled blank back sides, even on the back of poems already typed. Later drafts usually appear on a light rag bond.

One other thing. From the armature light that extends over the desk hangs a sign, about 8 × 12 inches. It is bright red, with white letters that read

Sorry We're
CLOSED

Here at Eagle Pond Farm, Kenyon found her personal space to write, to be herself as a poet. Here she first handed "Perkins" a few poems for his comment, beginning a lifelong tradition. Here she found a subject matter in the land and people she grew to love profoundly. And here Kenyon also found her spiritual home.

PERSONAL EXPERIENCES of major importance — the increasing depth of her marriage, her growing community of poets and friends, her travels abroad, her struggles with illness — occurred during Kenyon's twenty years at Eagle Pond Farm. Yet Kenyon's spiritual reawakening is a singular event among them. It formed a framework for living *through* whatever else occurred. I use the word in the same way Kenyon did in her poem "Trouble with Math in a One-Room Country School." In a reminiscence about the years she, Kenyon, and Joyce Peseroff spent discussing each other's writing, Alice Mattison recalls their effort to find the right word for a passage in this particular poem. The scene depicts young Jane leaning over the aisle to ask her neighbor, Ann, how to do a division problem. Thinking she was cheating, the teacher (identified as Miss Moran here; compare to the prose reminiscences where the teacher is called Miss Sikima or Miss Irwin) "sprang from her monumental desk/and led me roughly through the class/without a word." Then she shut Jane in the furnace closet for punishment. When Kenyon brought an earlier draft of the poem to the writing group, she was

32

dissatisfied with the prepositions she had used to describe the teacher's rough handling of her, but she was stymied about how to change it. Mattison describes the conversation:

> How was she to describe the teacher leading her from the classroom to a closet? She'd already used "from" and she didn't want the double preposition "out of." I am afraid I remember this conversation because I was the one who came up with the answer: "through." The line remains, "And led me roughly through the class." Jane liked "through" because it had only one syllable, a syllable she hadn't employed before, but also because it made the humiliation worse. She wrote down the word with a satisfied flourish.[10]

This is the sense in which I use the word *through* in connection with Kenyon's spiritual life. It's a tough word, a rooted word that bears authority. Events go from or out of her life, all leaving their mark on her spiritual life, but Kenyon's spiritual faith is what led her through the experiences themselves.

The basic facts of Kenyon's spiritual awakening are recorded in several places. The Sunday after they moved to Eagle Pond Farm, Hall surprised his wife by saying, "I suppose we ought to go to church."[11] In a late notebook Kenyon records her reaction: "Oh, no, I thought. Stockings and a skirt." They went to honor custom: Hall's ancestors were among the founders of the church. His cousins would be there. The pew that his maternal great-grandfather had purchased in South Danbury Christian Church was waiting.[12] Call it a social obligation.

10. Mattison, "'Let It Grow in the Dark Like a Mushroom': Writing with Jane Kenyon," *Michigan Quarterly Review* (Winter 2000): 127.

11. See also *A Hundred White Daffodils*, pp. 67-69, 94-97; and *Life Work*, pp. 5-6.

12. South Danbury Christian Church has retained its original name throughout its history, with one exception. When the church joined the Congregational Church, it called itself "Congregational Christian" for a time, even though it

During that first service, both Hall and Kenyon were impressed by the minister, Jack Jensen. At first it was simply the fact that he quoted Rilke during the sermon. That made them decide to come again. And they kept coming. "Something unlooked-for began to happen," Kenyon recalled.

> Beyond the social pleasures I took from church, I started to take comfort from the prayer of confession and the assurance of pardon. I was twenty-nine years old; by now it was clear to me that I wasn't a good person all the time. I was sometimes irritable, selfish, and slow to forgive. It eased my mind to acknowledge my failings and start over.[13]

Jack Jensen was the farthest thing from the stereotype of a country preacher. Holding a Ph.D., he also taught philosophy and religion at Colby-Sawyer College. His sermons were a revelation to Kenyon: "I listened to Jack's sermons week after week, discovering to my astonishment that my soul had been starving. He had what I needed, and I could accept it from him because I respected his mind and his training." Jack, wrote Kenyon, "was the shepherd of his sheep, and he slipped his crook around my neck so gently that I was part of the South Danbury fold before I knew what had happened."[14] In short or-

---

never officially changed its name. Congregationalism is a Protestant form of church organization effectively brought to America in 1620 by the Pilgrims. In Congregationalism, each local church exercises free governance of church matters under the lordship and authority of Christ. The central belief is that through prayer and study, congregants will be open to the wisdom and leadership of Christ. Since there are no presbyteries or synods, particular emphasis is placed upon the fellowship of the individual church. In 1957 many Congregationalist churches, including South Danbury, merged with the United Church of Christ, thereby adopting the name "Christian Church" in years following.

13. Kenyon, *A Hundred White Daffodils*, p. 68.

14. Kenyon, *A Hundred White Daffodils*, p. 95. In *Life Work*, Hall also testifies to the impact Jensen made upon his religious beliefs (pp. 121-23). In fact, in Ann Arbor, Hall and Kenyon had been married in a judge's chambers; but after five years in New Hampshire, they renewed their vows in the church with Jack's guid-

der, Kenyon was reading the Gospel of Mark, at Jack's suggestion, with William Barclay's commentary, and she and Hall joined a Bible-study group that focused largely on the prophets, Isaiah in particular.

But Kenyon needed a spiritual mentor to personalize what she read and studied. Just as Akhmatova later validated her artistic aims, now Jensen helped validate her faith. He directed Kenyon to female mystics: Saint Teresa, Julian of Norwich, Simone Weil. She also read Augustine's *Confessions,* Thomas à Kempis's *The Imitation of Christ,* and Evelyn Underhill's translation of *The Cloud of Unknowing.* In Kenyon's words, "Jack gave me a spiritual life — it's that simple. Over the years my poetry changed to reflect my awakening. Life changed profoundly."[15]

Jensen and South Danbury touched Kenyon's life in many ways.[16] She reveled in the fellowship of the church, with its annual potlucks and baked-goods sales. (She herself was a splendid and creative cook.) She loved the calendar of the church year, and would read through the four Gospels every Advent season. She also felt called to give of herself, serving as a Hospice volunteer for years. And as she herself pointed out, her spiritual awakening had direct implications for her poetry.

Kenyon's essay "Childhood, When You Are in It" hints at this awakening. It ends unfinished with these words: "In 1980 I had an

---

ance. Hall recalled this event in a recent letter he wrote to the author: "We had a private get together with our minister Jack Jensen, Saturday afternoon in the church, and Jack brought flowers and three glasses and half a bottle of wine and we went through the marriage ceremony, unofficially, together. By this time we had become regular church-goers."

15. Kenyon, *A Hundred White Daffodils,* p. 96. Years later, when Jack lay dying of cancer, both Hall and Kenyon spent hours by his bedside. See Kenyon's poem "In Memory of Jack" in *Otherwise* (Saint Paul, Minn.: Graywolf Press, 1996), p. 204.

16. Not everything about the church pleased her. For a number of years she remained troubled by the fact that women didn't have a larger pastoral role in the church. Eventually South Danbury did have a female pastor, Alice Ling, who ministered to Kenyon and Hall during Kenyon's illness and who officiated at Kenyon's memorial service.

experience that changed my understanding completely, changed my way of being in the world."[17] This is a monumental statement for anyone to make. On its own, the unfinished essay leaves us in the uneasy realm of speculation. But certain chronological events help identify the event and her "way of being in the world."

In his introduction to *A Hundred White Daffodils*, Hall comments on the experience that Kenyon is referring to: "I came home after three or four days away and found Jane in a quiet, exalted, shining mood. She told me that something extraordinary had happened while I was away. She had felt a presence with her in the room that lingered with her. She associated it with the Holy Spirit, and it seemed to her female."[18] In her interview with Bill Moyers, Kenyon herself commented further on this experience. She told him that "Once There Was Light," part five of "Having it Out with Melancholy," draws on that event:

> I really had a vision of that once. It was like a waking dream. My eyes were open and I saw these rooms, this house, but in my mind's eye, or whatever language you can find to say these things, I also saw a great ribbon of light and every human life was suspended. There was no struggle. There was only this buoyant shimmering, undulating stream of light. I took my place in this stream and after that my life changed fundamentally. I relaxed into existence in a way that I never had before.[19]

"Relaxed into existence" is a telling phrase. Kenyon's spirituality was never a means for escaping existence. Rather, it enabled her to embrace reality with all its gritty beauty and intrusive suffering.

What she did discover, however, was the existence of a spirit that superseded mere reality — one certainly more familiar and comfortable than Grandmother's fear-inducing specters. Now it

17. Kenyon, *A Hundred White Daffodils*, p. 69.
18. Hall, introduction to *A Hundred White Daffodils*, p. x.
19. Kenyon, *A Hundred White Daffodils*, p. 160.

was not uncommon for Kenyon to speak of the Holy Ghost as her muse. "Briefly It Enters, and Briefly Speaks" exemplifies the speaking of the muse at all hours, in all places:

> I am the one whose love
> overcomes you, already with you
> when you think to call my name. . . .

Similarly, "The Bat" demonstrates the supernatural quality of the Holy Spirit's presence. The narrator introduces herself as reading about rationalism in the dusk of an early winter evening. She speculates, "Maybe the world *is* intelligible/to the rational mind." But then again, she speculates that maybe she lights the lamps for nothing. Does order prevail or not? "Then I heard wings overhead" — a bat has flown into the room. She and the cat leap into action, chasing it from room to room. This is not the rational mind operating, to be sure. The bat successfully eludes them:

> At every turn it evaded us
>
> like the identity of the third person
> in the Trinity: the one
> who spoke through the prophets,
> the one who astounded Mary
> by suddenly coming near.

No rational articulation can fully express the poetic vision, the inner seeing. It is more like the flicker of the bat's wings, or the coming near of the Holy Spirit. If the Holy Spirit became Kenyon's muse, Mary became her guide.

In arranging the contents for *A Hundred White Daffodils*, Donald Hall estimated that Kenyon wrote "Childhood, When You Are in It" during 1991, and he placed the previously unpublished "Gabriel's Truth" immediately following it. Even if the date of this piece is indeterminate, "Gabriel's Truth" follows naturally from "Childhood." There the unfinished manuscript ends with an homage to Julian of Norwich and Saint Teresa as spiritual guides. A nearly evolutionary pattern brought Kenyon to Mary's side in "Gabriel's Truth."[20] Here she is exploring not just the relationship to the mystical presence of the Holy Ghost but the relationship to the persons of Jesus and Mary. Kenyon's premise in the essay, and one that would repeatedly be tested in her own life, is this: "The lives of God's holy ones are subject to major interruptions."[21] In the case of Mary, it was Gabriel's startling announcement — an event that changed her life forever. As troubling were Simeon's ominous words at the temple: "Behold, this child is set . . . for a sign which shall be spoken against; (Yea, a sword shall pierce through thy own soul also)" (Luke 2:34-35, KJV). The sword in Mary's soul, going ever deeper during Jesus' earthly life until it plunged all the way at Golgotha, riveted Kenyon's attention. Mary, she wrote, "followed Christ through everything — through his scrapes with the religious establishment, through the humiliation and apparent defeat on the cross. She never failed in her love for Jesus, no matter what personal disappointment or horror it led to."[22] Mary became Kenyon's model for following Christ through "confusion and torment."[23] And she provided practical lessons for the spiritual life:

> Mary teaches us to trust God always, to live in hope, to respond with love to whatever happens, to give and not count the cost, to be faithful in the worst circumstances. She teaches us, women

20. In her interview with Bill Moyers, Kenyon specified a relationship between "The Bat" and Gabriel's appearance to Mary: "What I had in mind was being broken in upon, the way Mary was broken in upon by Gabriel. You think you're alone and suddenly there's this thing coming near you, so near that you can feel the wind from the brushing of its wings. Why this experience with the bat made me think of Mary and Gabriel, I don't know, but it did" (*A Hundred White Daffodils*, p. 165).

21. Kenyon, *A Hundred White Daffodils*, p. 70.

22. Kenyon, *A Hundred White Daffodils*, p. 71.

23. Kenyon, *A Hundred White Daffodils*, p. 72.

and men alike, not to insist on ourselves, on our own comforts and satisfactions. And she shows us, finally, that her strenuous love was able to defeat death.

Blessed be Mary, the mother of our Lord, who suffered so sharply for our good.[24]

To think that Kenyon's spiritual faith bestowed a calm and equanimous spirit, a power to face any challenge personally undiminished, would be mistaken. The very appeal of Mary as a spiritual mentor was her lesson of faith through uncertainty and suffering.

The sudden intrusion of suffering, in fact, became a frequent subject of exploration in Kenyon's poems. "Evening Sun" from *The Boat of Quiet Hours* exemplifies the pattern established fairly early in her mature poetry. The light of evening sun itself is always evocative for Kenyon, a suspension between daylight and darkness upon which life's shadows dance. The poem begins with a recollection of childhood, when she danced, spinning in circles in a yellow dress. As the skirt of the dress flared out in the "ochre light" of the June evening, she herself seemed to become the sun: "Turning and turning/until it flared to the limit/was irresistible. . . ." But even then she knew

> that I would have to live, and go on
> living: what a sorrow it was; and still
> what sorrow burns
> but does not destroy my heart.

The colon suggests that living itself would be a sorrow. The metaphor of the little girl dancing like a twirling sun shifts to a sorrow that burns like the sun. But, she affirms, it does not (cannot?) destroy her heart. Kenyon's entry for 6 December 1961 in her schoolgirl journal proved prescient: "In Mary Martin's, or Peter Pan's words 'I won't grow up.' There are too many responsibilities in con-

24. Kenyon, *A Hundred White Daffodils*, p. 72.

nection with adulthood. I want to have an excuse for the way I act. I want to have fun, fun in ways most people would consider childish." The burden and heartache of those responsibilities, as the little girl twirling in this poem discovers, are inevitable.

In another evening poem, "Twilight: After Haying," Kenyon evokes this same sense of the sudden intrusion of suffering. The first stanza begins with a stoic inevitability:

> Yes, long shadows go out
> from the bales; and yes, the soul
> must part from the body:
> what else could it do?

In the second stanza Kenyon describes the weary workers, who sprawl in the field by the baler. Too tired to get up right away, they talk and smoke while night overtakes them. In the third stanza the moon comes out "to count the bales." The pale moon is like the shadow soul, casting the scene in eerie relief. The fourth stanza consists of this single, striking observation:

> These things happen . . . the soul's bliss
> and suffering are bound together
> like the grasses . . .

A moon-like enigma hazes the metaphor. Which "things" happen? Those physical events described in the previous three stanzas? The ellipses at once conjoin and separate the "things" and the following statement. In fact, these "things" — the natural order of the hay reaching its prime, then being cut and baled — are also like the natural spiritual order of bliss and suffering bound together. In this life they are unavoidably interwoven — baled together into one whole like the simile of the grasses bound together.

The intrusion of suffering on life supplies a major theme in Kenyon's poetry; it also serves as subject for several of her essay reflections. "The Shadows" is one such piece. Kenyon begins the essay by describing the way an annual summer storm always smashes the voluptuous peonies she so dearly loves. As she often does in her poetry, Kenyon moves from natural events as a frame to the essential subject within it. In this case that subject is her husband, who is just recovering from his second surgery for cancer, just two-and-a-half years after his first surgery. Kenyon describes this "smasher" in their lives, then comments, "The luckiest, sunniest life invariably includes tragedy, if I do not overstate these matters by calling them tragic. To lose your health, your strength, your ability to work, and to take pleasure in life — that is tragedy. It's no less tragic because it happens to everybody."[25] Even so, Kenyon refuses to wallow in tragedy. Her enormous resilience of spirit battles back, searching for light. This year, she explains, she outwitted the storm by going outside before it struck and cutting "every full-open peony in sight, quantities that I would never permit myself under other circumstances." She brought them into the house so that she and Hall could savor their beauty and their scent. "We are getting an education this summer," she comments, "in the humanities, I would say — in love despite fear. . . . And daily we grow in the determination to cast off trouble like a garment in the heat and keep going, keep living, and living abundantly, with more awareness of each moment and more joy."[26]

Those are brave words, tested often in Kenyon's searching for "a great goodness." Kenyon used a portion of Psalm 139 as an epigraph to *Constance*, perhaps the volume that most clearly evidences her searching. About the epigraph she commented, "The psalmist says, darkness and light, it's all the same. It's all from God. It's all in God, through God, with God."[27] One should not misunderstand her comment, for Kenyon is not saying that darkness and light alike emanate from God. Rather, the pronoun "it"

---

25. Kenyon, *A Hundred White Daffodils*, p. 118.
26. Kenyon, *A Hundred White Daffodils*, p. 26.
27. Kenyon, *A Hundred White Daffodils*, p. 166.

alludes to God's steadfast presence in whatever earthly condition one finds oneself. Kenyon clarifies that in her next sentence paraphrased from the psalm: "There is no place I can go where Your love does not pursue me."

One finds Kenyon's faith, first of all, deeply rooted in the matter of this life, as opposed to mystically abstracted from life. In terms of meditation practices — and it could be reasonably argued that her poems are meditations in the way that the poems of Gerard Manley Hopkins are — Kenyon would ally with Saint Ignatius of Loyola rather than Saint Francis. Ignatius, also the spiritual mentor of Hopkins, advocated beginning *in* this world and moving toward God or discovering him here in common things, rather than attempting to cloister oneself from the world. In much the same way, Kenyon's faith and her work root firmly in this world and earnestly seek God's presence in it. Perhaps that directly affects a second quality of her faith and, consequently, her art — that is, a grappling for certitude.

Indeed, the great risk of any engagement of faith with reality arises from the fact that the world is a messy place. Unquestionably, Kenyon's increasing struggle with depression contributed to her own sense of the world's messiness. As Alice Mattison observes, "Jane had deep pessimism interwoven with her unmistakable delight in life, a pessimism that I think was her birthright as a depressive."[28] An analogy with Emily Dickinson in this regard is not far off the mark. Kenyon read Dickinson with great enthusiasm, primarily for Dickinson's syntactic structures. But in a letter to Mattison, Kenyon also remarked, "I can tell you that she knew *her* Bible, by gum. Her struggle with God is constant in the poems."[29] Each time Kenyon lifted a pen to yet another blank page, whether it was the back of a church bulletin or the blank side of a postcard, she was carving an inscriptive testimony to that struggle. Is this where messiness, evil, and suffering end? And at what point does the

28. Mattison, "'Let It Grow in the Dark Like a Mushroom,'" p. 136.
29. Mattison, "'Let It Grow in the Dark Like a Mushroom,'" p. 134.

"great goodness" begin? Or are they forever bound by co-existent struggle?

The questions collided as she sat in her Eagle Pond farmhouse, surrounded by the splendor of a world wrapped rich in green or layered in white, but also infiltrated by interior doubt and, at times, unspeakable pain. The answers to the questions were never clear when she wrote. She just kept carving words into lasting forms that might lead others to answers.

The struggle manifests itself in many of Kenyon's poems. In "With the Dog at Sunrise" she ponders what to say in a letter to Sarah, a widow at thirty-one. How, in words, can one lift the pall of darkness? As she reflects on possibilities, the dog runs on ahead and urinates against a hemlock: "The snow turns the saffron of a monk's robe/and acrid steam ascends." It is almost as if this most mundane of earthly events transports her to spiritual vision — but not quite. Too much suffering intrudes; nonetheless, she keeps searching:

> Searching for God is the first thing and the last,
> but in between such trouble, and such pain.[30]

But far up the hill in the woods, she knows with certainty that deer are at ease under the sheltering pines, "nose to steaming nose. . . ." Like so many of Kenyon's poems, this one ends with some ambiguity. Perhaps the ease of the deer, these creatures untouched by any searching after God, merely mocks the pain she feels for her young friend. They have no need, no rational urgency to justify suffering and searching for God. Perhaps, on the other hand, the deer themselves symbolize souls at rest ("nose to steaming nose") far up in the woods, where they are free from earthly troubles. Whichever

---

30. These lines underwent significant changes in drafts. In the first nine drafts of the poem, the lines begin with "Loving God," which certainly has an affirmative voice. The next eight drafts, however, have "Looking for God," which is more tenuous and uncertain. Finally "Searching for God" appears.

way one reads this poem, the narrator stands suspended, alone in her search for answers.

In an interview with David Bradt held in March 1993 and later published in *The Plum Review* in 1996, Kenyon was asked how she felt about being referred to as a contemplative poet and compared to Emily Dickinson. Kenyon's answer reveals much about her ongoing spiritual quest:

> To be mentioned in the same breath with Emily Dickinson makes my day. If by contemplative you mean one who meditates on religious matters, I guess we both do that in our work. Dickinson thinks a lot about her soul, and I think a lot about mine. She thinks about her relation to God — a God who is distant, and rather cruelly arbitrary. In many of my poems I am searching, clumsily, for God. We are both full of terror, finally, and puzzlement, at the creation.[31]

Living in the creation, engaging it fully, Kenyon nonetheless found herself full of terror and puzzlement when trying to locate God's place in it. Nowhere in her poetry is this more fully demonstrated than in the posthumously published "Woman, Why Are You Weeping?"

Several stories lie behind the poem, and these shape our understanding of it. Kenyon and Hall had gone to China and Japan in 1986 as visiting writers sponsored by the State Department Cultural Exchange. They visited India under similar auspices in 1991 and 1993. The poem "Woman, Why Are You Weeping?" derives from a daily journal Kenyon kept during the 1991 trip. The journal entry for Wednesday, November 20, begins matter-of-factly. Kenyon had as her guide a Brahmin named Rajiv, who worked for the U.S. embassy. It was a sunny morning, and they breakfasted on toast and tea on the verandah before Rajiv took her to the place "where the Yamuna and Ganges Rivers converge, one of the holiest

---

31. Kenyon, *A Hundred White Daffodils*, p. 175.

places in India."[32] To get there, Rajiv engaged two boatmen to row them upcurrent.

> We sat, shoes off, on a white sheet, propping ourselves up with our arms. We passed a huge white ashram on the shore. After perhaps twenty minutes we arrived at the place where the boatmen moored the boat. Rajiv got out on a little dock. He scattered the flowers he had brought and a priest blessed him. Then he got back in the boat, and we lingered there for a moment. The colors of the two rivers were distinct — one green, one brown, making a roiling line where they met. People jumped out of other boats to bathe in the water. It is here that Mahatma Gandhi's ashes were scattered. Anyone who can manage it brings the ashes of their dead here. If they are too poor to buy wood for cremation, they bring the bodies, or, if they could afford wood, but not enough, the partially burned bodies are put into the water here. We stopped talking. The boat rose and fell gently. Then Rajiv said something in Hindi and we were off again.

It seemed a bucolic day — sun shining on the water, birds darting to catch scraps of bread tossed overboard. But then, tragedy broke jarringly into the scene:

> I glanced off to my right, to a shoreline littered with detritus. Among the sticks and junk I saw the body of a newborn, lapping against the shore. I looked away. That is a chicken, not a baby, I said to myself. Looked again. Baby, legs still not uncurled from the womb. To the right of it, perhaps a dozen feet, a snake sunned itself, raising its upper body as we passed by. To the left, a garland of marigolds. What I say is true. You will not believe me.

32. This and subsequent observations from the journal are found in the Kenyon Archives, Box 29, Folder 28.

Kenyon recalled how she sat, stunned, in the boat — "I wasn't sure I could talk without coming apart."

When she told Rajiv what she had seen, he "explained that this was the holiest place the child's mother could have come to with the corpse. She might have walked a long way to get here. The most devout thing she could do she did. I stopped crying, and I stopped feeling horror, and some kind of quietness came over me." When they got back, the taxi was waiting. Appointments had been scheduled. Events came like train cars. Nevertheless, the sight that morning left a deep imprint on Kenyon's mind and emotions.

Not until she and Hall returned to New Hampshire did she begin working on the poem, and she worked on it through much of 1992, only to set it aside to return to later. Soon her own illness was upon her. In his introduction to *A Hundred White Daffodils*, Hall recalls how he and Kenyon began work on selecting poems for *Otherwise* on 12 April 1995, the day after they learned that Jane was definitely going to die. They worked together that day and the next, while she was still able to concentrate. Hall suggested including "Woman, Why Are You Weeping?" and wanted to read it to her so she could decide. She firmly refused. After her death, the poem was first published in *The Atlantic Monthly* (April 1999) and then in *A Hundred White Daffodils* as the concluding entry. Kenyon's closest readers — Gregory Orr, Joyce Peseroff, and Alice Mattison — agreed with Hall that it should be included there.

But why did Kenyon feel otherwise? Especially since, in Hall's estimation, "This poem of spiritual loss includes some of Jane's best Christian writing, as well as brilliant images from India, a country she loved."[33] Truly, it is a poem that engages suffering head on; it struggles with the relative merits of other religious beliefs when placed alongside Christianity; and it explores powerfully a range of Kenyon's own emotions.

There is yet one more story behind the poem, however, one told with remarkable candor by Kenyon's longtime friend Alice

33. Hall, introduction to *A Hundred White Daffodils*, p. xii.

46

Mattison. (The two of them, along with Joyce Peseroff, gathered several times a year to critique each other's work.) During the winter of 1992, Mattison visited Eagle Pond Farm, taking delight in Kenyon's slides of India and her new skill in preparing Indian food. But, she adds, she also felt uncomfortable:

> It seemed that she was suddenly rejecting everything in her life that had preceded the Indian trip, including her religion and the very way she thought. Much later I understood that she was troubled to discover that Indians seemed to have a religion that felt true; how then could her own, different belief also be true? At the time, when she expressed doubts about subjects I knew had always been important to her, and doubts about her own life, I thought she was indulging in intense rejection of herself. She talked and talked about seeing a dead baby in the Ganges, and how a new Indian friend allayed her dismay by explaining what his religion and culture made of that baby. I was wildly jealous of this man, Rajiv. I suppose I thought she didn't love me anymore, and only wanted Indians for her friends. At one point in the visit she insisted I was angry with her. I was, but denied it. I said she was angry with me, and she denied that.[34]

About a month later the next workshop was held at Mattison's house in New Haven. Again an argument flared, this time over the poem, which Kenyon had brought along. "I was burning with jealousy and rage," Mattison wrote, "that my Jane should be rejected and dismissed — by herself." By "my Jane," it is clear that Mattison refers to the woman of faith and fortitude she had known in the years before the trip to India. There was reconciliation — as there must be between close friends. Mattison notes that Kenyon later "made some clarifying changes and I saw that I had misunderstood what she had in mind." And about a week after the workshop argument, Mattison called Kenyon at Eagle Pond Farm: "She [Kenyon]

---

34. Mattison, "'Let It Grow in the Dark Like a Mushroom,'" p. 134.

said it had been the worst week of her life. We cried. We calmed down."[35] There is little question that one reason for Kenyon's firmly negative response to having "Woman, Why Are You Weeping?" included in *Otherwise* was that it reminded her of the terrible argument she had had with her friend.

The poem is nonetheless central to the purpose here — probing the full contours of Kenyon's spiritual beliefs. These shaped the nature of the writer and her work for twenty years, and demand close scrutiny. "Woman, Why Are You Weeping?" is a part of that. Indeed, still another reason why she refused to publish the poem, with all of its spiritual disquietude, may have been that she felt it didn't reflect what she ultimately believed. But it can be argued that that belief is honed here — as it is in many of her other poems — on the edge of doubt and anguish.

The first two stanzas are extrapolated from the account in John's Gospel of Mary Magdalene's encounter with the two angels at the empty tomb. The narrative is an interesting drama for several reasons, not the least of which is that Jesus' first post-Resurrection appearance was to Mary Magdalene. According to Matthew's Gospel, Mary was one of a group of women who followed Jesus to the cross "to care for his needs" (Matt. 27:55). Mark's Gospel places Mary Magdalene among the women who witnessed the crucifixion (Mark 15:40). No compelling biblical evidence suggests that Mary Magdalene was the harlot caught in the act of prostitution, or that she is the Mary who anointed Jesus' feet with nard. Biblically, she stands out as a woman of pure faithfulness to her Lord. Kenyon sharply departs from Scripture, however, at the end of stanza two, with Mary's plaintive lament, "They have taken away my Lord, and I don't know where they have laid him." In Scripture, Mary's bewilderment is immediately dispelled by the appearance of the risen Christ; in Kenyon's poem, bewilderment and loss hold sway.

The following stanza transports us from the Judean grave to the familiar pew in South Danbury Christian Church. Communion

35. Mattison, "'Let It Grow in the Dark Like a Mushroom,'" pp. 134, 135.

is about to be served — but, Kenyon notes, "The old comfort does not rise in me, only/apathy and bafflement." Why? India, she claims, "has taken away the one who blessed/and kept me." The loss of the narrator's Lord is as thorough as the loss Mary faced before the empty tomb. Only a yawning hole greets them. The narrator confronts only desolation, which we hear in her echo of Mary's lament:

> Men and women with faces as calm as lakes at dusk
> have taken away my Lord, and I don't know
> where to find him.

She is referring to the men and women of India and her conflicting experiences among them.

Part one of the six-part poem thereby lays out the conflict of loss and certitude. The following parts flare back and forth from the time Kenyon spent in India to the present — focusing specifically on the moment of confused contemplation as she sits in the church pew awaiting communion but more generally on the shape of her faith in the months following the trip to India. Part two, in which she affirms again that "I only know that I have lost the Lord/in whose image I was made" — a loss not only of belief but also, consequently, of self — draws one into the world of Hindu beliefs. Instead of a belief in the one Lord, she has encountered a belief in multiple deities in various forms and emanations — a belief the people clung to as tenaciously as she had clung to her Christianity. Fundamentally, the issue is an old one. Is all religion simply culturally relative, shaped according to a people's experience and practice in different regions? If that is the case, then are all of them valid — or are none of them valid? Ultimately the question must redound to the validity of one's individual belief system, heretofore assumed to be the one true religion.

Part three returns us to Mary Magdalene, beginning with these haunting words: "They have taken away my Lord, a person/ whose life I held inside me." The lines are suggestive of Mary, mother of Jesus, but in fact they express the central tenet of the Christian religion that the person of Christ, through the work of the Holy Spirit, dwells within the believer. But then we discover that the *speaker* of part three is not Mary Magdalene herself but the narrator, for she is picturing what happened to Mary through her own reconstruction of biblical events: "I watched him reveal himself risen/to Magdalene with a single word: 'Mary!'" The word, then, is not to her or for her. No one calls her name out of the absence. The past tense of the final stanza evokes an aching sense of loss:

> It was my habit to speak to him. His goodness
> perfumed my life. I loved the Lord, he heard
> my cry, and he loved me as his own.[36]

In "Gerontion," T. S. Eliot provides a portrait of enormous spiritual loss suffered because of the compulsion to scrutinize everything from a rational viewpoint. Gerontion admits,

> I that was near your heart was removed therefrom
> To lose beauty in terror, terror in inquisition.
> I have lost my passion . . .

Gerontion, however, accepts this as irreducible and irremediable fact. It is the direct consequence of "thoughts of a dry brain in a dry season." The narrator of "Woman, Why Are You Weeping?", on the other hand, writes in spiritual anguish over her sense of loss.

In part four the scene shifts abruptly to India. Sharp, contrasting images of the streets, the flowers, and the people emerge. In the second of three stanzas, the narrator confesses that she feels alien

---

36. Cf. Psalm 6:9. One of Kenyon's adult notebooks (undated) reveals her love for the Psalms. Among random lines and quotations from other poems, brief quotations from the Psalms appear. The lines from this poem make one mindful of several Davidic psalms. See, for example, Pss. 28:6, 40:1, and 61:1 as other echoes of this passage.

among the Hindu gods also. It is not that she is forsaking one religion for another; rather, the issue is whether any religion, including Christianity, has any claim for priority in this world.

Part five continues the images and the bewilderment, but also
narrows to her own place in the world. Is it merely by random circumstance that she lives in New England rather than India? Not
only her religion but also her personhood has been distorted. She
has lost her Lord; she has lost herself.

Part six relates the culminating event, the same one rendered
in prose in her journal. The emotional tone now is flat, devoid of
drama. The scene is rendered matter-of-factly, mirroring the narrator's complete helplessness:

> Rajiv did not weep. He did not cover
> his face with his hands when we rowed past
> the dead body of a newborn nudging the grassy
> banks at Benares . . .

The tone is matter-of-fact for a simple reason. This — the giving of
the infant to the river — is as much a reality of Indian life as the
soaring images of the street life, the flowers, the gods. The fact is
that the family of this baby was too poor to cremate the corpse; thus,
the Ganges received it. The shaken narrator turns inward:

> "What shall we do about this?" I asked
> my God, who even then was leaving me. The reply
> was scorching wind, lapping of water, pull
> of the black oarsmen on the oars. . . .

Instead of the assurance of God's presence, the question is an-
swered by the harsh present.

It is an unnerving poem. Powerful in its imagery and careful
syntactic movement, haunting in its emotional evocations, the
poem seems to be Kenyon's last testament of unbelief. She shakes a
small but very angry fist at an empty sky. This reality has taken her

Lord, and she can no longer find him. It is not mere capitulation to the inevitable but an anguished, Job-like plea.

Although Kenyon finds no necessary and sufficient answers in the poem, she grapples bravely with the significance of Christian belief and *her* belief in this world. Every step of her Christian walk over the last fifteen years led her to this climactic and dangerous point of arduous testing. The Gospel of Mark records the story of a boy ill with convulsions. The boy's father comes to Jesus seeking help. Jesus responds with a challenge: "Everything is possible for him who believes." To which the father cries out, "I do believe; help me overcome my unbelief!" (Mark 9:20-27). One could not say that in this poem Kenyon is pleading, "I believe; help me overcome my unbelief." It would be accurate to say, however, that she struggles with the meaning of belief in her life, and the sometimes overwhelming feeling of unbelief.

External factors may qualify her particular feelings at this point in her life. For example, her depressive episodes, which will be discussed later in the context of several poems, were growing ever more frequent and dark. Perhaps the questions surrounding "Woman, Why Are You Weeping?" may best be resolved by her friend Alice Mattison, who had originally raised angry questions about the poem. When Kenyon traveled to Seattle for a bone-marrow transplant and endured the vicious pain of radiation, the two talked on the phone. They had talked previously about the phenomenon that when one acquires bone marrow, one also acquires a part of the donor's blood type and immunity. Mattison recalls the conversation and the two old verities by which she tested the personhood of her friend:

> When Jane said she felt like someone else, I couldn't quite take her seriously, but I also did take her seriously. "Do you still believe in God?" I asked her.
>
> "Yes."
>
> "Do you still believe that the natural object is always the adequate symbol?"

52

"Passionately," said Jane.

She hadn't changed all that much, so I asked if she still loved me. That week, we thought she'd live.[37]

The dialogue speaks powerfully about Kenyon's belief, as much as she struggled with it. It is the human process, as she said in her interview with Bill Moyers, of searching for "a great goodness."

JANE KENYON'S LIFE cannot be weighed by one work. Rather, one sees her life as a tapestry woven by threads of enormous vitality and compassion. Although shy by nature, she entered readily into the fellowship of her church. She relished nature, particularly the surrounding emerald fields of the farm and the blue eye of Eagle Pond. Walking the north trail of Eagle Pond, standing near the downward rush of cold water over granite boulders in the heart of the stream, one can see Mount Kearsarge, starker and grayer than the surrounding hills, shouldering upward in the distance. Standing by the birdfeeders alongside the farmhouse, watching the dip of an oriole past the barn, one can sense that this was Kenyon's true world — a refuge from the realities she bravely confronted. But it was also a safe place from which to deal with the realities of personal loss as well as loss in the world.

If there is any true testimony to Jane Kenyon's spirit and person, it lies in the legacy of her art. "For me," she once said, "poetry's a safe place always, a refuge, and it has been since I took it up in the eighth grade, so it was natural for me to write about these things that were going on in my own soul."[38] She made that comment specifically in regard to *From Room to Room*. But it also held true for the years thereafter, when she continued to roam the rooms — often giddy with pleasure, sometimes troubled and disconsolate — of her

37. Mattison, "'Let It Grow in the Dark Like a Mushroom,'" p. 137. Mattison describes the slogan "The natural object is always the adequate symbol," taken from Ezra Pound's *Make It New*, as "the closest thing we had to a group creed" (p. 127).

38. Kenyon, *A Hundred White Daffodils*, p. 145.

soul. In a sense, Kenyon sought to lead a very unremarkable life — to be close to the husband and the daily routines she deeply loved.[39] But life wouldn't have it that way. Not when bipolar disorder twisted her brain chemistry like the jerking of a giant roller-coaster; not when the world unveiled its hard secrets — a dead baby floating in the Ganges. Still, she could always come back to the safe haven of her poetry.

Like her favored Keats, Kenyon packed all the living she could into her brief lifetime. She once remarked that Keats's "Ode to a Nightingale" was the most "nearly perfect" poem in the English language. Certain lines from that poem seem to echo Kenyon's thoughts. Keats addresses the bird as its song fades away into the woods with these words:

> Fade far away, dissolve, and quite forget
> What thou among the leaves hast never known,
> The weariness, the fever, and the fret
> Here, where men sit and hear each other groan . . .

But the great affirmation for Keats in the poem is this: to escape the pain of this world is also to escape its beauty. That beauty holds one to this place. To this world Kenyon constantly returned, seeking its beauty, finding it in surprising places, and capturing it in her poems.

---

39. She and Hall did grow closer after they moved to the farm — something that Hall commented on specifically: "It was here that the marriage particularly flourished and blossomed and became magnificent."

CHAPTER THREE

The Poet at Work

When Jane Kenyon told Bill Moyers that "Let Evening Come" was "given" to her by "the muse, the Holy Ghost," she was not suggesting that the poem derived from some rhapsodic inspiration and that she was a mere vessel through which the words flowed.[1] It is true that Kenyon herself was surprised at how "rapidly" the poem came, a word she used to describe its process to Donald Hall. From the start it held a conceptual wholeness and tonal unity that guided the stages of drafting and revision. Nonetheless, Kenyon still invested the full resources of her poetic craft in that drafting and revision. Writing poetry demanded hard and routine labor on a regular

---

1. While discussing her writing methods with David Bradt, Kenyon explained,

> If I showed you a poem with all of its drafts, you could see for yourself how the language changes, how the poem grows and comes into focus, pulls together. At first it's a kind of blind activity. Things come to me when I'm in a certain frame of mind. I sometimes have the feeling that I'm taking dictation. Words suggest themselves. Sometimes I'm not entirely sure of their meaning myself, so I look them up and find that maybe on some deep level I *did* know what that word means, and it just happens to be the *perfect* word. There's a tremendous sense, when I'm working well, that I'm getting a big boost from somewhere. I couldn't tell you where. (*A Hundred White Daffodils* [Saint Paul, Minn.: Graywolf Press, 1999], pp. 176-77)

basis. It meant that she gave herself up to her tools — perception and language — for the sake of the reader. Poetry was nothing less than an offering of her very best.

In his scrambled religious state, Robert Frost wondered several times if poetry would be a sufficient offering on the altar to get him into heaven. He feared that even his "best offering may not prove acceptable in his sight."[2] T. S. Eliot had similarly lofty — albeit more humanly directed — goals for the poet's task. The "familiar compound ghost" of *Little Gidding* asserts,

> Our concern was speech, and speech impelled us
> to purify the dialect of the tribe
> and urge the mind to aftersight and foresight.

For Eliot, each word encapsulated truth; the poet erected the structure of words in such an architecture that, as the reader examined it, he or she grew mindful of the truths the poet had discovered.

Perhaps Kenyon's goals were less loftily stated. She did not see her poetry as a divine act — an offering unto God. Nor did she see her poetry as a conveyor of truth to the general mind (that is, a didactic tool). She sought above all penetrating lyrics of passionate beauty, words that the poem could not live without, imagery so crystalline that the reader could trace his or her own life in it. Above all, she cherished honesty. These goals informed her labor. Nevertheless, in interviews, addresses, and letters she did construct specific principles and guidelines for that labor. Before engaging those principles, however, it may be best to examine Kenyon's craft, considering her use of imagery, literary devices, melody, and language.

Kenyon's imagery may well be described as elemental. Although her poems often trip the reader into speculation, the imagery itself roots solidly in the material things of this earth. This pat-

2. Frost, *Selected Letters of Robert Frost*, ed. Lawrence Thompson (New York: Holt, Rinehart & Winston, 1964), p. 525. This quotation is taken from a letter to G. R. Elliot, and is only one of several in which Frost expresses a similar sentiment. See, for example, pp. 413, 530, 555.

tern is well demonstrated in the volume *Let Evening Come,* which moves through the seasonal cycles of life at Eagle Pond Farm. Since the experience of seasons belongs to all of us, we as readers find the poems very accessible. Through them we experience what is intuitively felt to be true because the imagery is grounded in the world we know. Once homed in such familiar patterns, we more willingly assent to where the poems lead.

Precisely at this point the "luminous particular" that Kenyon sought comes into play, for by it Kenyon locates the reader in this world with meticulous particularity. Kenyon used the term to describe Anna Akhmatova's poetic art and its startling ability to capture the reader by means of a sharply defined image or metaphor. The "luminosity" is that casting off of light through the concrete, that illumination of the reader's mind.

Early in the writing process, Kenyon added words and images and tried out options in margins, providing the fullest portrait possible. In the later stages of revision, the process dramatically reversed. Kenyon crossed out words, details, and entire lines as she narrowed the focus to the essential. She polished the work of all rough edges, focusing particularly on the precision of the imagery.

The fundamental attitude of nearly all poets toward imagery is encapsulated in the caveat "Show, don't tell." Instead of naming emotions, incarnate them in things or events. In "Ars Poetica," Archibald MacLeish put it like this:

> A poem should be palpable and mute
> As a globed fruit . . .
>
> A poem should not mean
> But be.

Often, however, this attitude toward imagery is simply accepted without demonstrable reason. Why has this opinion become a fundamental article of faith among modern poets? And how did it shape Kenyon's craft? The answer may be found a century earlier among the American Fireside Poets.

For nearly a full century, these poets — William Cullen Bryant (1794-1878), Henry Wadsworth Longfellow (1807-1882), John Greenleaf Whittier (1807-1892), and Oliver Wendell Holmes (1809-1894) — held sway over the American literary scene. They were the Literary Men of Importance, the Czars of Culture. Their tasks were to entertain and to instruct. Because they held the prominent chairs by the fireside for almost a century, there was little room for dissenting voices. Dissent to what, though? First, to the loose and sprawling narrative, often driven by the chugging engine of strict metrics and rhyme patterns. And second, to their frequent use of didacticism (reducing reality to simple nuggets of moralizing) and sentimentality: using feelings and emotions in the work for their own sake — putting them on display, if you will.

Precisely such issues fueled the turn-of-the-century American modernists — T. S. Eliot, E. A. Robinson, Ezra Pound, and, arguably, Robert Frost. Each wanted to return the work to reality. Not surprisingly, Kenyon herself cites Eliot as a model: "Almost always if I search I can find something in the natural world — an objective correlative in Eliot's phrase — that embodies what I'm feeling at the moment. That's when a poem really takes off."[3] But the issue requires qualification in Kenyon's case, for she realized that employing sentimentality was a far different thing than expressing sentiments — one's beliefs, disquietude, joy, sorrow, and so forth.[4] In fact, the ever-increasing readership of Kenyon's work is due in part

3. Kenyon, *A Hundred White Daffodils*, p. 177.

4. In an interview with Dave Barney, Donald Hall provided a useful definition of sentimentality:

> When I use the word "sentimentality," I mean the appeal to an emotion without foundation for it. I find much narcissism in contemporary poetry, the notion that anything that happens to the poet is automatically interesting. Any anecdote of one's life can become a narcissistic inwardness. I don't put down inwardness, but it becomes perverted. I guess I tend to find narcissism more of a pervading vice in contemporary poetry than sentimentality.

See "Happy Men in Desert Places: An Interview with Donald Hall," *Southern Humanities Review* 22, no. 3 (1988): 233.

to the way she admits readers to the emotional experiences and beliefs of her world. Rather than throwing sentiments at the reader, Kenyon asks, "Do you see anything of yourself in here?"

The Poet's Craft

Concerned to avoid sentimentality, Kenyon was adamant that the emotion be embodied in the particular. Donald Hall observed that this belief solidified during Kenyon's work translating the great Russian poet Anna Akhmatova: "As she worked with Akhmatova's early lyrics, condensations of strong feeling into compact images both visual and aural, she practiced making the kind of poetry she admired most — an art that embodied powerful emotion by means of the luminous particular."[5] In "The Suitor," for example, Kenyon moves from the concrete reality to emotions bound in a tight harness of similes. The brief, eleven-line poem flashes like serendipity. Indeed, that is its subject matter.[6]

In "The Suitor" Kenyon uses simile not simply for poetic effect but also to direct the action of the poem itself. The poem opens with two people lying in bed in early morning light. At the open windows, curtains "lift and fall,/like the chest of someone sleeping." In this sentence (three lines) the simile directs the poem just slightly outward to the windows, but sleep is still heavy in the room. In the next sentence (four lines), the narrator's vision moves beyond the immediate and concrete visual setting of the bedroom to an imaginative vision beyond the window. In fact, the very wind that lifts the curtains becomes her guide, drawing her out. Beyond the window the wind moves the leaves of the box elder:

5. Hall, introduction to *A Hundred White Daffodils*, p. x.
6. Even though I propose a tie to beliefs that solidified during Kenyon's work on Akhmatova, which she did in New Hampshire, it is very likely that Kenyon wrote "The Suitor" while still in Ann Arbor.

> they show their light undersides,
> turning all at once
> like a school of fish.

The simile itself is light and delicate, like the wind. Then the wind, in the final four lines, blows lightly back upon the narrator, who seems of a piece with the airy imagery. "Suddenly I understand that I am happy," she announces. The emotion of happiness has already been the subject of the poem through its descriptive imagery. The narrator's statement simply confirms that for the reader. More significant, however, is her complete surprise at the emotion, evident in the way Kenyon shapes the final simile:

> For months this feeling
> has been coming closer, stopping
> for short visits, like a timid suitor.

This is not a poem of ecstatic release of emotion; rather, it reveals the delightful discovery of happiness through the unveiling power of the similes. That crafting permits the reader to say, "Yes, I see. This is what it is like for me also."

Kenyon employs the metaphor as artfully as the simile. Indeed, she will use a metaphor of such intensity that it nearly captures the entire poem in one breathless moment. In "Cesarean" she writes,

> The surgeon with his unapologetic
> blade parted darkness, revealing
> day.

Here the act of the cesarean is concentrated in three quick lines, but the suggestiveness of the metaphor carries the rest of the poem. The surgeon's parting of darkness and day is a God-like act. The blade is "unapologetic" because the surgeon-God has no need to apologize for bringing forth the gift of life. And as the poet's "small clay" is lifted from her mother's "large clay," the microcosmic world of the operating room erupts into white light and shouting. Kenyon wisely leaves it unstated, but at this point the reader senses an angelic choir heralding the new light of this life.

Because Kenyon concentrated on the lyric form in her poetry, a variety of sound patterns also appear in her work. One of Kenyon's favorite technical devices is enjambment. It permits a line to stop both meaningfully and syntactically, then surprises the reader by carrying both meaning and syntax into the next line, effectively making the lines work double time — as a whole moment and as an ongoing movement. The technique, very likely influenced by Kenyon's training in music, often opens a whole new way of seeing the situation she is describing or provides a clever response to the presumed situation of the prior line.

In "Three Songs at the End of Summer" we find these lines:

> The cicada's dry monotony breaks
> over me.

Read as a complete unit, the first line merely suggests that the cicada's monotonous noise finally ends. But the enjambment into the second line changes the meaning entirely. It places the poet directly on the scene, where the monotony breaks over her like a cloud of sound. Similarly, Kenyon will use enjambment to extend an image. In the first stanza of "February: Thinking of Flowers," she describes the windswept, snowy fields. In the second stanza she then moves from a rather abstract declaration to a specific picture, then to a metaphor:

> Nothing but white — the air, the light;
> only one brown milkweed pod
> bobbing in the gully, smallest
> brown boat on the immense tide.

Here the enjambment of the third line startlingly turns the reader's expectations. "Smallest" seems at first reflexive to the milkweed

pod. And it is — but it also turns into the adjective for the concluding metaphor.

Also clearly observable in Kenyon's poetry is the musical lyricism that creates moods ranging from the intense and rhapsodic to
the quietly pastoral. Several things contribute to this lyricism. Most
important, of course, is Kenyon's own acute sensitivity to sound.
She liked to work with assonance and consonance. From "No" we
have these lines:

> It was time to turn away
> from the casket, poised on its silver
> scaffolding over the open hole
> that smelled like a harrowed field.

The lines are quiet, yet the agony of grief infiltrates them as the
casket is about to be lowered into the ground. The major pattern is
the s sound in many of the words chosen: *was, casket, poised, its, sil-*
ver, scaffolding, smelled. With the exception of *casket* and *scaffolding,*
where the s is hardened by the following *k* sound, all the sounds
are soft and comforting. A tension works within this predominant
pattern, however, through the harder *r* sound in *turn, silver, over,*
and *harrowed. Silver* is something of an anomaly, since it starts soft
and ends hard, but the other words are all suggestive of threat. To
"turn away" is to suggest that something is over. The simile of the
harrowed field is rough and disturbing. Most powerful, however,
is the strategic third line, when the casket is about to be lowered
into the ground. Here Kenyon employs the sinking, long *o* four
times, dropping mercilessly into the "hole." Here is the unavoidable reality, conveyed as much by the sounds of the words as by
their meaning.

Kenyon also employs both interior melodies and strategic repetition as musical devices. Seldom does she use end rhyme. When
she does, it sometimes seems almost coincidental, as if she is
rounding off a pattern established interiorly. At other times, the end
rhyme repeats a word in a prior stanza to provide response or clo-

sure to the previous idea. Most frequently, the melody of the poem is carried by variations of vowel sounds.

In *From Room to Room* the poem "In Several Colors" exemplifies many of Kenyon's familiar devices, already well in evidence early in her career:

> Every morning, cup of coffee
> in hand, I look out at the mountain.
> Ordinarily, it's blue, but today
> it's the color of an eggplant.
>
> And the sky turns
> from gray to pale apricot
> as the sun rolls up
> Main Street in Andover.
>
> I study the cat's face
> and find a trace of white
> around each eye, as if
> he made himself up today
> for a part in the opera.

One immediately notices her characteristic use of enjambment in the first two lines. End-stopping the first line suggests a self-defining event. Every morning *is* a cup of coffee. The second line, however, broadens the portrait to include the narrator, holding her cup of coffee in the morning, looking out at the mountain. With the lines pushing one's reading of the poem through enjambment, one hardly recognizes the skillful evocation of mood through interior melody.

The predominant vowel sounds in the first stanza are *o* and *u*. Nearly all are short or attenuated sounds, and they are strongly varied by consonant placement. Such variation makes the one consistent interior rhyme, which is only a variation on the same syllable, all the more pronounced: *morning/ordinarily/color*. Each instance also occurs early in the line like a major note, with the variations following in quick succession to the end of the line.

The second stanza continues the same vowel variation: *turns/ apricot/sun rolls up/Andover.* In the third stanza, however, the musical variations on a single theme suddenly tighten to a finale with a playful and explosive series of perfect rhymes interwoven: *I/face/ trace/white/eye.* For the first time Kenyon works the long vowel sounds. Then the last two lines carry this playful poem to its conclusion by picking up the varied sounds of the first two stanzas. And Kenyon adds a few more deft touches. *For* in the final line picks up the regular interior rhyme of the first stanza. *Today* in the penultimate line also closes off the poem by repeating that end-word from the first stanza.

"In Several Colors" does not stand alone in its careful use of melody. Convincing examples can be found throughout Kenyon's work. The last stanza of "Things" from *The Boat of Quiet Hours,* for example, combines heavier *l* sounds with lighter *a* sounds to create a sense of falling. The play is perfect to the argument of the poem: all things fall into light. The drafts of Kenyon's poems do not show a sustained or even conscious effort to construct such melodic patterns. It seems an intuitive skill, the gift of a brilliantly tuned ear and the felicities of language sounds.

Kenyon uses repetition with the same seemingly intuitive skill. She repeats lines or phrases to produce several powerful effects: to evoke a sense of supplication, to provide a sense of repose and acceptance, or to express and try to understand a baffling struggle with difficult events. John Unterecker was the first, to my knowledge, to make critical observation of this technique. In a review essay that included *The Boat of Quiet Hours,* he comments on "At the Summer Solstice":

The artistry is essentially one of concealments in a poem of this sort: inconspicuous repetitions (when you think of it, the purest form of rhyme) move through from top to bottom, but even in these last few lines we can feel their presence (hot/hot; lightly/

lightly) along with the hidden internal rhymes and partial rhymes (today/stay/shades; room/you; eyes/my/thighs) that account for the most definable elements of its quiet, satisfying music.[7]

Writing about Kenyon's second book of poetry, Unterecker did not have the advantage of seeing the flowering of this musical technique in Kenyon's career. But later poems only prove that his perception was accurate.

In "Inertia" from *The Boat of Quiet Hours*, the initial repetition in the first line of the poem — "My head was heavy, heavy" — not only evokes a mood for the poem but echoes the weighted vowel sound as onomatopoeia to encapsulate the mood itself. Not until line 21 is the repetition fulfilled in meaning: "muddled and heavy-hearted." Here the implied mood is specified to the narrator. A secondary pattern of repetition also moves through the poem, supporting the primary mood of heaviness. In the first stanza the narrator comments that her hands are so heavy that "I had to ask two times/ before my hand would scratch my ear." In the second stanza she juxtaposes her hands with the "enterprising feelers" of the centipede that crawls out from the spine of her dictionary. In the third stanza she returns to her own befuddled and inept hands, then in the final stanza notes how quickly the centipede slithers away. The repetition in the secondary pattern is disjunctive, underscoring the psychological distance of the narrator.

In his essay "Our Lady of Sorrows," Gregory Orr says that Kenyon's use of repetition goes beyond poetic craftsmanship. In fact, much of the dialectic and meaning of the poem lie in the repetition itself:

Certainly story is at the heart of Jane's poems. Incantation is also central to Jane's poems: the magical repetition of phrases

7. Unterecker, "Shape-Changing in Contemporary Poetry," *Michigan Quarterly Review* 27 (1988): 491.

like the rhythmic moans a grieving mother might make. The repetition of a phrase has survival power: "Let evening come. Let evening come." "It might have been otherwise. It might have been otherwise." These incantatory orderings are set against enormous possibilities of disorder.[8]

Perceiving the possibilities of disorder not only in the story of the larger culture but also in the story of her own life renders Kenyon highly vulnerable. Survival, as Orr points out, is both her personal aim and her aim for the reader. She constructs a story in which others may see and read their lives.

Repetition, then, may be seen as a struggle against disorder, a pattern most pronounced, perhaps, in *Let Evening Come.* "Three Songs at the End of Summer," a poem from that volume discussed more fully later in this study, illustrates the pattern. The first song opens with a listing of commonplace events at Eagle Pond Farm. The first stanza of the second song begins with an apparently optimistic repetition: "The days are bright/and free, bright and free." Indeed they are. The narrator has just described them as such. The reader is lulled by the melody before the second stanza cracks like a whip:

> Then why did I cry today
> for an hour, with my whole
> body, the way babies cry?

The conflict between the bright day and her weeping accentuates her vulnerability.

This pattern continues throughout the volume. "Now Where?" shapes an eloquent dirge on melancholy, directed by three introductory repetitions:

8. Orr, "Our Lady of Sorrows," in *Bright, Unequivocal Eye: Poems, Papers, and Remembrances from the First Jane Kenyon Conference*, ed. Bert Hornback (New York: Peter Lang Press, 2000), pp. 31-32.

It wakes when I wake, walks
when I walk, turns back when I
turn back. . . .

Similarly, the third stanza echoes "I lie down," "I lie down," as the narrator fights against succumbing.

The most notable use of repetition occurs, of course, in "Let Evening Come" itself. Here the rhetorical shadings of the lines are so supple that, although the repetition is obvious, the levels of connotative meaning emerge only after the lines have been savored many times. Examination of that exquisite play with language will be reserved for the full discussion of the poem in Chapter Seven. But here it is worth noting how Kenyon employs yet another shading of repetition to offer solace and benediction.

MELODY IN PARTICULAR is directly linked to word choice, and an examination of Kenyon's poetic diction leads to surprising conclusions. In her writing workshops with her friends Joyce Peseroff and Alice Mattison, the three writers often searched for the "right" word. But what characterizes the right word? Appropriateness to context, surely. One might also mention the emotional weight of the word and its precision of description. For Kenyon, however, rightness went beyond these fundamental matters to an exact linguistic fittingness between word and image and hence between word and reader.

Marie Borroff's illuminating study *Language and the Poet* provides a helpful paradigm for considering Kenyon's selection of words and to what ends she uses them. Since the argument here will require some linguistic tabulation, I accept Borroff's caution: "It is not my view that tabulations of linguistic detail will of themselves yield an understanding of the all-important relationship between what a poem expresses and how it is expressed."[9] That latter

---

9. Borroff, *Language and the Poet: Verbal Artistry in Frost, Stevens, and Moore* (Chicago: University of Chicago Press, 1979), p. 24.

understanding is essentially a matter of style, meaning, and method, and includes such matters as imagery patterns, literary devices, character, and setting. Nevertheless, tabulation of word origins does reveal something of the poet's mind and art. Why this word instead of another that might work just as well? For a poet who labored as assiduously over revisions as Kenyon did, it is not an empty question.

Two defining qualities of Kenyon's language should be established to frame this discussion. First, readers are often struck by the conversational tone and accessible settings of the poems. The familiarity of language and setting, in fact, often disguises the sophisticated technical artistry. The reader moves into the story and is hardly aware of how he or she entered it. Borroff makes the same point about Robert Frost's poetry:

> We [readers] see that the story being told is "true" in the sense that it could have happened to us in the world as we know it. The scene in which it takes place is familiar to us, whether at first or second hand, and can be easily visualized. The manner of the telling is not realistic (the poem does not sound like a tape-recorded anecdote) . . . it is too clear and concise for that. Yet the details of the narrative are presented in a simple, down-to-earth manner, by a speaker who does not set himself apart from us.[10]

These qualities apply almost uniformly to Kenyon's poetry. Even when we are in places that are not familiar to us, either by circumstance or by setting — such as in "Having it Out with Melancholy" and "Woman, Why Are You Weeping?" — the nature of Kenyon's clear, direct, realistic telling allows us intimate access to the events of the poem.

Second, the language of the poems — even when they deal with complex issues — appears to be quite simple. It is not bookish or eru-

10. Borroff, *Language and the Poet*, pp. 7-8.

dite; it tends toward the vernacular. Clearly this lends emphasis to Kenyon's delight in the present experience. But a closer examination of the actual word stock she is using reveals the close deliberation involved in her language choices.

Simplicity in language can be defined in several ways. As Borroff points out, "The most obvious objective correlative of 'simplicity' in language is word length — the frequency, for instance, of lines made up wholly of monosyllables, and a corresponding infrequency of words of three syllables or more."[11] Syllable count, however, is of limited worth in examining a poetic work, and only acquires relative merit when other technical elements are factored in. For example, "Credo," Part 8 of Kenyon's "Having it Out with Melancholy," has an unusually high percentage of monosyllabic words. The entire poem is spare as the emotions unravel, but this section strikes the reader as particularly jarring. Linking the spareness of worn emotions to the spareness of language appears to be an easy connection to make. "Credo" contains a total of 83 words. Of these, 63, or 75.9 percent, are monosyllabic; 17, or 20.5 percent, are disyllabic; and only 3, or 3.6 percent, are polysyllabic. The spareness of the syllabification is extraordinary.

In and of itself, however, syllable count is too limited a tool to be very useful in this analysis. It is when we look at syllable count in combination with something like word arrangement that it is more substantively revealing. The majority of the multisyllable words in "Credo," for example, fall in the first stanza, starting with the long, five-syllable "Pharmaceutical" followed by the disyllabic "wonders." In the second stanza things fall apart at the predicted coming of the "Unholy ghost," and here the monosyllabic words pile up, in sharp, short phrases, verb structures, and descriptive units that hit like machine-gun fire. We meet the ghost through whiplash adjectives: "Coarse, mean." Then the narrator spits out the trinity of actions the ghost will take when it comes to possess her again:

11. Borroff, *Language and the Poet*, p. 23.

you'll put your feet
on the coffee table, lean back,
and turn me into someone . . .

Each of the verbs describing the ghost's actions are monosyllables. But what will the effect be on the narrator? She will be possessed by a being she doesn't want to be — a being with no being. The three negative verbs that follow match the monosyllabic action of the ghost: "can't take," "can't sleep," "can't read." It is the chant of hopelessness.

Merely counting syllables, then, is not enough. Many variables — such as the strategic placement of different-syllabled words, the author's use of rhythm and pacing, and internal conflicts — guide the poetic process and give it pattern. It is true, nonetheless, that Kenyon uses a slightly higher percentage of monosyllabic and di-syllabic words to achieve a conversational tone. In this regard, she more closely resembles Robert Frost than, say, Wallace Stevens; Elizabeth Bishop than Marianne Moore.

A more profitable way to define simplicity in poetry is accord-ing to word choice, particularly choices between the two primary contributors to our word stock: Old and Middle English on the one hand, and Romance and Latinate derivatives on the other. As one examines Kenyon's word choices, one discovers an overwhelming pattern of Old and Middle English derivations. In fact, the pattern is so striking that it almost seems that Kenyon deliberately screened the Romance-Latinate diction. Someone might point out that Kenyon was a French major at the University of Michigan before she became an English major. With that background, she would be aware enough of the word stock to screen it at will. Why would she want to? First, to mine the fundamental simplicity of the basic word stock of our language; and second, to use language with an elemen-tal quality to match the elemental quality of her imagery. Kenyon's imagery is earth-rooted; so too is her poetic diction. According to Borroff, percentiles of ten or lower from Romance-Latinate stock indicate a very low or plain style — deliberately so in the modern era. Borroff says that such numbers represent the "extreme low."[12] And this describes Kenyon's poetry: extremely high use of Old and Middle English derivations (with the exception of occasional use of Greek, Sanskrit, Old Norse, and other derivations), and extremely low use of Romance-Latinate stock.

Consider an abbreviated statistical analysis of several poems that will be discussed elsewhere in this study. "August Rain, After Haying" has a total of 101 words. Of these, 82 are Old English, 2 are Old English compounds, and 1 is Middle English — a total of 84.2 percent. Words with Romance-Latinate origins make up 10.9 percent. The percentages are in keeping with the elemental images of farm life described here, but also with the baptismal imagery of the middle and final stanzas. "Briefly It Enters, and Briefly Speaks" is an interesting poem linguistically because it reveals a substantially broader word base, including Greek, Sanskrit, and Gaelic. The total word count of 144, however, still includes 82.8 percent of Old and Middle English words and 11.1 percent of Romance-Latinate words. "Evening Sun," a poem evoking Kenyon's childhood and filled with the most elemental imagery and description, should not surprise us with its percentages of 81.4 for Old and Middle English words and a scant 8.1 for Latinate words. Finally, the plaintive "Otherwise" creates its wistful tone with an elegant simplicity of idea and language. The poem moves through staggered accents and irregular lines, the longest of which is only seven syllables. One senses the feeling of mortality in its very structure. That feeling is reinforced by the language. Of the 103 words in the poem, 86.4 percent are Old English or Old English compounds, and a mere 7.8 percent are Latinate.

SEVERAL POETIC TOOLS, then, are critically important for Kenyon. Her imagery is inescapably earth-bound, thus creating an accessible world for her readers to enter. The bridge to her poetic world is enhanced by the literary devices of simile and metaphor. And almost all of her poems reveal her skill with such devices as

---

12. Borroff, *Language and the Poet*, p. 24.

enjambment, caesura, assonance, consonance, and repetition to shape melodious patterns. Finally, Kenyon matches her diction to her imagery for a consistent poetic experience by relying heavily upon a "plain" style, marked predominantly by an Old English and Middle English word stock. Instead of relying on the more refined and abstract Latinate-Romance diction, Kenyon derives the stunning power of her poems from the vivid image, the clear, cutting portrait, and the always inviting tone of her narrative voice.

The Poet's Purpose

While several key elements shaped the craft of Kenyon's work as a poet, she also held certain fundamental beliefs about poetry and the poet. The first was her abiding belief that poetry matters. It is worth the labor of writing; it is worth the pleasure and insight given. Kenyon described this "mattering" of poetry at some length in her 1993 interview with David Bradt:

> It matters because it's beautiful. It matters because it tells the truth, the human truth about the complexity of life. As Akhmatova says, "It is joy and it is pain." It tells the entire truth about what it is to be alive, about the way of the world, about life and death. Art embodies that complexity and makes it more understandable, less frightening, less bewildering. It matters because it is consolation in times of trouble. Even when a poem addresses a painful subject, it still manages to be consoling, somehow, if it's a good poem. Poetry has an unearthly ability to turn suffering into beauty.[13]

Kenyon made her own emphatic commitment to bring poetry to the people, to demonstrate that it "matters," by giving gratis readings in schools and libraries. She encouraged other New Hampshire artists

13. Kenyon, *A Hundred White Daffodils*, p. 175.

to follow suit in "A Proposal for New Hampshire Writers," which she wrote in 1992. "Art," she argues there, "is for everybody." And to other writers she offers this challenge: "Our job is to see that the flame not only doesn't go out, but that it shines in the windows of the libraries or town hall or grange for one or two or three evenings in the coming months."[14]

One might be tempted to summarize Kenyon's view as "art matters because it is." An insufficient apologia, to be sure, and one that she thoroughly tempered in her thoughtful comments in the Bradt interview. There is little question that Kenyon elevated the task of the poet and of poetry itself. Already at the University of Michigan she was forcibly struck by Robert Bly's view of poetry as a "public moral force."[15] Indeed, Kenyon herself once explained that she had for many years seen the poet as having "an almost priestly function."[16] It is not surprising that she made such a statement. A tone of the intercessory and confessional lilts through many of her poems.

Kenyon felt strongly that it was not for her to elucidate the "poet's task" as a theoretician.[17] Her task was to make that climb up to her study and write. Yet her occasional reflections on the subject, often whimsically stated, shape a fascinating road map of her perceptions. In "Poetry and the Mail," for example, she writes,

> What a weird impulse writing is in the first place — to make something out of memory and observation, out of emotion and thought, utterance and silence, the stated and the implied. *Out of nothing*, as a woman once said to me at a cocktail party. Yes, I thought to myself immodestly — just as God created the world.

14. Kenyon, *A Hundred White Daffodils*, p. 137.

15. Kenyon, *A Hundred White Daffodils*, p. 133.

16. Kenyon, *A Hundred White Daffodils*, p. 162.

17. Donald Hall's place in literary theory and criticism was, of course, well established before their marriage. His most important essays on art are collected in *Poetry and Ambition*. One could safely assume that Kenyon was fully aware of these theories as they critiqued each other's poems.

We try to say exactly what we mean, to put the exact word in the
exact place — and then we take it out to the mailbox and put up
the red flag.[18]

If the impulse is "weird," the product is not — which Kenyon acknowledges when she describes literature as "the garden of our inward life." Again, she notes, "Artists report on the inner life, and
the inner life distinguishes us from centipedes, although I may un-
derestimate centipedes."[19] Kenyon nurtured her own inner life
through the natural beauty of Eagle Pond Farm, and her aim in her
poetry was to recreate this place — and the sense of wonder it in-
stilled — for the reader: "Poets renew for us the awe we feel at creation."[20]

Kenyon also believed that poetry has a corporate and com-
memorative function. In her interview with Bill Moyers, Kenyon
commented, "One of the functions of poetry is to keep the memory
of people and places and things and happenings alive."[21] This is
not merely the preservation of the poet's own experiences, although it surely includes that. Rather, poetry serves a larger purpose: like Greek drama, it becomes the voice of a nation's experiences. "Art," Kenyon said, "is the mirror of the soul, individual and
national. It tells us who we are, where we're going, what's valuable
and what isn't."[22]

These are lofty beliefs. Common to all of them is the sense
that poetry constitutes a "going forth" to others, an opening of one's
own perceptions and emotions to encourage others to find corre-
spondences there. If Kenyon saw poetry as a "public moral force"
and the poet serving "an almost priestly function," the purpose of
each was to enter the lives of others, if only for a moment. If she
saw poetry as the garden of the inward life, it was to help others dis-

18. Kenyon, *A Hundred White Daffodils*, p. 129.
19. Kenyon, *A Hundred White Daffodils*, pp. 136, 138.
20. Kenyon, *A Hundred White Daffodils*, p. 181.
21. Kenyon, *A Hundred White Daffodils*, p. 164.
22. Kenyon, *A Hundred White Daffodils*, p. 173.

cover the beauty or discern the weeds in their inward lives. And if she sought to keep memory alive, it was to mirror those memories — sometimes joyful, sometimes filled with fear and pain — in others. So Kenyon had clear — though unprogrammatic — beliefs about the poet's place and purpose. These were complemented by several very specific principles she held for herself as a poet.

The Poet's Principles

In her interview with David Bradt, Kenyon was asked, "What's the poet's job?" One might expect a routine answer to the question — but that's not what Kenyon gave. With remarkable precision, she outlined a set of principles that guided her artmaking:

> The poet's job is to tell the whole truth and nothing but the truth, in such a beautiful way that people cannot live without it; to put into words those feelings we all have that are so deep, so important, and yet so difficult to name. The poet's job is to find a name for everything; to be a fearless finder of the names of things; to be an advocate for the beauty of language, the subtleties of language. I think it's very serious stuff, art; it's not just decoration. The other job the poet has is to console in the face of the inevitable disintegration of loss and death, all of the tough things we have to face as humans. We have the consolation of beauty, of one soul extending to another soul and saying, "I've been there too."[23]

This statement is so compact, in fact, that we need to break it down into its constituent parts in order to appreciate the whole.

Five key elements appear. The first is that the poet is a truth-teller. Kenyon would settle for nothing less than absolute honesty in her work, a principle that in itself set her apart from the senti-

---

23. Kenyon, *A Hundred White Daffodils*, pp. 183-84.

mentalist. Even when her personal anguish is most evident, as in "Having it Out with Melancholy," her poetry is superbly controlled so that the truth of the *event* is foremost.

The second task of the poet is to render the truth in beauty. If one hears an echo of John Keats's "Ode on a Grecian Urn" here, it is not coincidental. Kenyon gloried in the beauty of Keats's verse. Her point, however, rises above the echo to a more general aesthetic principle: art is something we cannot live without. This is not simply because it enriches our lives but because it is essential for our well-being. Without it, life is sterile and gray.

One of the reasons that art is essential is that it rescues us from routine and automation. It resurrects feelings in us that we often bury in slavish devotion to daily tasks and demands. Hence the third task of the poet is to locate and evoke those feelings that are important to us because they define us as humans rather than robots. In her writing, Flannery O'Connor sought to fight against the deadening effects of robotic routine. In *Mystery and Manners*, she distinguishes between mere routine and what she called "troubled seeking." She sought the latter, she said, because if the artist gives only the routine, it serves merely to perpetuate people's manners, which express their deep-seated problems — their unanswered questions, their quiet desperation, their essential human hollowness. While Kenyon had something of the same idea, her method steered to a polar opposite from that of O'Connor. While O'Connor painted disturbing portraits of the grotesque to jar readers into "troubled seeking" after the mysteries of life, Kenyon sought to create an art of such profound and expressive beauty that it would create in readers a longing for lives that are meaningful beyond routine.

To that end, the poet's fourth task is naming. Not only does she stimulate longing through beauty; she also directs that longing through naming. In Kenyon's aesthetics, suggestiveness is insufficient. But neither does she simply declare. Didacticism is at odds with everything she does as a poet. Naming, then, should be understood as capturing the force of a specific emotion in a specific situation. If imagery universalizes sentiment, event particularizes it —

hence the infinite care Kenyon pays to the particular. It is not just any garden; it is a garden of peonies. They are not just any peonies; they are white peonies smashed by a hard storm and now trailing avenues of ants. If naming lies in the particular event, it also lies in finding the exact word. With a nearly religious sensibility, Kenyon evokes the essences of things by seeking out the right words for them. This is not merely a matter of glossing a dictionary — although half a dozen of them headed her desk. Rather, it is the act of finding the precise words that bring meaning to life in the poem.

Finally, the poet's job extends beyond the poem to bring consolation. "Extends beyond" implies a poet-reader connection, but it is the poet's job to establish that connection within the poem itself. Here is where, in Kenyon's words, the poem gets to be "very serious stuff." Poetry enables a communal meeting of sensibilities; through it the poet gives expression to a psychological or spiritual state that the reader can recognize and share in. As Kenyon put it, "We have the consolation of beauty, of one soul extending to another soul and saying, 'I've been there too.'"

Here we see the specific poetic principles guiding Kenyon's work: emotion embodied in the particular, the supremacy of the luminous image, and the pentad of truth, beauty, naming, evocation of feelings, and consolation. A discussion of such principles, however, is insufficient without a consideration of the poet and her work — her work habits and her rich but challenging relationships with her closest critics.

The Poet at Work

Unless unusual events such as a trip or an illness intervened, Kenyon's daily routine was firmly established. Awakening early, she would leave the house with Gus, her dog (a mixed breed who was mostly retriever), to walk a few miles up Mount Ragged or around Eagle Pond Farm. On her return, she might do a few chores, eat breakfast, and then climb the back stairs off the kitchen to her study. She would work there all morning, dividing her attention among three or four poems in progress rather than working on just one for the long haul. If the writing went well, she would break for lunch, then head back to the study. If she felt she had exhausted the muse for the day, she would turn to chores. If it was a nice day, she would work all afternoon in her gardens. And, of course, she reserved plenty of time for reading and correspondence.

After Kenyon had completed numerous drafts of several poems, she always gave them to Hall as her first reader.[24] She would reach a point in the creative process where she would want his opinion in order to move forward. "I reach the point where I just can't see one more thing to do with a poem," she explained in an interview. "I've poked and poked. Yet I sense that it needs more. Even if I think it is finished, I still want Don to confirm my opinion."[25] Hall would give Kenyon his poems to read as well. But this was not an exercise in which they simply praised one another's work. Each read the other's poems with a critical eye and made suggestions for improvement. The fact is that they were both extraordinarily gifted poets, but in their own highly individual ways; they were fundamentally different as writers. Nonetheless, each often provided the other with that random insight that opened a door for refining or completing a poem. Inevitably, of course, there were times when they disagreed about the work. In his introduction to *Bright, Unequivocal Eye,* Hall recalls such an instance:

> It was natural that we did not always like each other's poems. I remember Jane sitting on the sofa reading through the manuscript of a collection of mine, with tears in her eyes, saying, "Perkins, I don't *like* it." I wept also, saying, "It's all right. It's all right." It had to be all right.

24. A detailed description of the working relationship between Hall and Kenyon appears in their joint interview with Marian Blue. See *A Hundred White Daffodils,* pp. 185-88.

25. Kenyon, *A Hundred White Daffodils,* p. 188.

78

We loathed it when others compared us as poets: Comparisons violated boundaries. When we were first married and few people knew her work, men (it was always men) condescended to her. "Have you *published?*" Once an English professor asked Jane, "Don't you feel *dwarfed?*" Later, a few let us know that Jane's poems were better than mine. This observation was as chauvinist as the other: "She's younger, she's female, and she's *still* better. Ha, ha."[26]

Their relationship may best be understood as a *community* of two writers who held in common their mutual calling as poets. Within the safe precincts of that community, the rare ability to trust, to speak critically but not unkindly about each other's work, flowered.

What kinds of comments might Hall make on Kenyon's work? His practiced eye always picked out certain words and constructions: "I cross out a line or a word. I'll take out all her particles. She isn't allowed to say 'was making.' I write in 'made.' That's one of my tics."[27]

But Kenyon didn't show her work to Hall until she had worked her way through many drafts replete with her own marginal and interlinear comments. When Kenyon worked on "The Bat," for example, Hall's input was critical and substantive — but she did a great deal of revising on her own first. Through all the versions of it, Kenyon retained the first-person narration, but in the early drafts she worked hard to replace mention of that narrator with concrete, objective description. Thus, in the third draft, she made a critical change in the first lines of the second stanza:

> I really do hope that the universe
> is intelligible to the rational mind —

becomes

26. Hall, introduction to *Bright, Unequivocal Eye*, p. 2.
27. Hall, in *A Hundred White Daffodils*, p. 27.

> Maybe the universe is
> intelligible to the rational mind —

Shifting the weight from the mystified narrator to the larger mystery of the universe itself sets up the ambiguity of the final stanza, where the reality of the bat and the mystery of the Holy Spirit fuse. But that fusion itself provided Kenyon with considerable challenges. In the same draft, the final stanza appears like this:

> It [We] seemed to be getting us nowhere.
> [It was about] like trying to understand
> the third person in the trinity,
> the one who spoke through the prophets,
> the one who even now
> is in our midst.

In the fourth draft, the focus shifts from "we" to the bat as agent. Again, the narrator removes herself from center stage, letting specific events speak for the poem. The fifth draft bears only minor internal changes, but Kenyon has heavily inked the margins with alternative possibilities. In subsequent drafts, she turned her attention repeatedly to the final stanza, "poking," as she said, for possibilities. She finally submitted the thirteenth draft to Hall for reading, with the final stanza now shaped like this:

> Like the identity of the third person
> in the trinity: the one who spoke
> through the prophets, the one who
> even now is in our midst.

In Hall's handwriting two suggestions appear. First, to omit "in the encyclopedia" in the first stanza of that draft. Second, to omit or revise everything after "prophets" in the last stanza. His marginal notation reads, "Omit? Or make it clearer. As it reads, it seems as if the third person is just the bat. But this isn't mysterious, rather low.

It should be the bat *plus* something else."[28] That "something else" arrived when Kenyon added the Holy Spirit's astonishing appearance to Mary. In so doing she also crafted her own expression of the Spirit's prophetic voice along with the manifestation to Mary.

Kenyon's revision work on "The Bat" consisted largely of sharpening and refining a concept that was there from the beginning — the conflict between the rational mind and the mysteries of imagination and spirit. Consequently, she focused her attention on image, diction, and line pacing.

Her poem "The Little Boat" from *The Boat of Quiet Hours* presented challenges of a different sort altogether. One is the mystery of the title; another is the convoluted genesis and development of the poem. Although Hall's commentary was always important to her, the development of this poem is interesting because it shows how good a self-critic Kenyon was, how tirelessly she worked to find just the right images and just the right words.

The first random lines for the poem appear among two drafts of other poems she was working on, both of which remain unpublished. One of these, "Hidden Damage," is a complete and independent poem (three seven-line stanzas) about a student whose husband "beats her when she tries to study." When the woman boards a bus to go home, she sees the driver loading baggage, one carton advising the recipient "to check for hidden damage." As she rides home on the bus, she thinks "about the violence of men toward women." This is actually a tight, well-crafted poem.[29] The second poem in this folder, also complete unto itself, is titled "Cold Day in August," a brief descriptive poem about nature. Here the first notes for "The Little Boat" are found.

On the original version of "Cold Day in August," Kenyon scratched out the last three lines, then added a series of notations in the lower margin. Some are random phrases; others move toward

28. Kenyon Archives, Box 6, Folder 9.

29. Drafts of "The Little Boat" are in Box 6, Folder 32 of the Kenyon Archives. I was able to find only one draft of "Hidden Damage."

full lines. At the bottom of the page a stanza emerges that shows how Kenyon worked, deleting words and adding phrases (here using brackets):

> One night in early September was the night
> before [the first day of] school. We'd been to Ward's
> on State Street with mother. Each of us had a stack
> of books, lined tablets, blank paper. Each had a new pink
> eraser — nubile — and a few
> perfect pencils, and crayons. It all smelled
> wonderful like crayons — like wax — it was all complete and
> unmarred by disappointed disappointment ambition. [no
> small thing
> even in a child. . . .]

Clearly, the lines intrigued her, and further annotations in the margins add detail. For example, arrowed behind "paper" on line 4 is a list of additional items she might include: "a reader, a speller, an arithmetic book"; "a jar of paste with a brush fastened to the lid"; "a penmanship book in which we would practice loops across the pages that looked to me like the galvanized culvert [that went] under the road. (It was large enough to run through on a dare.)" Suddenly a whole new poem began to evolve at the bottom of the page, and Kenyon, always captivated by writing about her childhood years, pushed the memory farther.

The poem continues on a new page in the vein of nostalgic recollection as Kenyon accumulated scenes and assembled memories. She liked to find titles early, as if to nail down a focal point for the poem. On this second sheet she tried four possibilities: "Lines Written After Sleeping in a Sleeping Bag," "Sleeping on the Porch," "The Sleeping Bag," and "Sleeping on the Porch in Sleeping Bags." She then drew boxes around the second and third to narrow the choices. In the first typed draft, the title became "The Sleeping Bag." A new verse added in this draft expanded a second memory:

When we were children
my brother and I used to sleep on the big screened porch
of our house ~~when~~ [as soon as] the peepers sounded from
   the stream
and boggy lower barn yard across the road
mother would get out the cots with wooden ~~legs~~ [frames],
and the sleeping bags — red and gray and black plaid flannel
inside, and battleship gray outside — the ~~same~~ gray
of the U.S.S. Walker, on which ~~he~~ [brother] would later serve
as sonar technician.
The peepers were the audible signal of spring —
Their singing meant we were allowed to go to the porch for
the summer.
~~And the difficulty of~~
How hard it was to sleep the first night out.

Kenyon made two additions. After "house" in line three, she added in the margin, "brother had his side; I had mine. He slept near the chimney and I near the steps to the garden." Here one observes Kenyon's near obsession with accuracy, telling the truth and getting it right even in the smallest details. The second addition — about the peepers — appeared as the penultimate line of this draft.

This draft of free writing continued to a second page, taking the children to the first day of school. The stanza here became the final stanza in the finished version. The children walk to the top of Foster Road and wait under "Riemers' big maple" for the bus to come. Although the poem is still heading in several different directions at this stage of invention, the basic dialectic of the finished poem is beginning to emerge — the evocation of the sleepy ease of freedom in summer counterpointed by the rigor and routine of the school year. In this draft the narrator is making observations in her present voice:

Because I have just spent the night in a sleeping bag for the first
time in twenty-five years I remember how we heard the bus
driver . . .

That soon changes in subsequent drafts as Kenyon lets the events speak for themselves.

In working to eliminate her present voice, the one that intrudes upon the memory and is tempted to extract lessons or turn didactic, Kenyon cut one long stanza entirely. The stanza, reproduced below, demonstrates the kinds of choices she made early in a poem's development:

> Home again . . . graham crackers and butter,
> [conversations with Willie the cat,]
> later supper, then out to the porch in earlier dark,
> crickets, a train, and sleep . . .
> By October I [used to] come in — brother was manly and
> [always] stayed a few weeks more . . .
> Why do I tell you this? What is it to you
> with a life of your own particulars? Only ~~this . . .~~
> ~~It is in them that~~ [that] much of what was lost
> is found [in things]. Why my life was as it was
> no one knows, ~~or whether it is a sleeping bag~~
> ~~on a porch is part of eternity.~~
> But [some part of] what it was I now remember.

By means of the crossed-out lines in this early, handwritten draft, one can sense Kenyon's unease with the open-ended nature of the stanza. Clearly she needed an image or a solid physical base in which to root her ideas. Nonetheless, the first typed draft duplicates much of what she has in the handwritten draft. But this was not unusual. At this stage, Kenyon wanted to commit it clearly to paper, to have a *form* before her to start revising.

The revisions on the first typed draft are typical. Here the ruthless attention to line pacing and deleting repetitive or extraneous material begins. In the first stanza Kenyon cut two-and-a-half full lines:

> When we were children
> my brother and I slept on the big screened porch

all summer. [~~The porch went around two sides~~
~~of the house — brother slept near the chimney~~
~~and I near the steps to the garden.~~]

She also cut extraneous lines about herself. For example, in a later stanza about the strictures of school and the classroom, Kenyon deleted the line "What a bad democrat I was; this offended me." The line refers to the fact that all the children in her class had to practice penmanship in the very same patterns, but as it stands in the poem the line is vague and so detracts from the situation described.

Although the ending of the poem shows evidence of pruning too, it is still fixed upon the vague notion of particulars:

[What is it to you with your own life]
Why do I tell you this? You have your own life
of particulars? Only that much of what was lost
is found again in things. Why my life was as it was
no one knows, but part of what it was I now remember.
[I still don't know]

But Kenyon had also found her solution, undeveloped at this point, in the preceding stanza of this draft with the lines "All day in my imagination my body floated/above the classroom. . . ." This would develop into the perfect image of dissociation — between herself and her classmates, between present and past. By the very next draft she had seized upon that image and started to shape it into the concluding stanza.

The next draft continues the revisions but contains two anomalies. Still under the title "Sleeping Bag," the poem is now dedicated to the memory of Elizabeth Bishop, a poet Kenyon once listed as one of her favorites. In the right margin is a handwritten epigraph: "Now I live here, another island, that doesn't seem like one, but who decides? . . ." "Crusoe in England." Several drafts later, both the dedication and the epigraph are crossed out. Several drafts after that, the title is crossed out and changed to "The Little Boat."

The title might seem curious since, save for a brief reference to her brother's service on the U.S.S. Walker, there is no mention of a "little boat," but in the right corner Kenyon wrote, "Keats's little boat." Thus the new title, and the allusion to seasons of change and the course of one's life in Book I of *Endymion*. Although it was dropped for publication, later drafts include the epigraph from *Endymion:*

> And, as the year
> Grows lush in juicy stalks, I'll smoothly steer
> My little boat, for many quiet hours,
> With streams that deepen freshly into bowers.

By this stage Kenyon had also worked out the final stanza as a parallel to the image of the floating little boat. The poem had jelled, both conceptually and formally. In that pattern of hovering between the physical and the abstract that Kenyon would often use, she now developed the image of her body floating above the classroom. In the final draft, her body is "navigating easily between fluorescent shoals." The image of the little boat becomes her floating self, but, more than that, it becomes the floating of the poetic imagination:

> floating, watching. . . . The others stayed below
> at their desks (I saw the crown of my own head
> bending over a book), and no one knew I was not
> where I seemed to be. . . .

Although there are other poems that have more extant drafts ("The Little Boat" has fourteen), this is one of the most heavily revised poems on manuscript and demonstrates Kenyon's process of discovering the poem and shaping it toward its final form. What began as random lines about childhood events evolved into a tight portrait of her poetic mind emerging from childhood. Moreover, the heavy revisions, particularly the work on the final stanza, reveal Kenyon's process of selectivity. Page by page through the drafts, one observes the decisions: this stays or must be added; that must go.

The additions work to develop that living essence of a Kenyon poem — the image. The deletions, sometimes the hardest work of revision, eliminate the overtly personal from a poem already firmly embedded in a particular situation, any hint of the didactic or sentimental, and any extraneous or redundant detail that might muddy the essential portrait.

IN HER PROCESS of revision, Kenyon's close relationship with several readers proved critical. Although she did not always agree with them, their serving as sounding boards for her ideas was essential. The most important reader was Hall, of course. But Joyce Peseroff and Alice Mattison were also invaluable critics.

Kenyon and Peseroff had known each other for some years before Mattison met Kenyon in 1979, at which time Kenyon was working on her Akhmatova translations and on the poems that would make up *The Boat of Quiet Hours*. At that time Mattison was living in New Haven, where she was writing and teaching. She had had several poems published in the little magazine *Green House*, edited by Kenyon and Peseroff. All three would, in the space of a few years, have books published by Alice James. It was, in fact, at a reading of Alice James poets that Kenyon and Mattison met. Then Mattison arranged a reading in Hamden to which Hall, Kenyon, and Peseroff were invited. This was the beginning of what became an intimate circle of writers.

It wasn't until January 1983, however, that the actual workshop, at Kenyon's proposal, began taking place, the first time at Peseroff's house in Lexington, Massachusetts. The friends alternated meetings at each other's homes, and twice met at an inn in Amherst. Typically they would read their work aloud, make comments in discussion, and take pencil to paper. Alice Mattison recollects that "in all our meetings we worked hard on diction, trying to be brief and clear."[30] This is the necessary distilling action of the

---

30. Mattison, "'Let It Grow in the Dark Like a Mushroom': Writing with Jane Kenyon," *Michigan Quarterly Review* (Winter 2000): 127.

poetic labor, squeezing the orange so that only the living essence remains. The essential sweetness lies in the precise word, the clean phrase rightly placed. Such was the activity of this workshop. It took friendship and bravery — that rare combination — to make it work. "As a workshop," Mattison wrote, "we pushed one another's writing as far as it would go."[31]

FROM HER CONCEPT of the task of the poet to her strenuous revision process, Kenyon approached her art with a clear-eyed precision about her aims and practices. Holding a high view of the poet as intercessor, Kenyon sought first of all to intercede between the world — with its great beauty and great sorrow — and the reader. Indeed, she reached out to the reader by grounding her work in the natural world, the familiar event, and plain language. She crafted her poetry with forceful imagery, precision of line, sudden wit, and word play so that the reader would discover corresponding emotional and intellectual responses. Kenyon also believed that poetry kept a people's memory alive. The poet shapes events with an urgent vividness that enables readers to find their own memories alive in a poem.

Furthermore, Kenyon saw the poet as truth-teller, one who could accept nothing less than absolute honesty in her art. That truth, however, must be rendered in beauty, for beauty rescues people from the deadening routines of daily life. The poet directs people from those daily routines to a longing for mystery and meaning. And she directs that longing by naming those deep, important things that are often difficult to name. Finally, the poet grants consolation, the sense of reader and writer becoming one in a shared experience.

Surely there were other elements orbiting the periphery of Kenyon's writing world, exerting their influence at certain moments and seasons. For example, in her lecture "Everything I Know About Writing Poetry," which she delivered in 1991 at a literary con-

31. Mattison, "'Let It Grow in the Dark Like a Mushroom,'" p. 128.

ference in Enfield, New Hampshire, she made the point that one initially follows the poetic course of emotion like a baby, then revises like an adult. Metaphor embodies the emotion; fresh language makes it vital for the reader.

Still, the heart of Kenyon's writing — theory and practice — was not something she talked much about on the lecture circuit. She tended to avoid that as much as possible (although she did do free public readings, and loved reading with her husband). She had no interest in setting herself up as some sort of poetry guru, offering wisdom to the anchorites. Her theory and practice began off the back door of her kitchen, where she had to negotiate the adjacent door to the attic and find her way to her study. That's where it began and ended. In between were certain principles she cherished and events that called out for telling in her mind. In between were discussions with her husband, workshops with her friends. But it began and ended in the study. Were the door closed, one might imagine a sign: Poet at Work.

CHAPTER FOUR

From Room to Room

Finding a Place

Perhaps the only thing harder than writing a first volume of poetry is finding a publisher for it. The fierce competition to be among the few new poets published each year poses nearly insurmountable odds. Major presses generally stay with their "proven" authors — those who have won awards and recognition and can guarantee break-even sales in an industry where poetry seldom pays its own way. Generally, then, the first-time author enters competitions and makes inquiries of small presses as the only possible avenues for publication. Jane Kenyon, independent as she was, resolved to take this route; she also resolved not to tag along on her husband's coattails. And why shouldn't she do it on her own? Nearly all the poems in her first volume had been published independently, some in leading periodicals, a feat that would be the envy of any poet — *The American Poetry Review, Harvard Magazine, The Michigan Quarterly Review, The Paris Review, The Virginia Quarterly Review,* and others. This seemed to bode well for finding a publisher. Nonetheless, getting the volume published was not something that happened overnight, and Kenyon worked hard on a number of drafts with a variety of titles.

Multiple drafts of the complete volume are extant. One draft bears comments from fellow poet and friend Michael Benedikt. The volume was submitted for the Walt Whitman Award (and was one of fifty finalists) under the title "Changing Light." Three other complete drafts bear that title. Other titles of complete drafts are "Under a Blue Mountain" and "Cages Opening."

Kenyon's placing the volume with Alice James Books, then headquartered in Cambridge, Massachusetts, was fortuitous in several ways.[1] Alice James Books was founded as a writers' cooperative with an emphasis on publishing poetry by women. Aggressive promotion of books through writers' workshops, readings (particularly at universities), and grants virtually assured successful sales. In addition to participating in the workshops and readings, each poet published by Alice James donated time at the main office to prepare publicity mailings, fill orders, and the like. Alice James resisted the temptation to broaden its publications base too quickly, choosing instead to work with a small number of poets whose reputations were clearly on the rise.

Kenyon's involvement with Alice James provided her with several benefits in addition to the publication of her first volume of poetry. The cooperative formed a sorority of like-minded and dedicated poets. Indeed, Kenyon's workshops with Joyce Peseroff (who had earlier published with Alice James) and Alice Mattison (who would later publish there) grew out of meetings for the press. The cooperative also gave Kenyon a public forum for her work. The promotional activities often put two or three Alice James poets on a reading forum at the same time. Although initially shy about her public readings, Kenyon grew to love the quick and easy connection she made with her audiences.[2] Clearly it nurtured her further work.

1. Alice James (1848-1892) was a member of the famous James family, which was best known for her older brothers William and Henry. Alice endured a lifelong struggle with depression, and made several suicide attempts. Eventually she was confined to her bedroom, where, in 1890, she began to keep a diary. See *The Diary of Alice James,* ed. Leon Edel (Temecula, Calif.: American Biographical Services, 1991).

2. Wendell Berry, who had been friends with Donald Hall before his marriage to Kenyon, provides several interesting portraits of Kenyon during the early

During the mid-to-late 1970s, Kenyon was busy with another task that broadened her acquaintance with other poets, and that coincided with the release of *From Room to Room* in 1978. Along with Joyce Peseroff as co-editor (Rochelle Siegel was associate editor), Kenyon founded *Green House,* a poetry review which, for the duration of its six issues from 1976 to 1980, published many of the nation's leading contemporary poets. According to Joyce Peseroff, "We had decided to call the magazine *Green House* because we wanted to suggest a gathering place, a home for good poems, a shelter where writers could thrive and grow."[3] It was an ambitious effort, and both Kenyon and Peseroff undertook it with some trepidation. Their general aim was to publish a mixture of familiar and unfamiliar authors, but, as Peseroff explained it, they had another motive too:

---

years of the marriage. In "Sweetness Preserved" he recalls one of his first meetings with Kenyon during a stop at Eagle Pond Farm: "I remember being impressed by Jane's self-possession and dignity and quietness. These qualities continued to impress me after I knew her better. She was a writer, but she appeared to be watching 'the literary world' without anxiety or great excitement" (In *Bright, Unequivocal Eye: Poems, Papers, and Remembrances from the First Jane Kenyon Conference,* ed. Bert Hornback [New York: Peter Lang Press, 2000], p. 140). He also recalls the first time he heard Kenyon read her own work. The scene was a Saturday get-together of poets (Hall, Galway Kinnell, and Seamus Heaney, with Bert Hornback at the University of Michigan):

> Finally, late in the day, somebody — I don't remember who; it wasn't me — said, "Jane, why don't you read us a poem?" Jane, who had been sitting almost outside the room, saying little, perhaps nothing at all, during the conversation, fished up from somewhere a page that she had brought with her and spread it open to read. For me, this was the only uncomfortable moment of that day. I don't remember what I thought, but it would have been like me to have started trying to think of some ambiguous compliment to make in case I thought the poem was bad — something like "Well, Jane, you certainly do write poetry." And then that quiet woman read beautifully her poem "Twilight: After Haying." (*Bright, Unequivocal Eye,* p. 141)

3. Peseroff, "Green House," in *Bright, Unequivocal Eye,* p. 6.

As well as a literary explosion, the early 1970s began what would become known as the "second wave" of feminism in this country. Young women in our 20s, we were aware of what was going on about us. Each of us knew the gender ratio typical of many literary publications — often two men for each woman listed on the contributors' pages. Although we never did head counts, we tried to be especially open to the work of women. One of *Green House*'s special sections was "Women from Women's Presses." And we did make sure that half the names on our cover were those of women.[4]

For the first issue, Kenyon rented an IBM Selectric typewriter that she named "Horace" and typed every poem onto heavy stock to make camera-ready copy. All of the design work, including press-on lettering for the cover, was done by the editors themselves.

After the first issue — Spring 1976 — was circulated to bookstores, Peseroff joyfully wrote on a postcard dated 2 August 1976 that three bookstores she had checked had sold all their copies. The group printed a total of 500 copies of each issue, and were supported by 100 subscribers as well as bookstore sales.

Together, the publication of *From Room to Room* and the editing of *Green House* gave Kenyon a greater degree of confidence in her work. The fact of the matter is that she had vacillated in her opinion of her work. On the one hand, she could be her own sternest critic, and was often the first to denigrate her poetry in the workshops with her friends. Once she referred to three new poems as "shallow" and "10¢ poems."[5] On the other hand, Kenyon could be supercharged with poetic energy, enjoying times of superb confidence in her work. One of her trademark slogans in the workshops was "If you've got it, flaunt it."[6] Some of these conflicting attitudes and emotions were significantly ameliorated with the publication of

4. Peseroff, "Green House," in *Bright, Unequivocal Eye*, p. 6.

5. Mattison, "'Let It Grow in the Dark Like a Mushroom': Writing with Jane Kenyon," *Michigan Quarterly Review* (Winter 2000): 131.

6. Mattison, "'Let It Grow in the Dark Like a Mushroom,'" p. 128.

From Room to Room. She had published her first volume; she had earned a public reception.

From Room to Room constitutes a poetic journey. It shows Kenyon finding her place both at the farmhouse in New Hampshire and as a poet. The majority of the poems in the volume show patterns that Kenyon would use throughout her career — the intense image, the sparse, precise diction, the surprising turn of line, and the emotional movement up and down through the poem. But here she also experiments with the prose poem, a form that does not appear again in her later verse as she became more attuned to her own sense of poetic sounds and rhythms.

The volume is structured in five parts. Part One, "Under a Blue Mountain," refers to Mount Kearsarge, which from the distance of Eagle Pond Farm rises in a dark gray-blue bulk from the lesser hills. The fourteen poems in this section are all "settling in" poems, recording Kenyon's discoveries at the new place. The five poems in Part Two, "Edges of the Map," draw her closer in, suggesting that this is now "her place" as memories from her past begin to merge with what she experiences here. Part Three, "Colors," is an eclectic grouping. Only two of the nine poems in this section were included in *Otherwise*. Even though they do not represent Kenyon's most accomplished work, several of these poems — including "The First Eight Days of the Beard" and the wry poem "The Socks" — were audience favorites at her readings. The ten poems in Part Four, "Afternoon in the House," move to the "psychological room" of full acceptance and to the "physical room" of full appreciation for the beauty of Eagle Pond Farm. The final section represents Kenyon's early work on translations of Anna Akhmatova's poetry. The six translations here were all heavily revised for publication in *Twenty Poems of Anna Akhmatova*.

In subject matter the poems look in two directions — back to the life she left behind and ahead as she establishes a new life in a new place. In her interview with Bill Moyers, Kenyon said of her move, "I felt quite disembodied for a while. Someone said that when you move, it takes your soul a few weeks to catch up with you.

Of course, this house is so thoroughly full of Don's family, his ancestors, their belongings, their reverberations, that when we came here, I felt almost annihilated by the 'otherness' of it at times."[7] This search for place is seen particularly in two poems, the title poem and "This Morning." "From Room to Room" places the narrator directly in the house, standing among memorabilia. The image she adopts for herself is that of a fly:

> I move from room to room,
> a little dazed, like the fly. I watch it
> bump against each window.

As she bumps against the memories and artifacts held in this house, the image intensifies. Like the fly, she seems "Out of my body for a while,/weightless in space. . . ." She thinks of "my people," who "are not here." Dissociation sets in. Like the fly, she flickers, hovers, looking for a place to land. Recalling the hymn "Blessed Be the Tie That Binds," she can't remember the lines that follow the opening one. What ties bind her now? In the final stanza the flight of the fly changes to the flight of an astronaut outside his spacecraft, tethered to the oxygen hose but still dissociated, floating from some strange umbilical cord in search of a certain place.

The dissociative, hovering imagery that marks much of Kenyon's poetry is pronounced in this volume, suggesting her bewilderment in new circumstances. Observe the contrary actions in "This Morning," for example. In stanza one heavy snow presses down on the barn. In stanza two the breath of cows rises. In stanza four a "nuthatch drops to the ground" to get the seeds Kenyon has scattered. In stanza five the cats "lift their heads." While in this volume such images of suspension suggest her lack of sureness about place, Kenyon will use similar techniques in later poems to suggest, for example, the hovering of the poetic imagination, a withholding

---

7. *A Hundred White Daffodils* (Saint Paul, Minn.: Graywolf Press, 1999), p. 145.

95

of final answers to troubling questions, or an attenuated uncertainty in the midst of troubling circumstances.

Unlike the title poem, "Here" is about finding and having a sense of place. In the opening stanza, Kenyon addresses her husband's sure sense of belonging in the house. Not only was it his ancestral home, but he had visited it every summer since his childhood. It shaped his sense of place. She juxtaposes his certainty with her uncertainty: "I'm the one who worries/if I fit in with the furniture/and the landscape." But as the poem continues, she confesses to a growing familiarity and comfort with each. The house is becoming her home:

> I feel my life start up again,
> like a cutting when it grows
> the first pale and tentative
> root hair in a glass of water.

The image succinctly gathers her spirit. She has been cut off from one life, but transplanted here, she now begins to feel the new roots grow.

As Kenyon felt her life begin to grow into Eagle Pond Farm, her poetry opened increasingly to the imagery and events around her. In "For the Night," a poem eerily evocative of "Let Evening Come," she writes of night falling. There is a progression of light to darkness in the poem, but also a solidity of image. The first stanza pictures a mare in a "darkening stall" kicking over a bucket. In the last stanza, a bat lets go of the rafter in the barn, soundlessly, and "falls into black air." This pattern of suspension — whether ascending or descending — between light and darkness becomes far stronger in subsequent works, where it becomes allied with spiritual and psychological states. Here, it is as if Kenyon is discovering natural imagery from the farm that will later incarnate those states.

Like "Here," "Two Days Alone" shows the narrator finding her place. The two stanzas of the poem are closely paired. In the first she reads the newspaper in the living room by the wood stove, even though it isn't cold. The fire is a source of comfort. In an early draft of the poem, Kenyon wrote the third line as "feeding the stove like an animal," then crossed the simile out heavily. The simile placed all the despair and fear in her. The change to "feeding the stove-animal" draws a natural connection to the second stanza, where she has to leave the comfort of the living room to go out to the wood-shed for more wood. It is there that her despair and fear arise: "In the woodshed/darkness is all around and inside me." But she knows she has a safe place to return to. Although she wonders in the darkness, "Maybe/I don't belong here," she can go back to the house and affirm, "Nothing tells me that I don't."

In "Changes" Kenyon seems to have made peace with the ancestors whose pictures and possessions fill the home. It is a light-hearted poem of acceptance of differences, one that only someone who has found her place could write. In the first stanza she comments on the changes she has made:

> The cast-iron kitchen range
> grows rust like fur
> in the cold barn.

Of course she spots the irony of the range being out in the cold barn. The image of the rusty fur continues into the next lines with a reflection on her cats. Here too she has made *her* changes: cats that once roamed the barn are now kept in the house. In the second stanza these changes are accepted, just as she is. She imagines the "gallery of ancestors" on the parlor walls shaking their heads at her, thinking she has gone off the deep end of propriety just like the local character Charlie Dolbey, who used to chase bikes and cars while howling at the top of his lungs.

The acceptance of the ancestors eases into a quiet accommodation in "Finding a Long Gray Hair." Washing the floor as had other women who lived in the house, Kenyon finds the long gray hair, clearly not one of her own. But the connection is made: "I feel my life added to theirs."

As Kenyon deepened her connection to the farm, she began to

97

feel freer to reconnect with her past, a pattern that intensified greatly in later works. Here memories appear in evocative portraits, such as the prose poem "My Mother." "The Needle," about Kenyon's grandmother, is a poem Kenyon wrote during her junior year at the University of Michigan, but it finds an appropriate place here connecting past and present. Similarly, "Ironing Grandmother's Tablecloth" provides a moving recollection of things past. The poem begins with Grandmother's wedding, describing how the young bride smoothed the tablecloth, and how she ironed it for many years thereafter. It ends with a poignant scene of the granddaughter ironing the same damask and thinking about what her grandmother is like now:

> The streets of your brain become smaller,
> old houses torn down. Talking to me
> is hard work, keeping things straight,
> whose child I am, whether I have children.

Despite the discordance in subject matter, the poem itself brings past and present into accord.

All of these poems reveal a startlingly clear and original use of imagery. The power and grace of Kenyon's artistry — if not the masterful grasp of complex subject matter (that would come during her work on the Akhmatova translations) — flash in full brilliance. In "Full Moon in Winter," featured in Part Four, the now-familiar pattern of light and shadow works powerfully:

> The shadow of the house
> appears on the crusted snow
> like the idea of a house,
> and my own shadow
>
> lies down in the cold
> at my feet, lunatic,
> like someone tired

of living in a body,
needy and full of desire. . . .

Other images grasp a situation with acute precision. From "Year Day," this: "The clock's heart/beats in its wooden chest." The poem ends with these delightfully enigmatic lines: "Here are the gestures/of my hands. Wear them in your hair." What are the gestures? What but the images of the poem, held forth like imaginary flowers to adorn the reader's hair. Kenyon's imagery frequently evokes this sense of playful surprise.

Certainly the majority of the poems in *From Room to Room* fall, as I have explained, into two categories. One would be the poems expressive of the poetic and psychological act of separating oneself from the familiar and finding one's place in the new. The second category — and one that Kenyon never abandoned — are those poems of sheer playfulness in which she takes an almost grand delight in the scene she unfolds. Several stand out in this collection: "The Shirt," "The Socks," and "The First Eight Days of the Beard."[8] Although favored by audiences at her readings, such works were often confining for Kenyon. The works stood polished, final, and complete. But they failed to move beyond entertainment to capture that reflective quality that can pique the reader's reflection.

At this stage in her career, Kenyon's craft was largely shaped toward providing the lustrous image, sufficiently fresh and vigorous to awaken the reader's sensibilities. Persistently, however, one feels that there is more ready to break out, that the path of imagery wants to lead somewhere. In this volume, one poem in particular presages the metaphysical image that became a hallmark of Kenyon's later poetry: "Cages."

In "Cages" one senses the power of Kenyon's later work because here she moves from the concrete to the speculative. She

---

8. "The First Eight Days of the Beard" originally had nine lines and covered nine days. The original line four, "The spokes of a wheel," was cut in draft.

opens doors that invite the reader to pursue individual avenues of reflection. Part One, which sets the scene of the poem, is perfectly and smoothly executed, showing Kenyon's brilliance for metaphor. The first stanza opens with the narrator and her husband driving to Winter Park in March. They pass a dead beagle lying in the road, "his legs/outstretched, as if he meant to walk/on his side in the next life." At this point the reader hardly pays attention to "the next life"; the image of the dead beagle rivets the eye. In the second stanza, the couple continues driving into the night, through groves of orange trees, the oranges "breathing through their sweet skins." In the third stanza, which concludes the section on their travel, they see cattle staggering in the back of a truck pulling off the highway. The image provides an objective correlative for these travelers. Late at night, after many miles, they too finally "stagger" off the road.

The cattle in the back of the truck form a link to Part Two. When the travelers visit the hotel pool the next day, they discover an array of animals arranged in cages. A black swan floats in a few inches of filthy water; peacocks strut; flamingos stand on one leg "as if they loathed/touching the ground." But the narrator is particularly struck by the cage of monkeys. One of them reaches through the bars for her pen, as if to write a letter. "And one lies in the lap of another," the two strangely resembling the Pietà, seeking "some particle of comfort, some/consolation for being in this life."

What is the consolation for being in this life? Part Three breaks free from the concrete reality into speculation. What about the body itself as consolation? Sometimes, the narrator admits, it is her "favorite child," free and unhampered as the spider monkeys "loose in the trees overhead." And, one might readily assume, any poet who wrote such delightfully suggestive poems as "The Shirt" and "The Socks" would delight in the body. But there are also times, she adds, when "my body disgusts me." Like the caged monkey lying across the other's lap, or "like a goose with its legs/tied together," the body can seem too heavy in its reality. At such times, the narrator says, "I have to agree that the body/is a cloud before the soul's eye."[9] Herein lies the tension, then: if the poems in *From Room to Room* are generally about finding one's place in a geographical location, this poem in particular is about finding one's place as a human creature. Is one merely a physical being, not unlike the goose fattened for a tin of paté? Or is one a spiritual entity — a soul — held within that physical being? Kenyon calls this tension "This long struggle to be at home/in the body, this difficult friendship."

In response to the tension, Part Four transcends physicality in lyric song. It begins with the death of the body, suggested by old people walking on the beaches and mortuaries advertising on bus-stop benches. But then it shifts to the mystery of the nearby groves, where at night "unfamiliar constellations/rise in a leafy sky." Here the physical doesn't "cloud" the soul; rather, it elevates, lifting the soul to metaphysical wonder. Life here is profuse and celebrative, like the cannas blooming "their outrageous blooms,/as if speaking final thoughts,/no longer caring what anyone thinks. . . ." In this section one can almost see the poet slough off restraint. Kenyon herself was becoming comfortable with those "outrageous thoughts."

INTERSPERSED AMONG the lyric poems in *From Room to Room* is a sequence of prose poems, a form Kenyon never employed again after this volume. Nor, except for marginalia in her notebooks and papers, is there evidence that she had employed the form earlier. Why their place in this volume? How do they function?

It should be understood, first of all, that the prose poem was a fairly common form employed by poets during the 1960s and early 1970s. Basically, the form has all the qualities of the lyric poem, with intense emphasis on sound patterns, imagery, and brevity.

---

9. In an earlier draft of the poem, Kenyon attributed this image of the body to Bishop Cranmer:

> Then I have to agree
> With Bishop Cranmer, who called the body
> "a cloud before the soul's eye." (Kenyon Archives, Box 2, Folders 2-5)

While it is thus shaped conceptually as a lyric poem, it is presented on the page as prose in order to further concentrate the lyric intensity, to evoke a precise sense of setting, or to evoke a psychological state or state of memory. Immediacy and intensity are the poet's foremost objectives in the form.

Seven such prose poems appear in the volume. Like the volume as a whole, they capture the process of moving from one room, the old life, to the new room of Eagle Pond Farm. The first prose poem to appear is "Leaving Town," the second poem in the volume. In four brief, three-line passages, the poem recalls a couple's leaving behind their old way of life: the moving van departs, friends wish the couple well, and they begin the long drive east. Unlike many of Kenyon's poems, this one holds her voice, intense and immediate. The "I" reports the action — and the feelings. As the drive begins, the couple listens to a Tigers double-header on the car radio. During the second game they drive out of range of the signal, a metaphor for the fading reach of the old familiar place and the unknown they head toward. As the signal fades, a powerful image of dissociation intrudes and parallels the distancing: "I felt like a hand without an arm," the narrator says. The couple continues to drive all night and into the morning, a physical image for Kenyon's own journey through the dark of the unknown.

Other prose poems provide a similar nexus between the narrator's emotions and her adjustment to the new rooms. "The Cold" shapes a brief, intense lyric summons, contrasting the poet's preternatural joy in a season of bitterly natural cold. With the temperature dropping to twenty-four below in a day, she feels an unnamable happiness in seeing the pond ice over, and a strange gladness in finding the pillows in her bed cold just two minutes after leaving them. Here lies the mystery of acceptance, a feeling that one cannot label but that springs forth in the lyricism of the prose poem.

A similar acceptance occurs in "After an Early Frost," another of the playful poems that spring up at every turn in this collection. In this instance the narrator observes the cat carrying "her squealing mouse into the bathtub to play." What games, the narrator wonders. Monopoly? Twenty Questions? When she hears a sudden silence, she goes to remove what she expects to be a dead mouse. She sees nothing — until a corner of the towel moves and the mouse peeps out. Now what? Should she bring in the cat to "finish the job"? Instead she nudges the mouse into a coffee can, sets it outside, and goes about her work. Accommodation. She wonders if the mouse will survive or meet its end. "Somebody will carry me out of here too," she muses — then quickly adds, "though not for a while."

Two prose poems contrast past and present. "Hanging Pictures in Nanny's Room" tells of Kenyon's discoveries while rearranging the room. Perhaps the most memorable line occurs in her description of Nanny's photograph: "Her jaw like a piece of granite. You'd have to plow around it." Here the poet is in the present, considering the past. In "My Mother" she transports herself to the past, putting her present self into the mind of her childhood self. Her mother has just come back from a trip to the dime store in downtown Ann Arbor. At the time, Polly Kenyon had established her trade as a seamstress and was both taking in sewing and giving sewing lessons. Predictably, then, she returns with materials for her trade — spools of thread, zippers, and such. The narrator knows, though, that there will be a present for her. And there is — a wooden paddle with a small ball attached to it by an elastic string. Yet, for the narrator — as we see here through the child's eyes and mind — the significant gift is the simple fact that her mother returned: "Sometimes when she goes downtown, I think she will not come back."

"American Triptych" gives us the last two of the seven prose poems. It was one of the most heavily revised poems in this volume. From its earliest drafts the poem had a story-telling quality that appears already in Part One — a scene where people are gathered at a small-town store. Parts Two and Three function as lyric voice-overs on small-town life. The prose poem that forms Part Two appears straightforward — it describes children playing baseball. But it is also in thematic accord with other poems in this volume, touching as it does on the separation between youth and adulthood

in the line "No deaths or separations, no disappointments in love."
Children, as Dylan Thomas put it in "Fern Hill," go about their "sky
blue trades" while adults grow ever more aware of the distance between innocence and experience.

Significant here is the poetic voice or point of view. The narrator almost seems to be watching over these children rather than
simply watching them. So too in Part Three, "Potluck at the Wilmot
Flat Baptist Church," we get a third essential element in this communal life. Each detail, each moment of the potluck is recreated in
this longest of Kenyon's prose poems. And here she makes a declaration about it. She finds herself, she says, "among people trying to
live ordered lives." It is a remarkable contrast to the disorder of
parting recorded in "Leaving Town." Now she adds, "And again I
am struck with love for the Republic."

The temptation arises to pay only passing notice to the prose
poems in *From Room to Room*. They seem curiously at odds with the
far more concrete and organic poems that make up the rest of the
volume, almost as if the poet were indulging herself rather than illuminating the audience. But they are strategic to the whole. They
provide important links between past and present. Their intensely
lyrical and personal quality mark key transitions in the poet's leaving one place and learning to embrace another. They provide the
bridge that grants solidity to the other poems.

ONE OF THE INTERESTING THINGS about this volume is that, despite the challenging transitions Kenyon was making in her life,
her anxiety, save for several poems, is not pronounced. In fact,
playfulness, as well as searching and finding, may well prevail in
From Room to Room. Several poems strive to shape that nexus between past and present — a point from which she sometimes
seems to dangle like the astronaut attached to the lifeline. But she
is puzzling through just how that lifeline works. What is her place
in the long line of Eagle Pond ancestors? Does she still feel connected to her ancestors in Ann Arbor? As she settles into the
rhythms of natural life at Eagle Pond Farm, Kenyon adopts them

as her own and rejoices in the poetic landscape she has found. The concluding poem of the volume, "Now That We Live," richly affirms her joy in everyday existence, from the "fat spider by the door" to the blue swelling of the "imperturbable mountain" in the distance. This is the landscape in which she herself now lives, finding joy, confronting sorrow.

CHAPTER FIVE

Twenty Poems of Anna Akhmatova

Poetic Kinship and the Validation of Art

In her poem "Lines for Akhmatova," collected in *Let Evening Come,*
Jane Kenyon wrote of Akhmatova's life in Leningrad. Scenes of the
pastoral side of Leningrad — the narrow canals darkly gleaming
under "ornate street lamps," the golden leaves swept away by
women using birch-stick brooms — counterpoint the grimace of
tragedy:

> Husband and son, lovers, dear companions
> were imprisoned or killed, emigrated or died.

Akhmatova lived through the conflict, savoring the diminishing
beauty of her Russia, preserving it in her poetry, but also steeling
herself against the constant surge of sorrow:

> You turned still further inward,
> imperturbable as a lion-gate, and lived on
> stubbornly. . . .

In Akhmatova, Kenyon found not only a woman she admired profoundly for her poetic gifts but also a kindred soul. Kenyon too
struggled to preserve a delicate balance between her appreciation
for — and often joy in — the pastoral beauty of a routine life and

the surge of sorrow. The force of that conflict of emotions and perceptions, more than anything else, drove the force of Akhmatova's poetry through Kenyon's veins.

Furthermore, while it would not be accurate to suggest that Akhmatova gave Kenyon a model for a poetic style, it would be accurate to say that she reinforced and provided an imprimatur for a style that Kenyon was already very much at home with. The keenness of the telling image; the dancing movement among lines with unexpected openings of words, phrases, and ideas; the counterpoint of joy and sorrow — these were all techniques that Kenyon had employed since her college days. In Akhmatova, however, she met someone who had mastered the style and invested it with grace, power, and beauty. Kenyon's translation of Akhmatova's poetry validated what she intuitively sought. At a crucial stage in Kenyon's maturation as a poet, one observes these pertinent relationships with Akhmatova: an allied sense of poetic principles, a kinship of personality, and a shared spiritual faith.

THE STORY of how Kenyon first came to translate the great Russian poet is fairly well known. Robert Bly and Donald Hall's personal friendship extended over many years. Bly was a frequent guest at the University of Michigan when Hall was teaching there and when Kenyon was a student. As one of Hall's creative-writing students, Kenyon would frequently join the informal gatherings at Hall's house during Bly's visits. The visits continued after Kenyon and Hall married and moved to New Hampshire. Bly, as was his custom, would ask Kenyon what she was working on. On one of these visits, Bly made a suggestion that Kenyon recalled in her 1993 interview with David Bradt:

> I showed him some poems that I had been working on, and he read them thoughtfully, then looked up and said, "It's time for you now to take a writer and work with that writer as a master." I wasn't even sure what he meant, but I said, "I can't have a man as a master." He said without missing a beat, "Then read

Akhmatova." So I began collecting translations of Akhmatova, and I found, much to my dismay, that I didn't think any of the translations were good. So as a kind of exercise in close reading I began collecting all the versions I could of a given poem, and then attempting to write my own version. That's how the door opened.[1]

The door opened, but during the initial stages it opened onto a conflicted and confusing world.

As she began work on her own translations, Kenyon sensed that something remained hidden in prior translations. The soul of the poet had been veiled in words that Kenyon found to be too mechanical, lacking the force and power of the poet's personality. In the files of working drafts of Kenyon's translations, an example appears of her method of comparing previous translations. It is Poem 3 in *Twenty Poems of Anna Akhmatova*, "I know, I know" from *Rosary*.[2] In her working notes, Kenyon arranged four translations on a single page. On the upper left is Richard McKane's translation; on the upper right, Walter Arndt's; on the lower right, Stanley Kunitz and Max Hayward's; and on the lower left, her own. The positioning in and of itself is revealing, bringing to relief Kenyon's different poetic sensibility. For example, clockwise from McKane's translation the last two lines read:

In the snowy twigs black jackdaws,
black jackdaws shelter.

---

1. Kenyon, *A Hundred White Daffodils* (Saint Paul, Minn.: Graywolf Press, 1999), p. 178.

2. Kenyon's previous volume, *From Room to Room*, contains six early versions of her translations of Akhmatova. During her work on *Twenty Poems*, Kenyon started with the *From Room to Room* version (if there was one), focusing intensely upon nuances of sound and fidelity to lyric patterns, and making judgments accordingly. One of the first changes she made to "I know, I know" was to divide the poem into quatrains, following the pattern of the original.

On your snowy twigs for pillow
dawbirds, small black dawbirds rest.

Shelter the black daws in your snowy branches,
The black daws.

Shelter the black grackles, black
grackles among your snowy branches.

Comparatively, one notices that the first and third translations
seem confined by word meaning — that is to say, the *work* of translation. The second and fourth engage the poetry, the visual image
and the aural lyricism. It is notable also that in her version (the last
listed) Kenyon uses her own technique of enjambment in the first
line, making "black" reflexive to the prior "black grackles" but also
run on as an adjective for the next line. She also changes "daws" to
the more familiar "grackles." And she ends the poem not with the
desolation of the dark bird but with the lighter, more optimistic figure of the snowy branches.

KENYON'S NATIVE poetic sensibility was abetted by several guides
in what would become a five-year process of translation, beginning
in late 1979 through 1984. (*Twenty Poems* was published in 1985.)
Among these guides was Robert Bly's "The Eight Stages of Translation," a copy of which, bearing Kenyon's marginal annotations, is in
her Akhmatova files.[3] Perhaps chief among Bly's lessons was
"Choose the exact word." This is not necessarily the literal translation of the word but the word that captures the essence of the poem
and the poet's presence behind the poem. Thus Kenyon embarked
on a singular quest to reveal the hidden Akhmatova.

An understanding of the literal translation is nonetheless necessary to the process, as Kenyon well knew. So, in addition to find-

3. All files for *Twenty Poems of Anna Akhmatova* are in Boxes 3 and 4 of the
Kenyon Archives.

ing the "exact words," she entered the literal translations of lines in the margins of the drafts. For example, in one draft of "I know, I know," Kenyon typed in the right margin for line two: "Lit: will creak dryly." In her final draft the first two lines read

> I know, I know the skis
> will begin again their dry creaking.

Similarly, line six bears the marginal note: "Lit: removed by silence." Thus lines five and six in the final version read

> The windows of the palace burn
> remote and still.

It became a multilevel process: first to sense the spirit of the poem and the poet through close, intensive readings; next to draft a version capturing this spirit; and then to revise according to literal meanings to find the "exact" word and phrase.

Several other people guided Kenyon through the translation process. While working on her early versions, she began to wonder if they "had any real accuracy."[4] At that time she met Lou Teel, a Russian student at Dartmouth, who began to work with her to guide the process toward linguistic accuracy. Subsequently, when Bly visited again, he read the translations and immediately declared that he wanted to do a book of them for the Eighties Press (a small press he guided that was based in Saint Paul). Bly also put Kenyon in touch with Vera Sandomirsky Dunham, a Russian scholar and émigré who knew well the subtleties of both languages. In the following years Kenyon made frequent trips to Dunham's home on Long Island, where the two honed selected versions of the poems. Kenyon explained the effect this process had in her interview with David Bradt: "In working on the translations I became so close to those poems that I forgot they weren't mine. It was only after I got

4. Kenyon, *A Hundred White Daffodils*, p. 178.

that close that I could feel a bit of freedom in translation. Translation is a necessary evil, and especially difficult if you are uncomfortable with the notion of compromise." The important word there for Kenyon's development as an artist is *freedom,* for through the translation work her own confidence as a poet grew profoundly. The intricate and intense work with Akhmatova, Kenyon told Bradt, provided her with "this tremendous sense of freedom, and I began to feel some power in my own work for the first time."[5]

Akhmatova, then, validated Kenyon's own search for conciseness through intense revision and her need for the "exact word" that perfectly captured idea, sound, and meaning. Furthermore, the work gave Kenyon a sense of great confidence and freedom in her own writing. She was working on the poems for her next volume, *The Boat of Quiet Hours,* most of which she wrote during the five years she worked on Akhmatova. Not only in subject matter but also in poetic form, *From Room to Room* was a volume about finding one's place. It is often tentative, staking out small personal domains that Kenyon could claim as her own. But as time passed and work progressed at Eagle Pond Farm, that domain widened immeasurably. It did so largely through Kenyon's growing confidence in her use of imagery. Although Kenyon had always sought the vivid image — that which would, as Dickinson said, reduce the world to a graphic syllable — her approach received validation and encouragement from Akhmatova's battle against the Symbolists and her own striking use of concrete imagery.

Like Kenyon, Akhmatova began writing poetry early — when she was ten. In 1910, when she was twenty-one, Akhmatova married the poet Nikolai Gumilev, twenty-four, who had been courting her since she was fourteen. In 1912, Gumilev co-founded the Poets' Guild — the Acmeists — a society of about fifteen poets whose most outstanding members were Akhmatova and Osip Mandelstam. One of the early actions of the Guild was to renounce the prevailing poetic culture of Symbolism, inaugurated by such French

5. Kenyon, *A Hundred White Daffodils*, p. 179.

poets as Baudelaire, Verlaine, and others at the turn of the century. In the view of those who agreed with Acmeist principles, the Symbolists were simply too vague and ethereal, detached from physical objects as presences in and of themselves, and too casual with the literal meanings and suggestiveness of language. In the introduction to her translation of Akhmatova's work (which followed Kenyon's), Judith Hemschemeyer quotes from Mandelstam's essay "The Morning of Acmeism": "We do not wish to divert ourselves with a stroll in a 'forest of symbols,' because we have a more virgin, dense forest — divine physiology, the infinite complexity of our dark organism."[6] Instead of what they considered the vapor of Symbolism, the Acmeists wrote about the gift of life on this earth.[7]

The Acmeists celebrated the presence of this physical world and one's life in it. Their poems, and Akhmatova's in particular, are filled with concrete scenes that root the reader in reality. In the introduction to her translation, Kenyon notes another defining characteristic of the Acmeists that keenly interested her: "These poets announced that they were craftsmen not priests, and dedicated themselves to clarity, concision, and perfection of form. They summed up their goals in two words: 'beautiful clarity.'"[8] This goal opposed the Symbolist technique of deliberate linguistic opacity in order to trip the reader out of present reality, but it also affirmed Kenyon's methodology of searching out the "exact word."

As one reads extensively in Akhmatova's poems, eerie connec-

6. Hemschemeyer, *The Complete Poems of Anna Akhmatova*, 2 vols. (Somerville, Mass.: Zephyr Press, 1990), 1: 2. Hemschemeyer's translations, now accepted as authoritative, were published in 1990. The three translations that Kenyon had access to were those by McKane (1969), Kunitz and Hayward (1973), and Arndt (1976).

7. For the poet's own account of the history of Acmeism, see *Anna Akhmatova and Her Circle*, ed. Konstantin Polivanov, trans. Patricia Beriozkina (Fayetteville: University of Arkansas Press, 1994), pp. 31-35.

8. Kenyon, introduction to *Twenty Poems of Anna Akhmatova*, with Vera Sandomirsky Dunham (Saint Paul, Minn.: Nineties Press and Ally Press, 1985), p. 4.

tions arise: one almost thinks, "Here is a line Kenyon could have written." Consider the first stanza of "A Song" from Akhmatova's *Evening*:

> As the sun is rising
> I'm singing about love,
> In the garden on my knees
> I'm weeding out the goosefoot.[9]

Many of the patterns found in these few short lines are similar to ones that Kenyon had been working with for years. The first two lines hold the upward motion with the rising sun and the song about love. The third and fourth lines abruptly arrest the motion and bring it down to the poet on her knees, pulling weeds in the garden. Is that action the song of love? The tensions between rising and falling actions and the solid, earth-rooted imagery that appear here also figure prominently in *The Boat of Quiet Hours* and subsequent volumes of Kenyon's work. Clearly their poetic principles were strikingly similar.

ROBERT BLY'S SUGGESTION to Kenyon that she take Akhmatova as a poetic "master" was fortuitous for poetic reasons — but also for personal reasons. What was it that moved Kenyon so powerfully and personally about Akhmatova? Even a brief look at her life and work suggests answers.

The fact is that Akhmatova was still relatively unknown in the United States at the time Bly made his suggestion. Amanda Haight's *Anna Akhmatova* — the first substantial biography, and one that Kenyon read — was published in 1976, just two years before Kenyon began her work. Although it is far too involved to adequately summarize here, Akhmatova's life was full of austere and trying times, of constant threat to her poetic expression (at one time, fearing reprisal, she burned all the notes she had in her apartment), and of exul-

---

9. Hemschemeyer, *The Complete Poems of Anna Akhmatova*, 1: 241.

tant triumph through her art.[10] In a review/article in the *San Francisco Review of Books,* Emily Leider observes,

> [Akhmatova] sweeps through time, fusing past, present and future, joining her identity to other identities. Fusion, yoking opposites, marks Akhmatova as it does other great ones. . . . She combined concreteness and universality, the aristocrat with the peasant, conservatism with rebellion, sensuousness with asceticism.[11]

During the Regime of Terror, many copies of and notes concerning Akhmatova's poems were lost. (Friends of hers actually memorized lines of her poetry to keep it alive.) The Central Committee of the Commmunist Party outlawed the publication of her poetry in the early 1920s, and for almost twenty years none of her poems appeared in print. The Committee also sent her to Tashkent, in Uzbekistan, during World War II. After she returned to Leningrad in 1944, she still endured long periods of official antagonism. It wasn't until 1956, when Khrushchev delivered his speech to the 20th Party Congress, that she was given some degree of poetic liberation. If Khrushchev's speech restored her and fellow artists to a degree of official prominence, Akhmatova's true audience, the Russian people, had never left her. In the translation *Poems of Akhmatova* by Stanley Kunitz and Max Hayward, Hayward writes in his introduction of a singular event:

> By the time she returned to Leningrad in June 1944, she had regained some of the public standing she had enjoyed before the Party had deliberately tried to drive her into obscurity. In fact,

10. While several translations of Akhmatova's work summarize her life in their introductions, among the best such summaries is Kenyon's own. No doubt the translation that is most helpful in relating life events to the poems is the one by Judith Hemschemeyer, whose many endnotes effectively gloss the poems.

11. Leider, "Anna Akhmatova: A Clear and Elegant Howl," *San Francisco Review of Books,* September 1977, p. 27.

she had never been forgotten, and her enforced silence of the previous years only served now to heighten her moral authority. For many, indeed, she was quite simply the true voice of Russia. This was demonstrated by an extraordinary and fateful incident in Moscow, in May 1944, where she stayed for a while on her way back to Leningrad from Tashkent. When she appeared at a meeting in the Polytechnic Museum (the largest auditorium in Moscow, where Mayakovski had often declaimed after the Revolution) and read her poetry from the stage, the audience of three thousand people rose to their feet and gave her the sort of ovation normally reserved for the highest in the land. It must have seemed like an act of homage and reconciliation — in the spirit of the eager expectations many Russians now had for a better life after the victory over Germany.[12]

Even this brief overview of Akhmatova's life suggests the ways in which Kenyon would have felt a powerful kinship with her.

For one thing, each woman was a rebel in her own way. When Kenyon said to Bly, "I can't have a man as a master," the comment worked two ways. In fact, John Keats had long been at the top of her list of favorite poets (although the literary influence was minimal at best), as was Anton Chekhov as a prose master.[13] What Kenyon sought was a combination of a literary master and something of a spiritual and psychological older sister. She found that in Akhmatova — and Akhmatova's rebelliousness shaped part of that bond. Casual readers of Kenyon might not see the link at first. They think of Kenyon working in her dormer study in the picturesque farmhouse, or taking bucolic walks around Eagle Pond or up Mount Ragged. And it is true that in many ways Kenyon lived a quiet life.

12. Introduction to *Poems of Akhmatova*, trans. Stanley Kunitz with Max Hayward (Boston: Little, Brown, 1973), pp. 21-22.

13. In her 1993 interview with David Bradt, Kenyon commented, "He [Chekhov] really belongs at the head of the list. . . . His compassion, his delicate humor, and his profundity seem to me *most* enviable. And of course his brilliant use of physical detail" (*A Hundred White Daffodils*, p. 178).

But it was a life — like Akhmatova's — that was often twisted and conflicted by painfully difficult circumstances beyond her control: the illnesses and deaths of those she loved, her serious struggle with depression, and, later, her great battle with leukemia.

To recognize those circumstances, however, is not necessarily to submit to the onslaught. Akhmatova did not; neither did Kenyon. Both were by nature rebels. The journal entries Kenyon made in 1961 while she was a student at Forsythe Junior High School capture her rebellious spirit at an early age. For example, disgruntled with the "typical teenage novels" in the school library, Kenyon announced in a September entry, "I will go and check out [at the Public Library] profound, highly philosophical books, no matter how far beyond me they are. I am going to rebel!" She underlined *rebel* three times.[14]

One might be tempted to dismiss such comments as typical of an adolescent. The young Kenyon, however, was not a mere contrarian. Appearing throughout these youthful entries are an impatience with the status quo, a willingness to overstep conventional boundaries, and a willingness to experiment with her own sense of independence. These characteristics deepened as she matured, as did her mature sense of perseverance — her ability to face and address challenges and conflicts in her life. These traits closely allied her in a psychological kinship with Akhmatova.

Kenyon's adult rebellion against the status quo is often demonstrated in the columns she wrote for *The Concord Monitor*. Al-

14. She did go to the library, in fact. The entry for October 4 lists her prize selections: "My, my the books I did check out! *The Sundial* by Shirley Jackson, *A Man Called Peter* by Mrs. Peter Marshall, *The Price of Peace* by some very intelligent looking man (I can't think of his name) and *Science and Christian Belief* by somebody. I intend to read every last one, too. What personal triumph!" She started *A Man Called Peter*, a biography of Peter Marshall, Chaplain of the U.S. Senate, that same day, and it seemed to elicit the strongest reaction. On October 5, Kenyon noted, "I am going to be the black sheep of my family. . . ." She indicated that she was afraid that this book might influence her in a "favorable" way, "and I simply couldn't have that happen, could I." Nevertheless, she did finish the book — but admonished herself afterward: "I must start reading off-color adult novels."

though she sometimes wrote them during periods of depression when she didn't feel up to writing poetry (and consequently, according to Donald Hall, they were not always her best work),[15] the columns gave her the opportunity to explore a broad range of subjects and the satisfaction of accomplishing writing for the public venue.[16] When she was psychologically unable to write poetry, Kenyon found it satisfying to work with the broad palette, to be able to write on whatever topic she wished.

Many of the columns for the *Monitor* are nonetheless winsome, graced by Kenyon's humor and deft descriptive ability. In "The Mailbox," for example, she writes, "Our brick-and-stone post office is as homely as Larry Bird, and just as indispensable."[17] But there is also the column called "Snakes in This Grass?" where Kenyon skewers the plan of a neighbor to use "municipal sludge and industrial organic waste" to fill and reclaim a gravel pit. Kenyon gives examples of other failed attempts at this process in the area, laments the effects upon bodies of water, including Eagle Pond, and ends with an unexpectedly strident voice when addressing the effects on the youth camp on the far side of Eagle Pond:

> There is no way, *no way on earth,* that the stockpiling and spreading of sewage sludge and industrial waste will not compromise the very existence of the camp.
>
> This is the time to protest. About twenty days remain before our neighbor secures permission to move ahead. Once we hear

15. See Hall's comment in his introduction to *A Hundred White Daffodils*, p. xi.

16. Kenyon had experimented with the brief essay since her youth but didn't consider herself an essayist. Mike Pride, an editor of *The Concord Monitor*, recalls that "she was a little reluctant" (*A Hundred White Daffodils*, p. xi) when he approached her about writing for the *Monitor's* "Forums," a brief column to which different writers contributed several times a year. He first asked her to write about bipolar disorder, but she didn't feel up to that. Instead, she wrote about topics of concern to her neighbors, sometimes issue-oriented, sometimes descriptive and reflective. She came to enjoy writing these columns a great deal.

17. Kenyon, *A Hundred White Daffodils*, p. 82.

the sound of the first truck downshifting onto the pond road, any opposition will be too little and too late.[18]

Although often initially reserved with strangers, Kenyon had no difficulty speaking her mind when matters imposed upon her strong beliefs and values. And she had strong feelings about things far beyond Eagle Pond Farm. In her interview with David Bradt, for instance, she spoke passionately about how national support for the arts had suffered under the Bush administration. Her trips abroad with Hall, moreover, kindled Kenyon's awareness of global injustice. Particularly telling is her poem "Woman, Why Are You Weeping?", which she wrote after their trip to India in 1991. During this trip, despite the official functions she had to attend, Kenyon found ample time to travel with her guide, Rajiv, and to record her impressions in a journal. The scenes described in "Woman" — the destitute people, the dead infant's body floating in the river — are first detailed in prose that bears the throb of horror. These people, one realizes, suffer under their own Regime of Terror. Its name is poverty.

Clearly, Akhmatova's rebellion — against political strictures and against the status quo in Russia — appealed to Kenyon. Partly as a result of her rebellion, Akhmatova's life as person and poet was marked by numerous conflicts. Emily Leider summarizes just a few of the more significant ones: "During the Stalinist Terror Anna Akhmatova's poetry was denied publication and the books she had already published were attacked, removed from bookshelves and destroyed. Her former husband, the poet Nikolai Gumilev, was shot and killed [executed by the Bolsheviks in 1921], and their son sent to prison camp."[19] Leider observes that in such harsh times, "Poetry

---

18. Kenyon, *A Hundred White Daffodils*, pp. 124-25.

19. Lev Gumilev, Akhmatova's son, was released from prison on 15 May 1956. Isaiah Berlin reflects on Akhmatova's struggles as a poet during the Regime of Terror in "Anna Akhmatova: A Memoir":

Akhmatova lived in terrible times, during which, according to Nadezhda Mandelstam's account, she behaved with heroism. This is borne out by all available

turns out to be, for a poet, the basic necessity, more essential even than food, a place to live."[20]

Leider's comment should not be taken to mean that Akhmatova used her poetry as an escapist retreat from conflict. On the contrary, her poetry provided room for examination and testing. In *Anna Akhmatova: A Poetic Pilgrimage*, Amanda Haight correctly observes that during the self-destructive years of the Soviet Terror, "Values previously taken for granted were tested and many cast aside as inadequate or simply irrelevant."[21] As the lies of the regime came to light, Akhmatova became her own seeker of truth.

To FIND SUCH POWER, such a strong poetic spirit, in another female poet enthralled Kenyon. Yet, just as significantly, the kinship extended beyond art and personality to spiritual fervor. Like Kenyon, Akhmatova clung to her faith in times of trial. Amanda Haight notes that in her poems Akhmatova "traced the path of her own suffering without melodrama and without self-pity. In doing so she also recorded what had happened to her — her rediscovery of the meaning of life at the very foot of the Cross."[22] One can scarcely understand the kinship between these two poets without understanding this fundamental fact.

---

evidence. She did not in public, nor indeed to me in private, utter a single word against the Soviet regime: but her entire life was what Herzen once described virtually all Russian literature as being — one uninterrupted indictment of Russian reality. The widespread worship of her memory in the Soviet Union today, both as an artist and as an unsurrendering human being, has, so far as I know, no parallel. The legend of her life and unyielding passive resistance to what she regarded as unworthy of her country and herself transformed her into a figure (as Belinsky once predicted about Herzen) not merely in Russian literature, but in Russian history in our century. (Hemschemeyer, *The Complete Poems of Anna Akhmatova*, 2: 43)

20. Leider, "Anna Akhmatova," p. 26.
21. Haight, *Anna Akhmatova: A Poetic Pilgrimage* (New York: Oxford University Press, 1976), p. 194.
22. Haight, *Anna Akhmatova*, p. 194.

This is not to say that Akhmatova's religious faith was deeply orthodox or conventional. Nor was Kenyon's. Kenyon's religious belief was neither categorical nor doctrine-bound. Rather, it was a powerful force, a firmly rooted reality in her life. This was also true of Akhmatova, whose faith emerged most clearly in her late poems.

In Akhmatova's early years, it may be said that her god was poetry, her cause to keep poetry alive in the hearts of the Russian people, and her church the formality of verse. This was especially true in her first four volumes — *Evening* (1912), *Rosary* (1914), *White Flock* (1917), and *Plantain* (1921) — the very volumes from which Kenyon selected most of the poems she translated. These volumes were published in the years just prior to and including World War I, a time when the old Russian verities were shaken and the restrictions of the state began to muzzle poets and free thinkers alike. Akhmatova's religion of art came at a price. In 1959, Akhmatova reflected upon her career in one of her autobiographical journals:

> *Pro domo mea* [as for me], I can say that I never abandoned Poetry, though the frequent hard knocks of the oars against my numbed hands clinging to the side of the boat beckoned me to sink to the bottom. I admit that at times the air around me lost its moisture and ability to transmit sound. As it was lowered into the well, the bucket gave not a joyful splash but a hollow sound of striking a rock. In general, suffocating times began and lasted for years.[23]

But always there was that undercurrent of seeking after God.[24] Although more pronounced in her late work, it is also apparent in the early volumes. It is essential to understand that Akhmatova wrote

23. Polivanov, *Anna Akhmatova and Her Circle*, p. 23.

24. Akhmatova's long narrative poem "At the Edge of the Sea" provides a nearly chronological account of religious holidays in her youth. The poem is useful for understanding the religious atmosphere in which she was raised and which she accepted as her own.

for the Russian *people,* not to satisfy a bureaucracy or system or to win official approbation. She was a laureate of the common folk, and shared their religious sensibility.[25]

Following the Terror, Akhmatova's religious impulse and her tenacious yearning for God appeared more openly and dramatically in her poetry. In "The Last Rose," dated 9 August 1962, Akhmatova wrote,

> Lord! You see I am tired
> Of living and dying and resurrection.
> Take everything, but grant that I may feel
> The freshness of this crimson rose again.[26]

The living and dying and resurrection refer both to the stages of her life during the Terror and to the expectancy of a spiritual transition from this life, of which she is now tired, to eternal life. "Take everything" refers specifically to the things of this world, but that is followed by the petitionary prayer for "this crimson rose," a Dante-esque image. In fact, Akhmatova had read carefully in Dante (and had memorized sections of *The Divine Comedy*) and also in T. S. Eliot (particularly *Four Quartets*), and thus used the rose to represent the supreme fulfillment in divine love.

In several of the poems she wrote following World War II, Akhmatova's faith was not merely couched in a figure (like the divine rose) but became the overt subject matter of the poem. One of

---

25. Amanda Haight closes her biography of Akhmatova with the story of some of her close friends who came to visit her grave forty days after her funeral. According to Orthodox custom, this was the day when there was usually a special service at the grave. But because the day fell during the Easter season, no service was held. At first the friends thought they were alone in their remembrance. To their surprise, however, a set of footprints preceded theirs in the fresh snow. "When they arrived at the grave, the person standing by it turned and went away. No one knew her. She was one of those anonymous Russian women in a gray scarf and quilted jacket" (*Anna Akhmatova,* p. 197).

26. Hemschemeyer, *The Complete Poems of Anna Akhmatova,* 2: 317.

the most powerful of these appears in "Additions of the Cycle *Victory.*" The enjambment of the first two lines (a favorite technique of both Akhmatova and Kenyon) establishes the dialectic:

> The one people once called
> King in jest, God in fact. . . .

It is a poem of confession: Akhmatova writes, "The implement of torture/was heated by the warmth of my breast." She recalls the slaughter of the early disciples for the sake of Christ, but even then there was "the fragrance of immortal roses."[27] From the time of that early persecution and destruction, the world seems to have devolved to the point of decay: "Everything is on the verge of death," she says. She then proclaims her belief:

> The most reliable thing on earth is sorrow,
> And the most enduring — the almighty Word.[28]

"The Year Nineteen Thirteen: A Petersburg Tale," from *Poem Without a Hero,* may well be Akhmatova's stylistic tour-de-force. Formal variations flash and jar with the rising conflicts of the poem. It is especially interesting that, in lieu of expressing pure anger at the lies she uncovers, Akhmatova slyly inserts religious truths as a bulwark against the madness. "Poets/and sinning just don't go together," she proclaims.[29] Although the statement has religious significance, it also points to another trait shared by Kenyon and Akhmatova — the belief in the honesty of the artist.

In one of her memoirs, Akhmatova wrote, "I'm somewhat anti-Browning. He always spoke in another character, for another

27. The persecution of the early church fascinated Akhmatova, perhaps as a parallel to her own life. One of her final diary entries is on that very subject. See *My Half Century: Selected Prose,* ed. Ronald Meyer (Ann Arbor: Ardis Press, 1992), p. 66.

28. Hemschemeyer, *The Complete Poems of Anna Akhmatova,* 2: 619.

29. Hemschemeyer, *The Complete Poems of Anna Akhmatova,* 2: 29.

character. I do not let anybody else speak a word (in my poetry, it goes without saying). I speak myself and for myself everything that is possible and that which is not."[30] Honesty engages reality; honest poetry is authentic to its source and reveals that source — the events that have occurred, the poet's perception of them, and the poet's emotional interaction with them. In this way the poet also preserves a people's history. And indeed, Akhmatova's perception of her task as a poet was to preserve the memory of Russia.

Kenyon spoke in remarkably similar terms about her perception of art. For example, in her interview with Bill Moyers, she pointed out, "One of the functions of poetry is to keep the memory of people and places and things and happenings alive."[31] Fulfilling this function requires that the poet be scrupulously honest, persevering in the truth of authenticity, refusing the charms of romanticizing the event to soften its force for the reader. What better example exists than Kenyon's own "Having it Out with Melancholy"?

In her interview with David Bradt, Kenyon responded to the question "What's the poet's job?" by listing five things: telling the truth, using beautiful language, giving expression to deep feelings, giving everything a name, and providing consolation. She summarized the first four things by saying, "The poet's job is to tell the whole truth and nothing but the truth, in such a beautiful way that people cannot live without it; to put into words those feelings we all have that are so deep, so important, and yet so difficult to name."[32] Such convictions may be complicated when brought to the act of translation. Where does one poet's sense of authenticity impinge upon that of another? The question is an important one for the translating of Akhmatova's work, since one of her highest values in art was precision:

---

30. Polivanov, *Anna Akhmatova and Her Circle*, p. 48.
31. Kenyon, *A Hundred White Daffodils*, p. 164.
32. Kenyon, *A Hundred White Daffodils*, p. 183.

Today it has become customary to "introduce words," to "bring them together." After forty years, that which used to be daring begins to sound trite. There is another way — the way of precision; and something even more important — having each word in its proper place in the line, as if it were there for a thousand years, yet the reader hears it for the first time. This is very difficult, but when one is successful people say: "That's about me; it's as if I wrote it."[33]

For Akhmatova, *precision* consisted of both the tight formalism of her verse and the authentic experience expressed in vivid, honest language. To honor Akhmatova's intentions and the spirit of her work, Kenyon avoided mere *replication* of the poems through a mechanical form of translation and instead sought to recreate the poems altogether.

KENYON ANNOUNCED her method, but also her frustrations, in the introduction to *Twenty Poems of Anna Akhmatova:* "These translations are free-verse versions of rhymed and metered poems. Losing the formal perfection of the Russian verses — much of their 'beautiful clarity' — has been a constant source of frustration and sadness to me and to my co-worker, Vera Sandomirsky Dunham." Believing that it is "impossible to translate with fidelity to form *and* to image," Kenyon decided to "place the integrity of the image over all other considerations."[34] In a sense, she traded authenticity of one sort (a slavish replication of one language into another) for an authenticity of the experiences and the spirit of the poet.

The effect of Kenyon's work is to open our eyes to Akhmatova's world; we seem to see as the poet sees. Take "The Memory of Sun" from *Evening* (1912), which appears as the lead poem in

33. Hemschemeyer, *The Complete Poems of Anna Akhmatova,* 1: 23.
34. Kenyon, *Twenty Poems of Anna Akhmatova,* p. 5. Kenyon and Dunham translated from *Works,* 2 vols., ed. G. P. Struve and B. A. Filippov (New York: Interlanguage Literary Associates, 1965).

Kenyon's collection. The first line makes an overt claim, while the following three in the quatrain provide sensory images that abet and embellish the claim:

> The memory of sun weakens in my heart,
> grass turns yellow,
> wind blows the early flakes of snow
> lightly, lightly.

It is interesting to compare Kenyon's version with several others. For example, Kunitz and Hayward omit any first-person reference, thus abstracting the poet from the event:

> Heart's memory of sun grows fainter,
> sallow is the grass;
> a few flakes toss in the wind
> scarcely, scarcely.[35]

Richard McKane similarly objectifies the opening line, making it an impersonal claim, but he captures the lyricism of the last lines, which appear rather flat and vague in the prior version:

> The memory of sun weakens in the heart,
> the grass is more yellow,
> the wind flutters the early snow-flakes
> gently, gently.[36]

In its lyric beauty, this version is much closer to Kenyon's.

The next three poems in *Twenty Poems* are from *Rosary* (1914), Akhmatova's second volume of poems. In 1963 Akhmatova reflected on this work, perhaps the best-loved volume of hers: "You

---

35. Kunitz and Hayward, *Poems of Akhmatova*, p. 45.

36. McKane, *Anna Akhmatova: Selected Poems* (London: Oxford University Press, 1969), p. 20.

would expect that a small book of love lyrics by a beginner would have drowned in the sea of events. This is not what happened with Rosary."[37] They are "love lyrics," to be sure, but not at all in the traditional sense of romantic love, for these are poems of conflict, of temptation and choice, of powerful yearning, and of love for the land. As Amanda Haight observes, "The overwhelming mood of *Rosary* is of suffering and grief, of a woman abused and deserted, forced back out of necessity, not desire, to discover her own source of strength."[38] Thus, many of the conflicts in the poems are articulated but hardly resolved. The poetic beads of *Rosary* are often strained by such dialectic, a technique that Kenyon would also master in her art.

Perhaps that technique is what led Kenyon to translate "The Guest." If "Lot's Wife" has become one of Akhmatova's most popular poems in the West, "The Guest" is surely one of her most enigmatic. Typically, the poem begins with an unadorned statement: "Everything's just as it was." But just *how* was everything? The following two lines explain. The natural scene hasn't changed, for "fine hard snow" continues to beat against the windows. "And I myself have not changed," the poet declares. The last line of the first stanza, however, threatens everything: "even so, a man came to call." This is the disruptive figure, the guest who intrudes uninvited, disturbing the routine and the customary.

The second stanza reveals the guest's character. When the narrator asks, "What do you want?" his response is a jarring "To be with you in hell." At this point the narrator is able to laugh at his ominous response: "It seems you see/plenty of trouble ahead for us both." The third stanza, however, becomes more personal and cuts more sharply; there is a distinct sense of threat and fear. The guest lifts his "dry hand" to the flowers, bringing the image of death and decay to beauty, and commands the narrator to talk about her lovemaking. The threat intensifies in the fourth stanza as the guest's

37. Polivanov, *Anna Akhmatova and Her Circle*, pp. 40-41.
38. Haight, *Anna Akhmatova*, p. 37.

"half-closed eyes" — as if lidded like a serpent's — remain on her ring. Does his presence threaten the ring? Does he await its removal? Or does the ring serve to ward off the guest's temptation? His face, as he watches the ring, is described oxymoronically as "serenely angry," embracing the dialectic.

At this point in the poem, "the guest" may be interpreted in more than one way. It may indeed be Akhmatova's husband, who left for a six-month stay in Africa in 1910, right after the couple was married, and returned to Africa again in the spring of 1913. This led Roberta Reeder, who wrote the biographical introduction to Hemschemeyer's work, to speculate, "His constant desire to leave the domestic hearth to seek adventure dominated their marriage and helped destroy it."[39] Several readers have suggested that "the guest" is Alexander Blok, a young Russian poet with whom Akhmatova spent increasing amounts of time in the autumn of 1913. At that time, Blok had achieved fame as a poet and influence as the poetry editor of the journal *Love for Three Oranges*. In the journal, Blok had published poems addressed to Akhmatova as well as some poems she had addressed to him. And Akhmatova wrote several of the poems about Blok within a few weeks of writing "The Guest." Akhmatova insisted that she never had an affair with Blok, but the "serenely angry" face that the guest turns upon her ring certainly suggests the interior conflict.

The final stanza, however, opens the poem like a window flung wide, for it returns fully to the narrator:

Oh, I know it fills him with joy —
this hard and passionate certainty

39. See the introduction to Hemschemeyer's *The Complete Poems of Anna Akhmatova*, 1: 36. Reeder also quotes Valeriya Sreznevskaya, one of Akhmatova's closest friends, who viewed the marriage as an ongoing power struggle: "Their relationship was more like a secret dwelling — from her side, for her own affirmation of herself as a free woman; from his, because of a desire not to submit . . . and to remain independent and powerful. . . . Alas without power over this eternally elusive, many-sided woman who refused to submit to anyone!" (1: 34).

that there is nothing he needs,
and nothing I can keep from him.

Here one finds the theme developed in *Evening* and amplified in
Rosary: the unrequited love of the female poet. She is incapable of
withholding the power of her love even from one who appears not
to need it.

"The Guest" and *Rosary* as a whole can only fully be under-
stood, however, in light of the deepening religious patterns in this
period of Akhmatova's poetic life. In his study of Akhmatova, Sam
Driver points out that, instead of mystical language and symbolism,
Akhmatova used the religious language and artifacts of traditional
Russian orthodoxy.[40] And there is this supporting comment from
Roberta Reeder: "Nadezhda Mandelstam says that Mandelstam
spoke to her of Akhmatova in these terms before the revolution: 'In
Akhmatova's recent verse there has been a turn toward hieratic state-
liness, a religious simplicity and solemnity. . . . The voice of renunci-
ation grows stronger all the time in her verse, and at the moment
her poetry bids fair to become a symbol of Russian grandeur.'"[41]

In *Evening,* her first collection, Akhmatova frequently adopts
the voice of the abused Russian peasant woman. One might say
that she becomes their voice. Her voice is richer with possibilities
in *Rosary,* as "The Guest" shows us. In the final stanza of the poem,
the narrator is positioned in a Christ-like fashion, standing before
the guest, willing to give him everything but unable to give him
anything precisely because the guest doesn't need anything that she
has to give. The guest thereby wears many faces. He represents the
people who reject poetry and the poet's spiritual marriage to art; the
state that hardened its heart against the poet; and for Akhmatova,
with her unflagging interest in critical reception, those who
scorned the gift she had to offer.

40. Driver, *Anna Akhmatova* (New York: Twayne, 1972), p. 114.
41. Quoted in the introduction to Hemschemeyer, *The Complete Poems of
Anna Akhmatova,* 1: 64.

The next three works that appear in *Twenty Poems* are taken from Akhmatova's third volume, *White Flock* (1917). That *White Flock* continued many of the themes of Akhmatova's first two volumes is not surprising. Like an old shirt coming apart, her marriage grew increasingly tattered. In addition to Gumilev's prolonged absences, rumors of an affair were whispered about, nurturing the themes of the abused lover and unrequited love that Akhmatova had already explored. By this time she had become more of a public figure, and that no doubt fueled some of the rumors. By the late 1910s she was in the center of poetic life in Saint Petersburg, one of the celebrated members of the cabaret crowd. She was close to Osip Mandelstam, a fellow Acmeist. Vladimir Mayakovsky, another of the Acmeists, showed more than a passing interest in Akhmatova. And then there was Vladimir Shileiko, whom she married after she divorced Gumilev (after the revolution).[42] But this marriage was troubled too. Understandably, the dialectical battles continued to rage within Akhmatova's spirit and fueled her art during this period.

Not surprisingly, Kenyon selected poems that exemplify these conflicts. In "There is a sacred, secret line in loving," the narrator confronts the fierce temptation to engage in an adulterous relationship. "In loving," as Kenyon notes, literally means "in inloveness" or "being in love." That is the state of the heart, as the first line of the first stanza tells us, but it is opposed by a "line" that is sacred and secret — presumably a marriage vow, since, as the second line says, even attraction and passion cannot cross it. Indeed, the "line" is so powerful that it trumps the power of passion, "even if lips draw near in awful silence/and love tears at the heart."

The second stanza argues that the friendship of the past is no guard against the passion of this moment. Friendship is weak; prior happiness is forgotten. There is only the moment of terrible yearning toward an unseen void.

---

42. The marriage to Shileiko, as Kenyon noted in her introduction, was itself a six-year horror. Toward the end of it, Akhmatova lived in a ménage à trois with Nikolai Punin and his wife. After divorcing Shileiko, Akhmatova married Punin.

The third stanza begins by intensifying the moment. "Those who try to come near it are insane" — that is, if they believe they can edge up to the "sacred, secret line in loving" and remain unscathed. And those who do reach it are "shaken by grief," having trespassed their own vows. The narrator's resolution in the final two lines is to steel herself against the temptation:

> So now you know exactly why
> my heart beats no faster under your hand.

The resolution, one must admit, is somewhat infirm. Despite the narrator's resolve not to get entangled, the lover's hand does lie over her heart, taking its measure. The tension endures.

The transition from Akhmatova's first three volumes to *Plantain* (1921) is profound. World War I had shaken Russia, and there was a growing internal suspicion of Russian writers who might be subversive to the state. In her *Northern Elegies*, Akhmatova wrote,

> I, like a river,
> Was rechanneled by this stern age.[43]

The rechanneling began in the late 1910s, when the very nature of Russia began to change.

Kenyon captures the uncertainty and encroaching fear that marked that time in "Twenty-first," her first selection from *Plantain*. In the poem it is night; the capitol in Saint Petersburg is silhouetted in darkness. Out of the darkness comes this sharp statement:

> Some good-for-nothing — who knows why —
> made up the tale that love exists on earth.

The comment turns two ways, of course: to the savagery wrought by World War I, and to the wreck of Akhmatova's marriage. No won-

---

43. Quoted in Hemschemeyer, *The Complete Poems of Anna Akhmatova*, 2: 347.

der that she proclaims in the last line, "And now it seems I'm sick all the time."

This volume also contains vividly personal poems that mirror Kenyon's feelings in striking ways. One of the poems begins,

> There is a certain hour every day
> so troubled and heavy . . .
> I speak to melancholy in a loud voice
> not bothering to open my sleepy eyes.[44]

One wonders if Akhmatova's frankness emboldened Kenyon to write "Having it Out with Melancholy." Unquestionably, Akhmatova's authentic honesty about her experiences with emotional darkness helped Kenyon confront her own darker emotions.

The poems of *Plantain* capture the inexorable tide of change sweeping over Russia. They unmask Akhmatova's inner anguish during this time of personal and political upheaval. But they also capture a lingering sense of beauty in a profusion of natural images. Despite everything, it seems, the land prevails. That precious "Russian soil," which to a Russian represents a way of life, a historical rootedness as well as a pastoral beauty, endures. At times the fragile beauty seems threatened, however. One poem begins with a comment on birdsong:

> I hear the always-sad voice of the oriole
> and I salute the passing of delectable summer.

---

44. See also Poem IX from *Requiem:*

Now madness half shadows
my soul with its wing,
and makes it drunk with fiery wine
and beckons toward the black ravine.
And I've finally realized
that I must give in . . .

(Hemschemeyer, *The Complete Poems of Anna Akhmatova*, 2: 107)

The second stanza begins with an image of harvesters whose hitched-up skirts "fly in the wind like holiday flags." But this seemingly cheerful description is immediately countered by longing: "Now if only we had. . . ." In the final stanza, as if echoing the oriole's "always-sad" song, the narrator admits, "I sense unavoidable darkness coming near." The poem does not end on this note of darkness, however. We are not left with Yeats's rough beast slouching toward Bethlehem. Instead, the narrator admonishes us to

> come and see the Paradise where together,
> blissful and innocent, we once lived.

One might well say that one task Akhmatova set for herself as poet was to preserve in her artistic images that bit of Paradise we have left — and perhaps might reclaim.

Kenyon selected the final four poems in *Twenty Poems* from Akhmatova's later work. Significant among these, if only because it represents the longer autobiographical and dramatic poems that Akhmatova tended to write in her later years, is "Tale of the Black Ring." It is significant on several other levels as well, especially when one recognizes that the black ring symbolizes the poet's song, the ringing of her words, the dark mysteries disinterred from her soul.

In Part One Akhmatova explains how she inherited the ring from her grandmother. As a Tartar, her grandmother was "bitterly angry/when I was baptized." But because she "turned kind before she died," she gave Akhmatova the ring with this uncertain comment:

> "It becomes her,
> with this things will be better for her."

Why does it become her? Or will it *become* her, as if possessing her? And will the gift of song in fact make things better for her? The backdrop of Part One, then, provides the history of the ring, which raises many questions that play through the rest of the poem.

In Part Two the poet confronts the predicament of what subject to sing about: "There is plenty of grief, so little joy." Is the responsibility of the poet to sing of grief as well as joy? At this point the poet cannot confront that task; she turns her face from the truth and admits, "I lost the ring." The loss is metaphorical. It represents the poet's refusal to use her gifts to confront the reality of the full range of authentic human experience. When one of her friends attempts to encourage her to write anyway, she grows angry and sends them all away — an act of further separation.

In Part Three she returns to her "cheerful room," her hideaway from suffering. Nonetheless, she calls out "like a bird of prey" and falls back on her bed, remembering how she sat at supper, touching neither food nor drink, holding the black ring under the tablecloth. As she held it, she saw the dark eyes of her friends imploring her to write. Part Three ends with a final implicit question regarding the gift of song. It seems enigmatic, as if unattached to the rest of the poem:

> They won't come to me with what they have found!
> Far over the swiftly moving boat
> the sails turned white,
> the sky flushed pink.

Metaphorically, however, the implicit question perfectly resolves the poem. No one will bring the subject matter — here, the gifts — to the poet. Poetry is not merely a matter of receiving. It requires outward vision, looking beyond the "cheerful room" of one's own comfort. If the poet does this, she might discover, instead of impressions of great grief, the image of responsive joy in life — a boat moving swiftly, sails white, the beauty of a sky "flushed pink."

KENYON'S FIVE-YEAR immersion in Akhmatova's life and work, which included the daunting and often frustrating labor of translation, deeply enriched Kenyon's own growth as a poet. Perhaps most importantly, it bolstered her own confidence as a poet. In

Akhmatova, Kenyon found someone practicing the craft in the way she herself had already intuitively started to work as a poet. The careful attention to precise language, the dialectic of emotions, the unexpected delight of phrases and lines that changed meanings or gave birth to new ways of seeing — these hallmarks of Akhmatova's craft excited and emboldened her. The translation work also solidified Kenyon's own belief in the centrality of the vivid image as the starting point for the poem. Indeed, in her interview with David Bradt, Kenyon herself observed that "I came to believe in the absolute value of the image when I was working on these poems by Akhmatova."[45]

One way to measure Kenyon's growth as a poet is to compare the poems of *From Room to Room* with those of *The Boat of Quiet Hours*. The earlier volume contains poems about finding a place; the latter, about owning it. This volume, most of which Kenyon drafted during the years she was translating Akhmatova, also shows greater confidence in form and language.

Certainly, growing more confident in one's own literary style and achieving greater competence in using the tools of the poetic craft are valuable gifts. But the most valuable gift that Kenyon received from the translation work was undoubtedly the kinship of spirit she felt with Akhmatova. When speaking with David Bradt about Akhmatova's poetry, Kenyon said, "The images in a good poem come from a deep place."[46] The work of translation inevitably transports the translator (as opposed to the word-changer, who is focused on the mechanics of linguistic exchange) deep into the heart — the moods, experiences, fears and joys — of the poet. By her own native disposition Kenyon shared many of those deep places with Akhmatova. A spiritual kinship grew between them through the enduring tie of the poems.

Kenyon's translation work was not merely a labor of love in homage to Akhmatova, without question one of the greatest Rus-

---

45. Kenyon, *A Hundred White Daffodils*, p. 180.
46. Kenyon, *A Hundred White Daffodils*, p. 180.

sian poets of the twentieth century. Rather, it was a coming together of two poetic souls. From that encounter, Kenyon certainly received as much as she gave to the work of sorting through literal meanings to find the "right" meaning, capturing the lyrical intensity of a line, and focusing the image so clearly that one sees just as the poet saw. This experience was more than an expert schooling in poetic devices. It was the indissoluble meeting of great minds and a poetic sisterhood of beauty, power, and grace.

CHAPTER SIX

The Boat of Quiet Hours

The Poetry of Encounter

If *From Room to Room* acquired a reading public for Kenyon, her translations of Anna Akhmatova granted her a certain authority in the poetry world. During the time she was translating Akhmatova, Kenyon was also working on the poems that would constitute *The Boat of Quiet Hours*.[1] During those five years her confidence and sureness as a poet grew profoundly, permitting her to engage deeply personal topics in a very direct manner. *The Boat of Quiet Hours* is not only her longest volume but in all respects her pivotal work.

This is not to say that it met with immediate publishing success. She first submitted the manuscript to Scott Walker, founder of Graywolf Press, who informed her in 1982 that the press lacked the funds

---

1. The title and epigraph for the volume are taken from Keats's *Endymion:* "I'll smoothly steer/My little boat, for many quiet hours." Surely Kenyon also held in mind the famous first lines of the poem:

> A thing of beauty is a joy forever:
> Its loveliness increases; it will never
> Pass into nothingness; but still will keep
> A bower quiet for us, and a sleep
> Full of sweet dreams, and health, and quiet breathing.

The quotation Kenyon used for the epigraph first appears in her handwriting on the front of a manila folder.

to do a volume of poetry at that time. Alice Quinn at Knopf kept a copy of the manuscript, hoping to publish it, but urging Kenyon to submit it elsewhere in the meantime. Under the title "The Little Boat" she submitted it to Wesleyan University Press, Princeton University Press, and then W. W. Norton, which declined the manuscript in October 1983. She submitted it under the title "The Pond at Dusk" to Holt, Rinehart and Winston, which declined it in October 1984. Finally, Graywolf Press had some money again, and Scott Walker wrote to Kenyon, encouraging her to submit the manuscript again. When the volume was published in 1986, it was with the publisher Kenyon had first wanted.[2] Throughout this process, Kenyon had several readers comment on the manuscript as a whole, and the shape of the book as well as individual poems changed.

The volume appeared to reviews of generally high praise. In *Poetry* Linda Gregerson wrote, "The beauty of repose is a beauty most of us may only fitfully emulate or wistfully, and from a distance, behold. It is the chief beauty of Jane Kenyon's poetry and the informing ground of her vocal and speculative range." While praising Kenyon's sense of "song" or melody in the poems, Gregerson added, "Kenyon is self-reflective in the quiet of her contemplative book but never self-indulgent. Even when her perspectives are the recreated perspective of childhood, her voice is unwaveringly the voice of an adult; it cultivates no false ingenuousness."[3] Writing for *The New York Times Book Review*, Carol Muske observed that *The Boat of Quiet Hours* "seems more a condition of thought than a collection of separate poems."[4] If *From Room to Room* examines the "condition of thought" of finding a place, this volume examines the poet's condition in that place.

In "History and the Transpersonal Talent," a review/essay in the *New England Review*, Richard Katrovas observes of Kenyon's

2. These were not the only publishers Kenyon corresponded with. In fact, the archives for this volume include two files of such letters.

3. Gregerson, Review of *The Boat of Quiet Hours*, by Jane Kenyon, *Poetry* 151 (February 1988): 421.

4. Muske, Review of *The Boat of Quiet Hours*, by Jane Kenyon, *The New York Times Book Review*, 21 June 1987, p. 13.

work, "Meditating on the phenomenal world, its generative abundance, is the only stay against dread, which can never be annihilated but may be subsumed and placed in perspective. Kenyon's elegaic voice, poem after poem, belongs to one who regards the process of passings away in the midst of restorations." Yet his reservation (though not strong) also has to do precisely with Kenyon's poetic distancing from the event: "The lives of those beloved for whom she mourns are tethered to the great wheel of seasons; mourning her beloved, she mourns the world. If at times I find Kenyon's relentless sanity a little maddening, and grow a bit heavy-lidded from listening over an entire volume to beautifully restrained music in an inexorable minor key, I have perhaps discovered weakness in my own talent as a reader."[5] If reservations about Kenyon's poems in this volume do appear in reviews, they are generally of the sort that Katrovas expresses, having to do with Kenyon's personal equanimity in engaging an emotional event. Having examined Kenyon's poetic principles, however, one can well understand the reason. She relied on the lyric form and the image to do the work. With the exception of several of the intimately personal poems of later volumes, at this stage she relies upon her narrative to engage the event. She shapes the environment of that narrative through the images, sounds, and diction of her craft.

The Boat of Quiet Hours demonstrates advances in both technique and subject matter. The volume is structured in the following four sections:

   I. Walking Alone in Late Winter
  II. Mud Season (beginning with "The Hermit")
 III. The Boat of Quiet Hours (beginning with "Thinking of Madame Bovary")
 IV. Things (beginning with "Song")

5. Katrovas, "History and the Transpersonal Talent," *New England Review* 7 (Spring 1989): 346.

Alternate section titles appear in drafts of the manuscript: "Philosophy in Warm Weather" for I; "Killing the Plants" for II; "Ill Temper at Summer's End" and also "Near Water" for III. Each section roughly corresponds to seasonal changes at Eagle Pond Farm — Section I focusing on winter, Section II on spring, Section III on summer, and Section IV on late summer and early autumn. One way to measure the heightened craftsmanship in *The Boat of Quiet Hours* is by Kenyon's own criterion of the sharp, arresting image. By her own admission, the intensity of Akhmatova's imagery deeply affected her own artistry. In this volume the images emerge from their context with stinging clarity and with an aesthetic appropriateness that leaves the reader saying, "Yes, that's exactly the way to put it."

Typically, many of these images are elemental. In "Portrait of a Figure near Water," Kenyon writes of the calm of water as a restorative agent. In this poem the water counters the fire of anger: "Anger, the inner/arsonist, held a match to her brain." The images are always vivid and specific. In "Mud Season" she writes, "the first shoots/of asparagus will rise,/the fingers of Lazarus...." And in the same poem:

> Beside the porch step
> the crocus prepares an exaltation
> of purple, but for the moment
> holds its tongue. . . .

"The Appointment" repeats this pattern of personification:

> . . . the breeze
> made the heart-shaped leaves of the birch
> tell all their secrets,
> though they were lost on me. . . .

Such imagery is spare and sharp, with no wasted language or added embellishment. It demonstrates the work of a mature poet grown sure of her artistic touch.

In these poems Kenyon also begins to explore the major themes that would mark her future work. Each of these themes shapes a self-encounter and self-discovery. While signals of her anxiety and depression appear in *From Room to Room,* here for the first time we see her addressing her depression as subject matter. In addition, the interplay and tension between sudden sorrow and commonplace events, hinted at in *From Room to Room,* develop regular patterns here. Most profoundly, both her searching after God and her personal suspension of spiritual sensibility between earth and heaven are pronounced in these poems.

Most striking, perhaps, is her engagement of her own depression. While the personal effects of her illness will be discussed more fully in the context of "Having it Out with Melancholy," several general points about it should be established here, since it first emerges as a poetic topic in this volume.

ALTHOUGH KENYON said that her depression was not properly diagnosed until she was thirty-eight, she was well aware of the fact that she suffered from the illness throughout her life.[6] It was not unusual at that point in time to receive late diagnosis for the particular kind of depression she suffered: bipolar disorder (a more accurate clinical term for manic depression). It would often be masked by other symptomology and be diagnosed as attention deficit hyperactivity disorder, dysthymic depression, or simply a personality disorder.

According to Kay Redfield Jamison's landmark study *An Unquiet Mind,* published in 1996, bipolar disorder afflicts creative writers and other artists disproportionately to the general population. Other studies have since supported Jamison's claim.[7] It is not a fact lost on artists themselves. Robert Pinsky closes his poem "Essay on Psychiatrists" (1975) with an elderly professor addressing his

---

6. Kenyon, *A Hundred White Daffodils* (Saint Paul, Minn.: Graywolf Press, 1999), p. 153.

7. Jamison, *An Unquiet Mind: A Memoir of Moods and Madness* (New York: Knopf, 1996).

class of students. With the rise of Enlightenment thinking during the eighteenth century, the professor argues, the very logic these thinkers sought left a void. One had to fit everything into a category — each human, even God. Squeeze and shove and encapsulate until someone — a subject — fit the category.

When the old traditions of the intrinsic worth of humanity and God were capsized, "Poets were left/With emotions and experiences, and with no way/To examine them." Human creativity, like the human spirit itself, won't be squeezed into orderly cubicles or be reduced to logical categories the sum of which is a perfect and perfectly predictable human. As a consequence of society's effort to do so, the professor adds, "Poets and men/Of genius began to go mad." The old professor then begins to list the poets who come readily to his mind: Thomas Gray, William Collins, Christopher Smart, William Blake, Samuel Coleridge, Hart Crane, Ezra Pound. The list is partial, of course; it can be extended considerably. It includes such writers as F. Scott Fitzgerald and William Faulkner, both of whom were hospitalized, and Ernest Hemingway, who committed suicide. It includes such poets as Anne Sexton, Sylvia Plath, and Vachel Lindsay, all of whom committed suicide, and Robert Lowell, who was hospitalized. It includes the painter Vincent Van Gogh, who ended his impoverished life with suicide. And recent studies provide substantial evidence that the composers Handel and Schumann (who was hospitalized) were manic depressive. The names are like the tolling of bells at a memorial service. Their works are a legacy of exquisite but sometimes terrifying beauty. One is tempted to question whether, without the illness, we would have the works today.

What we receive from such artists — the value of their terrible legacy — is their uncanny ability to capture their own precarious moods and to translate them into terms that embody our own. In their work we find connections and embodiments of mood that we recognize even if we lack the blaze of creativity to set them forth ourselves. It is not just their own experiences but *our* experiences they capture.

Analogy helps us understand this disorder, if we accept the

qualification that some hypothetical "normal" brain chemistry for humanity exists as an ideal. Picture an even line — it may be a smooth path. That's the imaginary starting point for a normal person's life. Of course it has twists and turns, a few bumps, maybe even a pothole or two. Any life has its tension points and tragedies. But now imagine a path with a significant dip in it — this is the path of someone suffering from unipolar or "clinical" depression. The dip is so low, in fact, that one can't see the main path from its nadir. One just has to keep on going, slogging along until one finds the main path again. Sometimes the process requires the aid of medication or other treatment, but as time passes, the main path is usually accessible once again. In rare acute cases, the main path is permanently lost. For most people suffering from this form of depression, however, this provides a fairly accurate picture of the disorder: dips down into valleys of despair and anxiety, and an ongoing effort to regain the equilibrium of a "normal" life.

The picture for the person suffering from bipolar depression is completely different — because of the simple fact that for this individual there is no "normal" path. One exists in hilly country, even mountainous terrain. The bipolar depressive sinks like a rock into valleys that seem impossibly wide and deep precisely because she has been on the mountaintop. "Normal" life is impossible, because for her it is defined not by an even path but by the mountaintop. Her quirky brain chemistry, virtually unprompted, almost mockingly, will suddenly send her on a spiral upward. Under her own power she climbs up that mountainside, going faster every second. Finally she hits a high plateau where she stops to rest for a while. But even while she's resting, she is dizzy with euphoria, eager to finish the climb.

Now she dances where others fear to climb, feet clicking lightly on a thin sliver of rock that holds her head in the heavens. She is almost like a goddess, above everything — including human responsibility. Of course, there are no other humans at this height.

But then — as she always must — she trips while dancing and plummets down. Faster and faster. Through clouds that darken around her. Where did the sun go? And the farther she falls, the faster she falls. Newtonian laws are suspended; no friction, no resistance slow the plunge. And when she finally lands, it is not on the valley floor but in a dismal swamp where the water is green-scummed and the sides are steeply banked in rock, and the best she can do is swim hard, hoping she doesn't sink all the way.

Analogy, however, fails to fully capture either pole of the illness. In *Darkness Visible* (1990), William Styron laments the overuse of the word *depression,* calling it a "true wimp of a word for such a major illness." He adds, "For over seventy-five years the word has slithered innocuously through the language like a slug, leaving little trace of its intrinsic malevolence and preventing, by its very insipidity, a general awareness of the horrible intensity of the disease when out of control."[8] At other points Styron describes depression as a "brainstorm" — a tempest in the head where sanity shipwrecks.

The depressive pole of the illness exhibits a range of deepening symptoms. General indicators for the illness include standard criteria: loss of appetite; loss of interest in previously pleasurable activities; loss of energy, evidenced in long stays in bed and irregular sleep patterns; and general sadness. Depression is measured by the key word *loss;* its final state is loss of sanity in psychosis or suicide. The manic pole, on the other hand, is measured by excess: excessive energy, particularly of a creative sort; impulsiveness; feelings of superiority, even grandiosity; irritability ranging to rage; increased sexual appetite. Here, too, the excess can tip one into psychosis.

Several factors, singly or in combination, contribute to bipolar disorder. Genetic predisposition has received keen attention during the past decade of gene research. The emphasis here is on heredity and the increased incidence of the illness among those with a family history of it.[9] The second primary concern is biological — the

8. Styron, *Darkness Visible* (New York: Random House, 1990), p. 37.

9. In her interview with Bill Moyers, Kenyon explained her own genetic predisposition:

> There is a genetic component to this. My father had it, and I believe his mother had it. I really take after my father's people. I'm sure that it came down his

delicate dance of neurotransmitters in the brain chemistry. For a variety of reasons this dance may turn into a stagger. Brain chemistry is clearly a factor in both unipolar and bipolar depressive disorders, affecting the neurotransmitters dopamine, serotonin, and norepinephrene.

The standard psychopharmaceutical treatment for bipolar disorder includes two approaches. The first is using a mood stabilizer such as lithium, Depakote, Tegretol, or Topamax, all drugs initially used to control seizures but found to have psychotherapeutic properties. The second is using an antidepressant, ranging from the earlier tricyclics (Tofranil, Elavil, Norpramine, and so on) to the more recent selective serotonin reuptake inhibitors (SSRIs such as Prozac, Zoloft, and so on). Kenyon also tried Nardil, one of the more dangerous classes of drugs known as monoamine oxidase inhibitors (MAOI). Although Nardil, like all of the MAOIs, places severe restrictions on diet, Kenyon liked the effects of the medicine — one being that she was able to write extensively. She gave it up only because it prevented her from sleeping and made her exhausted. In "Having it Out with Melancholy," Kenyon spins off a partial list of the psychotropics she had used. In fact, in her interview with Bill Moyers, Kenyon confessed, "I jokingly call my psychiatrist my 'mixologist.' He's a good man."[10]

THESE FUNDAMENTAL clinical data indicate what Kenyon began to confront in a deeply personal way in the 1970s. At this time it was more a matter of her intuited sense of her mood than a clear medi-

---

lines. I'm trying to explain to people who have never experienced this kind of desolation, what it is. It's important for people to understand that those with endogenous depression, melancholia, don't do this for the fun of it. I'm no more responsible for my melancholy than I am for having brown eyes. Unfortunately, it's taken me a long time to really believe that it's not my fault. It's like having heart disease or diabetes. I've decided that I want to increase people's understanding about this disease. I want to ease people's burdens. (*A Hundred White Daffodils*, p. 159)

10. Kenyon, *A Hundred White Daffodils*, p. 159.

cal diagnosis. Several poems in the volume, however, indicate her growing awareness of it.

There are poems that focus on depression throughout the volume. Not surprisingly, several of them are found in Section One, focusing on the winter season, when the amount of light was reduced during the prolonged New England season of shadows. Psychology labels the depression induced by this lack of light Seasonal Affective Disorder (SAD); for Kenyon it was an inchoate longing for light which threads through several poems.

"Depression in Winter" is not technically about psychological depression at all but about a small depression on the south side of a boulder where sun has heated stone and melted snow. A "crescent" of earth has cleared, revealing the dried winter life beneath. The first stanza describes the physical setting; the second the poet's reaction to it. She has plunged through the snow, sinking "with every step up to my knees." Snow traps her, cages her, so that she has to throw herself forward "with a violence/of effort." Her unhappiness drives her; the battle with the snow makes her "greedy for unhappiness." Sadness is the rage that fuels more sadness. Then, "by accident," she finds the depression cleared of snow. It is analogous to human depression, chiseled out of cold, but here it is serendipitous, for it reveals bits of life even in the dead of winter. Thus it is that she "turned back down my path, chastened and calm."

The composition of "Depression in Winter" has an interesting history in its own right. The first draft was penned on the back of a Hallmark postcard. The first lines read,

> There is a little kingdom between the
> south-facing side of a boulder
> and the snow that girds the woods all around . . .

One of the first revisions Kenyon made in following drafts was to change "There is" to the active "There comes." In the untitled first draft, the poet is not present in the poem. The focus turns upon life at the base of the boulder, including "a mouse or a vole" hibernating there. In a later handwritten draft, Kenyon titled the poem "Ill-Temper in January" and added the first-person second stanza. Later drafts include her typical heavy crossing out as she searched for the right word or turn of phrase. One draft lists in the margin a series of alternative words for "unhappiness": trouble, wretchedness, affliction, anguish, suffering, desolation, despair, and tribulation.[11] In the final version, the poem as a whole is stripped down, and that bareness complements the subject.

If "Depression in Winter" suggests Kenyon's confronting her illness by means of metaphor, "Depression" shows her doing so so more directly. The poem is as stark as it is brief. The initial line evokes feelings of smallness, worthlessness, and insignificance: ". . . a mote. A little world. Dusty. Dusty." Then one realizes that by means of the ellipsis all these words function adjectivally to qualify depression. Here too Kenyon uses analogy to make the feeling concrete. She describes the women who followed Christ, ministering to his needs and loving him. They were first at the empty tomb, of course, and rushed forth with the joyful news. But the poem ends not with a bang of joy but with a whimper of despair: they "are not believed. . . ." The repeated ellipsis brings us full circle to the first line; in between lies depression, a severance from joy.

"Sun and Moon" focuses on the treatment for depression rather than describing the experience of it. The dedication, "For Donald Clark," refers to the doctor who first treated Kenyon for bipolar disorder. Now she has a name for the enemy; now too she has the means for combatting it. Yet, as she lies back "on the new bed" in the hospital, she has

> a vision of souls
> stacked up like pelts
> under my soul, which was ill —

11. According to Hall, both he and Kenyon used "a particularly excellent edition of Roget." In a letter to the author, Hall notes, "When you look up 'odor' you find 'spice.' When you look up 'miracle' you find 'prodigy.'"

so heavy with grief
it kept the others from rising.

Here is the soul's illness. But during a week of hospitalization and treatment, as the doctor's face "appeared/and disappeared/over the foot of the bed," she began to improve: "By slow degrees/the outlandish sadness waned." In the final stanza she is "restored" to her living room, but she is in an uncertain stasis between health and illness. She looks over the familiar furnishings and pictures "with something like delight,/only pale, faint — as from a great height." She feels a sense of distance, of not being connected to her "real life." These feelings remind her that daily activities go unheeded:

I let the phone ring; the mail
accrued unopened
on the table in the hall.

Here in "Sun and Moon," as in the two previous poems, Kenyon carefully monitors and poetically balances the encounter with depression, first by use of analogy and second by narrative. But in some other poems Kenyon had to work hard to keep the rage against the illness under control. Nowhere is this battle waged more powerfully than in the writing of "Rain in January" and "Bright Sun after Heavy Snow."

In earlier drafts of "Rain in January," the narrator reveals herself far more intimately than in the final form. Thus, in one early draft, the first stanza opens this way:

I woke before dawn still [/] in my body.
Water runs [ran] [/] down every window
like tears of lamentation.

The rain on the windows is a metaphor for the narrator's lamentation. Kenyon later revised the stanza to maintain the concreteness of the setting but withhold the direct emotional connection:

I woke before dawn, still
in a body. Water ran
down every window, and rushed
from the eaves.

Notice the interesting poetic touches here. The enjambment on
"still" creates simultaneously an emotional resting point and a
turning point: she awakened still; she is still in a body. Notice also
that it is now "a" body, not "my" body. By substituting the article for
the personal pronoun, she creates a certain emotional distance, unlike the intensity of involvement in the earlier draft.

An earlier draft has lines totally deleted from later drafts:

~~We~~ [I know I] live in the pause

Between blows of the axe

And nothing seems stranger to me

Than my life. . . .

Again, it may be that the first-person confessional narration
seemed too overt for Kenyon, for she discarded the lines entirely to
concentrate on the concrete image of the smoke from the chimney
that is the focus of stanza three in the final form of the poem. The
smoke "came down" into the yard and

brooded there
on the unlikelihood of reaching

heaven.

As she moved through the revisions, then, Kenyon displaced the inward confessional tone with poetic imagery that carries greater
weight and urgency. Here the personified cloud of smoke broods (a

perfect verb) "on the unlikelihood of reaching heaven," perfectly incarnating the despair of depression without ever naming it. Thus the poem's subject is universalized for all readers.

Kenyon did the same kind of refining work on "Bright Sun after Heavy Snow." The early drafts bear the title "After Heavy Snow: Bright Sun." In the first stanza, the image of snow sliding off the eaves gives way to this thought: "astonishing/how violence eases the mind." In the second stanza, "all seems flawed" under the sun's bright light. It reveals the forced bulb, just beginning to bud — but her response is a return to violence and impotence:

> I would dash the pot to pieces
> if I could raise my hand.

A later draft introduces the "small injury" of some affront over which she broods. But the violence edges more sharply inward. When she notices a cloud of chimney smoke downdrafted into the yard, an image comes to her, and "I assume my place/in the kingdom of hell."

Examining the drafting stages of "Bright Sun after Heavy Snow" reveals a poetic as well as an emotional modulation. Kenyon waged an inner battle through the poem as she turned from overt statement to her intuitive reliance upon suggestive imagery. She subsumes the heightened emotions of the earlier drafts in concrete portraits. The first two stanzas, except for pacing and word choice, remain substantially the same. The brilliance of the sun still reveals flaws; its light can be dangerous. But in stanza two the light reveals "forced bulbs on the sill/that refuse to bloom" instead of the narrator's sudden urge to smash the budding life. In the third stanza the neighbor's affront remains, but it is now given concrete image: "it rises in my mind/like the huge banks of snow along the road." Gone is the violent wrath of earlier drafts. And in the fourth stanza the shadow of the chimney smoke still moves across the yard, but instead of evoking images of hell, it points significantly to an objective correlative for her emotional state:

> The clothesline rises in the wind. One
> wooden pin is left, solitary as a finger;
> it, too, rises and falls.

That image — particularly with the discreet positioning of "one" at the end of the third line of the stanza, so that it dangles uncertainly — perfectly incarnates the mood. It is a triumph of art *over* emotion.

"Bright Sun after Heavy Snow" prevents the reader from mawkishly sentimentalizing Kenyon's artistry as if she were a complete victim of the illness she had. Rather, she dignified the illness by admitting she had it, but also by refusing to be defined by it, either as person or as poet. When a poet confronts her personal realities in such a forthright way in some of her poems, the danger for readers is to let that reality tincture all the other poetry she wrote. To do so is a disservice to a woman of such powerful vitality and capacity for delight.

Clearly the majority of poems in the volume are of the latter sort, extrapolated as they are from Kenyon's life at Eagle Pond Farm, which delighted her thoroughly and replenished her vitality. Several poems are kindled by specific events. "Evening at a Country Inn," for example, was occasioned when Hall's son Andrew had a car accident. This poem finds Kenyon and Hall at an inn, with Kenyon juxtaposing bucolic details of the country setting with Hall's distractedness. Pacing the downstairs hall, he thinks of the accident — of picking "the slivered glass" from Andrew's hair. The shards of tragedy lay before the couple — but there is comfort too. Commenting on a truck loaded with hay that has just pulled into the nearby gas station, Kenyon writes, "I wish you would look at the hay —/the beautiful sane and solid bales of hay." Here as elsewhere, the farm and country life represent order and restoration. The poem "November Calf" provides a tender scene where the farmer uses "a frayed and knotted scrap of rope" to pull a calf out during birth. The key to the poem is the moment when the whole herd comes to witness the birth, then frolics up the bank "flicking their tails," as if in revelry. The scene holds all the ironic comedy and gusto of a bunch of shepherds crowded around an infant in a manger. Not surprisingly, the spring and summer poems often turn giddy in their celebration of the return of light. "Thinking of Madame Bovary" is such a poem: it celebrates "the first hot April day." It is whimsical in its way, but reveals a truth from a hard-working crocus pushing through a dead oak leaf: "Everyone longs for love's tense joys and red delights."

IN THE SAME WAY that the poems confronting depression thread through the volume, so too do a series of poems encountering the divine. This action takes on two patterns in Kenyon's poetry gener-ally — a very direct assessment, as in "Woman, Why Are You Weeping?" or an indistinct hovering between the spiritual and the concrete worlds. Sometimes the latter pattern is resolved in the poem; sometimes it is left dangling in unresolved ambiguity.

Of the former pattern — that of direct self-assessment — "Back from the City" is surely one of the most overt in the volume. It is also one of the poems Kenyon revised most heavily, putting it through no less than eight fully handwritten or partially typed and handwritten drafts before she committed it to a fully typed script for textual revision. The final form is unrecognizable in the first draft. The first two drafts simply contrast her happiness "in the company of silent things" to the talk and heat of hotel rooms; na-ture is restorative of inner harmony. The third draft, typed but heavily overwritten in ink, is titled "Coming Home Alone." Al-though she has made changes, the conflict remains the same. In the fifth draft she changed the title to "Pastoral," suggesting fur-ther the ability of nature at Eagle Pond Farm to calm and soothe the spirit. Several more drafts follow; then a new, completely hand-written draft shifts the tenor altogether. After her stay at the hotel, Kenyon still takes obvious delight in the simple seasonal particu-lars of the farm: "The last red leaves fall to the ground. . . ./A nut-hatch spirals/down the rough trunk of the tree." But now the rich food and creature comforts of the hotel receive a sharp counter-point in the added third stanza. At the Cloisters the narrator has been gazing at a Pietà: "Mary holding her pierced and dessicated son/across her knees." In this way the narrator "indulged in piety" (in earlier drafts, "I enjoyed my purity" or "I felt pious"), but then a beggar beseeches her for a quarter. Now the conflict is not external — between city life and country life — but has turned inward. Her response to the beggar? "I quickly turned my back," she says. The juxtaposition of her indulgence in piety and her rejection of the beggar, the very one the emaciated Christ died for, drops like a weight into the heart of the poem.

Those who see the concluding stanza as only an exercise in self-recrimination — even self-abasement — miss the larger pattern of the poem. The concluding lines derive from the biblical context of John 21. Significantly, the scene takes place just after the resurrected Christ has provided breakfast by the miraculous catch of fish. Thus a tie is established first to the self-indulgence of the hotel's rich food; second, to the nuthatch feeding; and third, to the emaciated Christ given up as the bread of life. That is the poetic coherence. More important is the spiritual coherence, for in the lines quoted from Scripture, Jesus is blessing the repentant Peter — the one who denied Christ three times. Reflexively, the blessing extends to the narrator: she is forgiven for having turned her back on the beggar, for failing to have fed Christ's sheep. With the benediction of love, the poem celebrates restoration rather than despairing of harmony.

"Back from the City" finds an interesting parallel in "Coming Home at Twilight in Late Summer." Here again nature brings its restorative calm to a harried life. The first stanza depicts the travelers returning home. The portrait is precise and categorical. Gravel shoots from the tires "like sparks from a fire" as the car turns into the drive. The travelers think of the necessary tasks that await them — unpacking, going through the mail. They climb stiffly out of the car. Then, in the second stanza, they notice the pear tree, so laden with fruit that its limbs nearly touch the ground. Their steps making "black holes" in the twilit grass of the meadow, they walk to the tree and reap its bounty: "and we each took a pear,/and ate, and

were grateful." The echoes of the sacrament of the Lord's Supper —
"Take, eat, remember, and believe . . ." — create a new spirit, a re-
demptive cleansing offered by nature. Here the sheep themselves
are fed.

In a thoughtful review of *The Boat of Quiet Hours,* Kathleen
Norris argues that Kenyon's virtue as a poet is to engage spiritual issues without being overt or didactic. "Nature observed informs every
one of Kenyon's poems," she writes, but also adds, "and theology has
a physical presence as well." It works, says Norris, because Kenyon
"inserts theology into the ordinary." This act also shapes the general
appeal of Kenyon's work: "No matter what their beliefs, poets appreciate mystery: in a sense they are called to work with it. Kenyon
bravely insists on exploring events that most trouble the modern
mind, that can only be experienced in fear and trembling."[12]

WHILE SEVERAL such poems deliberate the author's encounter
with the divine, several additional poems configure the poet's place
between earth and heaven, the physical and the spiritual, between
joy and suffering. Introduced in *The Boat of Quiet Hours,* the pattern appears often in Kenyon's later work.

In "Ice Storm" Kenyon is staying with Hall at his mother's
house in Hamden, a suburb of New Haven. (Typically they visited
her once a month for two or three days.)[13] An ice storm has passed
through the area, afflicting most powerfully the "hemlocks and
broad-leafed evergreens." They exist, she writes, in "a beautiful and

---

12. Norris, "Exploring the Poetry of Doubt and Daring," *Books and Religion*
17 (1990): 32.

13. During these visits to Hamden, Kenyon would almost always take the opportunity to visit Alice Mattison, who lived in New Haven proper. Mrs. Hall's
house was the same one that Donald Hall had moved to in 1936, when he was a
child, and which his mother finally left in 1993, when the frequency of heart problems, ambulance calls, and hospital stays made her realize she could no longer live
on her own. She moved to an assisted-living center in New Hampshire, where she
lived for eight months before dying. She died two months after Kenyon became ill
with leukemia.

precarious state of being. . . ." Thereby we see the central metaphor of the poem, for humanity too exists tenuously in a beautiful and precarious state of being. Reflecting on the ice-laden trees, the narrator finds that she cannot sleep, although the others can. Instead, "The most painful longing comes over me./A longing not of the body. . . ."

But how to define this longing — unsettling, vague, and uncertain as it is. As Emily Dickinson had it, it is "a feeling of the air." Except in this instance, it is not Despair, as it is in Dickinson's poem. It hovers somewhere between that nothingness of despair and the soul-wrenching longing for beauty:

> It could be for beauty —
> I mean what Keats was panting after,
> for which I love and honor him;
> it could be for the promises of God;
> or for oblivion, *nada;* or some condition even more
> extreme, which I intuit, but can't quite name.

Like the hemlocks and evergreens in their perilous state, laden by an icy beauty that brings them close to the edge of destruction, the narrator herself dangles between the two poles. The poem ends in ambiguity: there is no personal resolution for this longing within.

Such suggestions of unresolved tension creep into even the most innocent pastoral portraits. In "Photograph of a Child on a Vermont Hillside," for example, Kenyon juxtaposes a "real child" with the "artificial child" the little girl becomes when the Boston journalist poses her. With the journalist, the child turns inward, looking down, careful not to let her inner self slip out. Yet she is indeed a child of these hills, at one with them and their stories. Kenyon wonders, if the child should speak, what words she would say to encapsulate her story. Perhaps these:

> *childhood is woe in solitude,*
> *and the bliss of turning circles*

154

> *barefoot in the dusty drive*
> *after the supper dishes are done. . . .*

Here again, woe and bliss intermingle. They hang in stasis at the center of the child's turning circles.

"Twilight: After Haying" also points toward that indeterminacy, again the tension between joy and suffering. The opening stanza is wistfully melancholy:

> Yes, long shadows go out
> from the bales; and yes, the soul
> must part from the body:
> what else could it do?

The diurnal pattern insists upon endings. That includes the laborer's long day of work, or the body's lifelong labor. Using the figure of the newly mown hay, Kenyon responds,

> These things happen . . . the soul's bliss
> and suffering are bound together
> like the grasses. . . .

In such poems as these Kenyon wisely refuses to provide the reader with pat answers or even possible alternatives. She provides the carefully etched setting along with the unsettling questions, leaving the reader to find answers. In this way she not only avoids didacticism but also permits the reader to own the poem. A sort of ethics of ambiguity hovers over many of these poems where she finds herself situated between physical reality and spiritual uncertainty. But the ambiguity is deliberate, permitting the poem to live on in the reflective reader's sensibility.

The final poem in the volume, "Things," also bears testimony to that aesthetic stance. Typical of Kenyon's work, the poem begins with a simple, concrete event in the first stanza — a hen flings aside a single pebble. The *sound* of the event, however, attracts the poet's ear:

Never in eternity the same sound —
a small stone falling on a red leaf.

So too is the poet's task in writing: to evoke the singular sound, the exactly appropriate sound to capture the event, so that it never again can be — or need be — duplicated in all eternity. The event and the words chosen to describe that event combine to form a moment seized out of eternity.

The next two stanzas are a paean to the sorts of common, everyday things that shape the timeless poetic event. Poetry is not a matter of catapulting one into a rhapsodic cycle of stars; it is a pattern of constructing stepping stones and images upon which one might climb, bit by bit, to glimpse eternity. Thus the second stanza focuses upon a very minute point in the natural world: the juncture of a twig and a branch. But look at it with the eyes of imagination, Kenyon encourages us. Then you might behold a "gate/we might enter, singing." Similarly, in the third stanza the concrete object is a mouse that has chewed a hole in a hundred-year-old quilt. Once again, Kenyon invites us to turn the eye of imagination on it. Quite literally the mouse chewed a hole through a blue star to get at the batting within the quilt — "and now she thrives." The anagogic imagination also reaches with the mouse through a blue star, reaching for something beyond that sustains.

Thus it is that the final stanza celebrates the light of the imaginative vision illuminating the corporeal body of reality. The first two lines are reflexive, referring to the concrete realities of the first three stanzas: "Things: simply lasting, then/failing to last." These two lines also figure into the final stanza's three parts, each separated but conjoined by a colon. The first colon after "Things" describes the nature of physical reality. It lives, then fails to live. The second colon follows "last" and steers the thought in a new direction:

failing to last: water, a blue heron's
eye, and the light passing
between them: . . .

In the world of physical realities that simply last and then fail to last, a miraculous life of light exists. The pronoun "them" is deliberately ambiguous, referring at once to the water and the blue heron at the water's edge, and to the light between simply lasting and then failing to last. This light is what the poet attempts to capture, even should it be as random and as simple as a pebble falling on a leaf, or the juncture of twig and branch. In each lies the light of life. The final colon in the third stanza falls after "them" and recapitulates the poetic experience of the life of the poem:

> into light all things
> must fall, glad at last to have fallen.

Several echoes emerge in these last two lines. The obvious one, of course, is of James 1:17: "Every good and perfect gift is from above, coming down from the Father of the heavenly lights, who does not change like shifting shadows" (NIV). Herein lies the "gladness" of falling into light in Kenyon's poem. A second echo emerges from the work of Kenyon and Hall's good friend Wendell Berry, who plays with the identical verse as the heart of his poem "The Gift of Gravity."[14] In his poem, Berry creates a metaphor linking divine grace

---

14. In one of the early drafts of the volume, Kenyon considered an epigraph from Berry:

> Not by your will has
> The house [survived] the night.
> — Wendell Berry

She then crossed the epigraph out.

The friendship between Kenyon and Hall and Wendell and Tanya Berry was of long standing. In his richly evocative and moving essay "Sweetness Preserved," collected in *Bright, Unequivocal Eye*, Berry traces some of the passages of this friendship. He also, it seems to me, provides one of the most trenchant observations about Kenyon's work that I have come across:

> Jane Kenyon's work . . . makes an unnegotiable demand upon a reader. It doesn't demand great intellect or learning or even sympathy; it demands quiet. It de-

and gravity, which causes the rain to collect and scour the earth into rivers, reshaping contours. Even though the rain "wounds" the earth, the narrator is

> newborn of pain
> to love the new-shaped shore
> where young cottonwoods
> take hold and thrive in the wound.

As Berry finds his grace in "the new-shaped shore," so too Kenyon finds hers in the fact that "into light all things/must fall." Like them, she too is "glad at last to have fallen."

THE BOAT of quiet hours, like Keats's elusive beauty after which the heart pants, may never be fully attainable. If it is, attainment is measured in moments rather than hours. In this volume Kenyon reaches forth to grasp those moments and often finds her hand full.

---

mands that in this age of political, economic, educational, and recreational pandemonium, and a concomitant rattling in the literary world, one must somehow become quiet enough to listen. Her poems raise unequivocally the issue of the quality of the poet's ear.

A true poem, we know, forms itself within hearing. It must live in the ear before it can live in the mind or the heart. The ear tells the poet when and how to break the silence, and when enough has been said. If one has no ear, then one has no art and is no poet. . . .

Jane Kenyon had a virtually faultless ear. She was an exquisite master of the art of poetry. Her voice always carries the tremor of feeling disciplined by art. This is what over and over again enabled her to take the risk of plainness, or of apparent plainness. Her ear controls rhythm and sound, and also tone. . . .

It is her perfection of tone that makes her poems able to accommodate sudden declarations of spiritual knowledge or religious faith, and that gives to so many of her poems the quality of prayer. It rules in her poems and passages of humor. . . . I am suggesting what I suppose cannot be demonstrated: that there is a practical affinity between the life of her soul and the technique of her poems. (*Bright, Unequivocal Eye: Poems, Papers, and Remembrances from the First Jane Kenyon Conference*, ed. Bert Hornback [New York: Peter Lang Press, 2000], p. 144)

Emily Dickinson wrote that "The soul has bandaged moments" but also that "The soul has moments of escape." One often finds Kenyon's poetry arcing like electrical current between these two poles. Life is made up of both kinds of moments, after all, and the enduring beauty of this volume is that synthetic energy that works the coupling into a whole. To anticipate a future poem, we might say that Kenyon leads the reader to believe it couldn't have been otherwise.

CHAPTER SEVEN

Let Evening Come

Watching the Shadows

The Boat of Quiet Hours may be described as poetry of encounter. There Kenyon explores her depression, her search for the divine, and her affirmation of — even playfulness and joy in — everyday things. These themes continue, but the poems in *Let Evening Come* and *Constance* seem to turn more intensely personal and introspective. Often the poems are touched with a tenor of sweet wistfulness. Impinging upon that are the hard realities of her personal experience with illness and death.[1]

During the late 1970s a substantial change swept over Kenyon's life with her father's illness and eventual death (in 1980). In fact, "Travel: After a Death" from *The Boat of Quiet Hours* was written following a trip to England and recounts, as Kenyon wrote to Alice Mattison, the depressive stage of grieving.[2] Unmistakable is the plaintive note of the last line: "Oh, when am I going to own my mind again?"

In the years following the death of Kenyon's father, Kenyon and Hall would have to deal with a series of family illnesses and

1. Patterns of diction inevitably suggest the themes in Kenyon's poetry. Thus it is not surprising that the two most frequent repetitions in this volume are "bright" and "light" with "dark" and "night."

2. Mattison, "'Let It Grow in the Dark Like a Mushroom': Writing with Jane Kenyon," *Michigan Quarterly Review* (Winter 2000): 125.

deaths. Kenyon lost both her aunt and her grandmother, and she herself had to face cancer of the salivary gland in 1985. Hall struggled with cancer for more than three years (colon cancer in 1989, and metastatic colon cancer of the liver in 1992), and his mother died in 1994. *Let Evening Come,* published in 1990, seems situated in the midst of these personal trials. At such times Kenyon tried both to understand the present suffering by confronting it poetically and to recall something of the enduring beauty and unspoiled innocence of the past.

With the generally very favorable reviews and solid sales of *The Boat of Quiet Hours,* Kenyon was now spared the agonizing search for a publisher. She felt comfortable with Graywolf Press, and obviously they were comfortable with her. In an early complete draft of the volume, it becomes obvious that Kenyon was thinking of connections to her prior volume. The working title she used for the draft was "We Let the Boat Drift" (also a title of a poem in the collection); subsequently she adopted the current title.

Reviews of the new volume were almost uniformly favorable. In *Library Journal* Louis McKee advised, "It is time we recognize that Kenyon is among the poets who stand tall among this new generation. Few writers see so well and speak so well of what they see. This volume belongs in any serious collection."[3] In *The New York Times Book Review,* Alfred Corn wrote that the volume "shows her at the height of her powers."[4] He went on to praise both Kenyon's descriptive skills and her dramatic skills. Writing for *Poetry,* David Baker was the only reviewer to take a largely negative approach to the volume. He associated Kenyon's poetry with a "poetry common to the minimal, primitivist impulses of the last three decades," where the poem tends to collapse inward toward personal density. Although Baker admitted that Kenyon was in clear control of the

3. McKee, Review of *Let Evening Come,* by Jane Kenyon, *Library Journal,* 15 May 1990, p. 80.

4. Corn, Review of *Let Evening Come,* by Jane Kenyon, *The New York Times Book Review,* 24 March 1991, p. 26.

style and language of her poems, it was not a style or language that suited him. While he praised "Father and Son" for its "quiet magic," he judged that "too many of her poems read more like merely private or mundane journals."[5]

Although many readers find more drama than mundanity in *Let Evening Come*, it is certainly true that the poems have a journalistic tone. The lyrical images that came so easily in the prior volume, showering the poems with spangles of light, here seem woven together with fingers that are bleeding. They are inward poems — not unlike those of Adrienne Rich and Anne Sexton, or Sylvia Plath's openly confessional poetry — but the reader also senses a resistance to the confessions. Kenyon insists on searching for the light, refuses the enveloping dark, and keeps working on the precise and vivid image that makes the poem belong to the reader rather than function as her private monologue. In doing so, she marks the volume with three large themes: evocations of youth, fear and despair in the present, and a sustained emphasis on spiritual searching.

WHEN David Bradt asked Kenyon about the sources for her poems, she referred first to the solitude of her rural upbringing. That had created in her a certain "inwardness," a reflective quality. This quality in turn fostered a keen sensitivity to emotions, both in herself and in others. How to deal with this sensitivity, how to express these feelings? For her, poetry became a "safe haven" at an early age, a place where she could explore those feelings. "I found," she says, "that poets are not afraid of feeling."[6]

Kenyon also commented specifically on the importance of her youthful exposure to the natural world. Reflecting further on Bradt's question, she added,

5. Baker, Review of *Let Evening Come*, by Jane Kenyon, *Poetry* 158 (June 1991): 161-63.

6. Kenyon, *A Hundred White Daffodils* (Saint Paul, Minn.: Graywolf Press, 1999), p. 176.

So where do poems come from? Primarily, I think, from child-hood. That's when I fell under the thrall of nature. I spent long hours playing at the stream that ran through my family's prop-erty. We lived on a dirt road near the Huron River, across from a working farm. I fell in love with the natural world. I use it again and again as a way of talking about something inward. If you read my poems you would not know you were in the twentieth century, because there are no airplanes or computers or E-mail.[7]

While many other artistic and personal experiences influenced Kenyon profoundly, she clearly believed that her childhood funda-mentally shaped the nature of the person who lived through those later events. It is not surprising, therefore, that in this volume, in which she does encounter significant stages of personal loss, she turns frequently to the past.

In one such cluster of poems, Kenyon follows what had by now become a typical approach to the subject matter of the poem: she begins with an immediate sensory perception and allows it to evoke memories of the past or meditative reflections on it. In "Waking in January Before Dawn," for example, the immediate context is clearly set in the first three stanzas. She awakens at the sound of the snowplow before dawn. In her groggy state, she makes a simple connection, simply stated: "There must be snow." This is exactly the connection the sleepy mind makes. But she also tries to make other connections: "What was it I fell asleep thinking . . . ?" Half-awake, she watches the Wolf Moon going down and the sky gradually lightening. Then she makes another connection as she lies in the half-light, burrowed under the covers. In the fourth stanza she remembers hiding under the covers at night during her stays at Grandmother's house, fearful that some animal across the room was ready to pounce. At Grandmother's, dawn brought the realization that the "animal" was only Grandmother's old sewing

---

7. Kenyon, *A Hundred White Daffodils*, p. 176.

machine. In the fifth and final stanza, the connection shifts back to her present bedroom, where "the dresser reclaims visibility."

Playing throughout the poem is the theme of light allaying fear, and of morning obliterating nighttime terrors. The narrator longs for light, and a poem such as this makes the quiet supplication of such a poem as "Let Evening Come" that much more profound. As she put it in "Things": "Into light all things/must fall, glad at last to have fallen."

Several other poems also evoke the past, recalling those events like scrapbook portraits. In "Catching Frogs" Kenyon recollects coming home after crouching by a pool, waiting for the opportunity to catch a frog. At the pool it grew dark; at home "I came into the warm, bright room/where father held aloft the evening/paper. . . ." The line stop and enjambment with "evening" plays nicely against the outside dark. That same interplay between light and dark, childhood and the present, marks "Insomnia," where the firefly she spots near the ceiling in the dead of night reminds her of catching fireflies when she was a child. She considers getting up to let the firefly out of the room but decides against it, "in case/it's my father, come back from the dead." "A Boy Goes into the World" evokes a memory of her brother Reuel heading off on his bike for a day of collecting precious odds and ends to mount on poster board. She starts to follow, but

> Mother called me back
> from the end of the sandy drive:
> "It's different for girls."

One thinks of the emphatic statement in Kenyon's junior-high journal: "I have always wanted to be a boy!" But here too a connection forms to the present as the poet mounts her own precious bits and pieces on the poster board of the poem:

> He has long since
> forgotten those days and things, but
> I at last can claim them as my own.

Kenyon's early rebellious nature emerges in one of these poems of recollection. "Learning in the First Grade" provides a whimsical account of a child taking issue with coloring instructions. The mimeographed sheet tells her,

"The cup is red. The drop of rain
is blue. The clam is brown."

These declarations are made in all the veracity of mimeographed purple ink. The poet, however, sees that "the cup was/*not* red. It was white,/or had no color of its own." She realizes that "my mind was finical." In a sense, the poetic mind is always somewhat finical. Or perhaps it should be better said that a "finical mind" produces a unique, individual perspective — a particular way of seeing. The first-grade student, of course, doesn't know this. She knows *the rules.* So when the teacher calls on her, she says the cup is red.

"But it's not," I thought,
like Galileo Galilei,
muttering under his beard. . . .

Only later does the thought become perception and the muttering become poetry.[8]

A DIVIDE ALSO carves its way between past and present in this volume, however. While the past often functions as both sustenance and subject for Kenyon's poetry, it is, finally, the past. Memories founder against the death of her father and her own struggle with depressive illness and grief. "Three Songs at the End of Summer" dramatizes both the connection and the divide. The first and third

---

8. Here the poet perceives herself as the child, for the child, of course, has no knowledge of Galileo. But precisely by making that connection Kenyon perfectly captures her youthful rebellion against authority. Like Galileo "muttering under his beard," she knows she is right, in spite of the rules.

songs of the poem function as poetic bookends for the middle song.
The first song occurs in the present at Eagle Pond Farm. The opening two stanzas begin with the lush physical detail typical of Kenyon's poems. They are rich with specificity as she looks out over the
newly mown hay field, noticing everything, right down to "five
gleaming crows" who "search and peck between the rows." In the
third stanza she hears the voice of the water-ski instructor at the
summer camp across Eagle Pond as he shouts at his young pupils,
"Relax! Relax!" The fourth stanza again picks up the details of the
scene, almost as if pasting photographs in an album of memories.
But the last stanza recognizes that summer is ending and that soon
all this will be left behind:

> Schoolbooks, carpools, pleated skirts;
> water, silver-still, and a vee of geese.

The juxtaposition of the two lines is keen — the first reading like a
"to do" list; the second an evocative picture of what remains behind.
　This dialectic carries into the middle song. The first stanza focuses on summer's fullness — an amplitude of light and sound:

> The cicada's dry monotony breaks
> over me. The days are bright
> and free, bright and free.

Should the poem have ended there, it would stand as a celebration
of summer's glittering fullness. One thinks of Emily Dickinson's
"These Are the Days":

> Oh, Sacrament of summer days,
> Oh, Last Communion in the Haze —
> Permit a child to join.

But in making the connection to Dickinson, one also remembers
these lines:

> As imperceptibly as Grief
> The Summer lapsed away —

Those lines in particular are telling, for between the first and second stanzas of Kenyon's middle song, grief strikes like an arrow:

> Then why did I cry today
> for an hour, with my whole
> body, the way babies cry?

From "bright and free" the poem plummets into inconsolable grief. Unlike the grief Dickinson writes about, the grief here does not "imperceptibly" lapse away. It stands against the brightness like a dark splotch of spilled ink.

The third song shifts the scene entirely. Picking up on the line of "things to do" to prepare the young campers for school, Kenyon evokes a scene from her own childhood. She recalls waiting for the school bus "with a dread that took my breath away." Physically, all nature seemed changed too. The days were not "bright and free"; the narrator remembers standing "under a dripping oak,/while autumnal fog eddied around my feet." If the first stanza of the middle song mirrors the emotions of the first song, then the second stanza of the middle song mirrors the emotions of the third song. Now all things seem gray; the oak drips like her own uncontrollable tears of the middle song. The third song ends this way:

> Spruce, inadequate, and alien
> I stood at the side of the road.
> It was the only life I had.

The stoic resignation of the last line responds to the question in the second stanza of the middle song. Why does she cry? It is unexplainable. It is, as Dickinson put it, "An imperial affliction/Sent us of the Air."

"The Pear" plays on a pattern similar to that of "Three Songs at the End of Summer." Here too the contrast lies between the extraordinary brightness of the external, natural world and the unnatural internal darkness. The first stanza introduces "a moment" in middle age when one grows bored, angry, and fearful. The "moment" here does not refer to a sudden, passing incident; rather, it suggests a stage or major life event. Paradoxically, the brightness of the day, as in "Three Songs at the End of Summer," simply makes the narrator feel "more desolate." Thus the analogy with the pear in the third stanza. The inward desolation works subtly, like a pear spoiling from the inside out. One may not be aware of it at first, like the spoilage in the pear, until it spreads to the point where "things have gone too far."

In several poems the past and present compress in a nexus of grief. "The Letter" refers to a letter from Tess Gallagher about Ray Carver's metastatic cancer. Kenyon begins the poem in typical fashion, with the declarative statement of fact: cancer, with its terrible side effects, has returned. The narrator's response, in the second stanza, is to snap the leash on the dog and head outdoors. In an earlier draft a different third stanza appeared, here with Kenyon's handwritten revisions in brackets:

> He'll be gone from us soon. We'll grieve
> for him, ~~but~~ [and] feel afraid for ourselves; turn
> back to the paychecks, appointments, and mowing
> the lawn. What wouldn't he give
> to ~~feel like mowing~~ [mow] the lawn?

Kenyon cut this entire stanza to continue the walk with the dog that started in the second stanza.

The natural scene, however, almost seems to mock her rather than comfort her. The vernal energy of "The trees have leafed out" stands in contrast to Carver's increasing frailty. "Sunlight penetrates in golden drops" as his light fails. Again Kenyon places us at that stark point where days "bright and free" collide with the question of why one cries for hours. Here in "The Letter" life goes on its routine way. The neighbor is cutting down trees on his property, reaping the bounty of the earth, while another's life leaks away. Even standing among her neighbor's stumps, the narrator understands that "The place will heal itself in time." For her it is time to call the dog and "go the long way home," back to the reality of a disease that cannot be healed.

In "We Let the Boat Drift," the title itself serves as metaphor for the poem. Just as the camp instructor shouted "Relax! Relax!" to the fledgling waterskiers, so Kenyon tries to command herself into relaxation. The first two stanzas set the scene in late autumn, after a hard frost. She walks the abandoned rails (across Highway 4 from the farmhouse) toward Eagle Pond. The water is "utterly still," and with its calm finality the thought of her father's death surfaces: "It's five years today,/and even now I can't accept what cancer did/to him. . . ." This is immediately qualified. It isn't so much the death of the body; such is inevitable. Rather, it is "the annihilation/of the whole man, sense by sense, thought by thought, hope by hope." The loss she mourns is one of personhood.

She reflects on one of their last discussions, which turned to the life to come. Attempting comfort, she had read Jesus' words in John 14: "I go to prepare a place for you." But her father retorted with Jesus' words in Matthew: "You, therefore, must be perfect, as your heavenly Father is perfect" (Matt. 5:48). Enigmatic words follow: "And he wept." Do these lines suggest the imperfection of her father's own life, measured against Grandmother's religious rules? But surely such an astute man would not have missed the barbed irony with which Jesus spoke about perfection in his Sermon on the Mount. There Jesus chastised those who thought themselves perfect simply because they kept the rules. Still, one can't help thinking, in a stanza packed with biblical allusions, of Jesus weeping (John 11:35). Is the father here weeping for forgiveness? In the end it is indeterminate, and perhaps that in itself continues to haunt Kenyon.

She is shaken out of her reverie by a neighbor's driving by. The woman honks her horn and waves. But she too, we discover, has suffered grief. Just in the past week Kenyon and this friend had canoed far out on the pond and let the boat drift. Kenyon describes the scene with a series of comforting images: the paddles "rested" across their laps; the light surrounding them "seemed alive"; "A loon . . ./let us get quite close before it dove." The natural rhythms offered solace even while the neighbor unburdened herself of disconsolation. In the drifting boat they were "well away from humankind." Such distancing becomes necessary to allay grief, but also to confront it inwardly.

Such poems examine various ways to ameliorate grief and its cousin, depression. Kenyon looks to nature and the restorative cycle of the seasons as healing agents. She longs for the quiet moment when "We let the boat drift." But in the poem "Now Where?" all such agencies seem to collapse. The poem incarnates depression itself as it feeds, succubus-like, upon the soul of the narrator. Depression is the subject of the poem, identified in the first stanza as "It." This "it" is inseparable from her, waking when she wakes, walking when she walks. It has come in its full diabolical presence, possessing the narrator to the extent that she becomes depression itself.

As if this possession of soul and body were not sufficiently menacing, the depression mocks all the old verities by which she has identified herself. Like the crowd jeering Jesus, the depression asks, in a grating voice, "Where is your God now?"

In the third stanza the transition to inward pain — the inevitable process of deep depression — is thorough. She lies down after dinner "like a widow." Separated from others by the veil of agony, she grows completely isolated, even from the husband who knows her most intimately. Ironically, she reflects, "To strangers I must seem/alive." Kenyon's careful use of enjambment here twists the meaning two ways. Does she appear as a mere vaporous seeming of self, or does she seem alive to those who don't know her? The crossplay here accentuates the idea that depression has stolen her self. As the poem closes, she is bereft. Without her keen vitality, she is left with only the capacity to measure passing days and seasons. She seems to have lost the ability to invest them with vivid significance. Now she measures only the presence of pain.

In a slightly different pattern, Kenyon addresses the dislocation caused by harm done to others in "While We Were Arguing." In this case it is anger, not the black onslaught of melancholy, that disrupts those routines that might have bestowed order upon the day.

The poem stands as one of Kenyon's most heavily revised works, as she herself underwent the turmoil of writing a poem about marital discord. Thus, in the early drafts, the poem starts with the stark *fact* of the matter:

> While we were arguing
> the first snow fell — or I should say
> it flew slantwise past the windows.[9]

In the final draft, Kenyon reverted to her regular poetic creed: "The natural object is the adequate symbol." Now the first snow, slanting past the window, opens the poem, creating an objective correlative for the coldness of arguing.

Similarly, emotions in early drafts are far more overtly expressed: "Bitter, bitter tears"; "Huge sighs escaped"; "The rage and hurt I saw/on your face I shall not soon forget." There are three handwritten early drafts in the poem's folder, unusual for Kenyon and an indication to her that she wasn't getting things right. Perhaps she sensed that in a poem about emotions, she herself was being too emotional.

In subsequent drafts Kenyon focused on making two kinds of changes. First, she began cutting those phrases and lines laden with emotional freight. "Bitter, bitter tears" in the second stanza became simply "tears." In the last stanza, she cut these lines:

> We had cut each other
> with envenomed swords — a hit, oh many
> palpable hits — and there is no
> Horatio to set it right.

9. Kenyon Archives, Box 8, Folder 22.

The allusion to *Hamlet* aggrandizes the destructiveness of the quarrel — and Kenyon sought to change this emphasis too. In later drafts, she worked away from this emphasis and started to work toward an emphasis on restoration — introducing the cups of tea, the arrival of the paper. But none of these, in and of themselves, grant restoration. That happens only when the narrator — in the final line — acknowledges the human fact of what happened: "'You see, we have done harm.'" The narrator speaks the line outside, in the dark, to the moon, as if in confession and understanding. That line, incidentally, is far more quiet, accepting, and forgiving than a variation that occurred in several of the late drafts: "As you can see, we have destroyed our life." With skillful wisdom she moves from angry denunciation to forgiving restoration.

LESS PROMINENT in this volume, yet not without strong presence, are those poems of spiritual searching. In particular, two works that precede the quiet acceptance of "Let Evening Come" are spiritually suggestive.

In "Last Days" Kenyon opens the poem with a scene of devastation during a hard rain. During the storm, apples fall "before their time," doors blow open and closed, lights stutter off and on. One thinks of young Jane and her complete bewilderment as Grandmother explained the Apocalypse and how one would be chosen and another left behind.

As the rain pelts down, Kenyon sits in a room where her mother lies "mortally ill." On the dresser, "among ranks of brown bottles from the pharmacy," lies a hymnbook open to "Safely Through Another Week." But safety here seems fragile and tenuous. Then comes the mocking incident. An "indifferent" housefly — the often-used poetic symbol of death — alights on her mother's "blue-white brow."

No spiritual answers are given; indeed, no clear questions are articulated. But the poem does haunt the reader, particularly because of the slightly macabre juxtaposition of the hymn title and the appearance of the "indifferent" fly. Also haunting is the way in which the scene of the first stanza turns inward in the second. The ambiguous opening line of the second stanza suspends the reader: "So I sat with her in a room made small." Does the "so" mean "in the same way" — like the storm pelting the orchard? Or does it suggest a quiet calm in the face of the inevitable? One might judge that the poem is disfigured by such intrinsic uncertainty, but uncertainty is precisely the point of the poem.

"Looking at Stars" contains a similar kind of juxtaposition — fearfulness and loss set against quiet assurance. The first two lines claim, "The God of curved space, the dry/God, is not going to help us. . . ." This is the God of things remote. But that declaration is followed immediately by the affirmation that help will come — from "the son/whose blood spattered/the hem of his mother's robe." The poem mirrors the great affirmation of a Savior close by, the same affirmation Kenyon makes in "Let Evening Come," the centerpiece of the volume and one of her most beautiful and beloved poems.

The first draft of "Let Evening Come" — handwritten — bears only a conceptual resemblance to later drafts. Here Kenyon set down in physical images the intermingling of light and shadow, that indeterminate time of day that always seemed to intrigue and puzzle her. She also established the supplicatory tone of the poem, with its prayer-like evocation, through the repeated use of "let." Following is a transcription of her first working draft, with the first emendations in brackets as they appear in the original:

Let the beam [light] of late afternoon sun/coming through
chinks in the barn boards
move up the hay bales as the sun
goes down. Let the cricket begin
to chafe (indecipherable) [in the long grass]
Let the dew gather on every blade and leaf and on [the
abandoned hoe]
Let the red fox turn toward
its sandy hole. Let the stars appear
from east to west. Let the moon display

its silver horn. Let songbirds cease
their song. Let evening come.
Let me learn to fear neither life nor death,
Let me learn to give without counting.

The first typed draft of the poem — the second draft — is considerably longer (27 lines). Here Kenyon accumulates images
grounded in what she sees on the farm. She observes carefully, adding concrete detail. She pays little attention either to stanzaic architecture or to diction. She allows the natural force of the poem as she
experiences it to accumulate. With the third draft she begins whit-
tling lines and sharpening diction to suit the image:

Let the light of late afternoon
come through chinks
        in the barn [boards]
moving up the bales as the sun goes down.
Let the cricket take up chafing as an old [as a woman]
woman takes up her knitting [needles and yarn]. Let evening
come.
    Let the dew bless [fall on] every leaf
and blade, let it bless [fall on] the abandoned hoe
Let stars appear from east to west,
[and] the moon display her silver horn.

Let [the] fox return to [its] sandy hole. Let wind
die down. Let the shed turn [go] black inside.
Let evening come to the bottle in the ditch,
to the scoop in the oats [to the air in the lung.
Let evening come.]

Let the arm slip from the arm of the chair,
let evening come. Let everything [it] come
as it will/and do not be afraid, [have a little faith,
and] let evening come.

Although the ending of the poem appears uncertain at this stage, one can observe Kenyon's process of sharpening and clarifying the imagery. For example, in lines 8-9 of this draft, she emends the rather vague "bless" to a very concrete picture of the dew falling on leaf and hoe. In the final version of the poem, she selected the more accurate verb "collect" instead of "fall."

Subsequent drafts of the poem demonstrate her relentless labor to sharpen images and find the right word. She also began to find the pattern of light rising and falling that mirrored the natural rhythm of work and rest.[10] The concluding stanzas of the poem, however, continued to give Kenyon problems.

The figure of the arm slipping from the arm of the chair perhaps bore too much of a sense of finality for her. She probably also remembered that the identical figure appears in the final stanza of "Rain in January" in *The Boat of Quiet Hours.* And no doubt she realized that the injunction "Have a little faith" ruptured the supplicatory tone of the poem. But it wasn't until the late drafts that she cut the image of the arm on the chair and changed the last line

---

10. It should be observed that, despite the frequent reading of "Let Evening Come" at funerals and memorial services, the poem reads as an affirmation of the natural rhythms of life — physically, biologically, and psychologically. If anything, it is a poem of great peace, regardless of whether the light rises or falls. In that sense, perhaps, it is appropriate to a funeral service. In his elegy "Life after Jane," Donald Hall says of the poem, "Jane speaks of 'evening,' and those who translate 'evening' immediately into 'death' are missing the poem's notion. Yet the mind leaps to find analogy — humans are symbol-seekers — and people read this poem at funerals. Someone has carved it into a gravestone" (in *Northeast: The Hartford Courant Sunday Magazine,* 27 August 1995, p. 8). Kenyon's own reaction to the poem is nicely summed up in a letter she wrote to Alice Mattison on 16 April 1986:

> I have written something new, which I am very excited about. While I was in A[nn] A[rbor] I heard my mother say, 'Let evening come.' We were talking about getting depressed as the day goes on, and wanting bedtime to come so you can become oblivious. . . .
>
> I think *Let Evening Come* is going to be my title. I have written the poem very fast. Of course you will have to see it before I know whether it is any good. (Mattison, "'Let It Grow in the Dark Like a Mushroom,'" pp. 131-32)

from exhortation to encouragement: "God does not leave us/com-
fortless, so let evening come." On the basis of that claim, the narrator can give herself to whatever evening brings in its natural
rhythm.

As Kenyon developed the poem into its final form, the tone
and melody emerged effortlessly. The lyric tercets carry varying
beats in a general approximation of eight-syllable lines. At the out-
set, with the first of the twelve supplicatory uses of "let," the reader
senses that "let" also suggests awareness of the fact that one really
can't do anything about what is coming anyway. "Let the light of late
afternoon/shine" — it will; it is nature's way. But here the natural
melody of the lines gently encourages the acceptance of nature's
way. One might contrast the tone of this poem, for example, to that
of Dylan Thomas's "Do Not Go Gentle into That Good Night."

The mellifluous acceptance of evening's coming is encouraged by the natural imagery of the farm that prevails throughout
the poem. With the exception of line 5, with its reference to a
woman knitting as a simile for the cricket's chafing, no direct human presence appears until line 14. Each of the natural portraits,
moreover, perfectly discloses evening's slide into darkness — un-
derscored by deft word choice. For example, the alliterative emphasis on the letter *d* in "Let the wind die down" in itself creates a sinking feeling in the line, abetted by the three strong, single-syllable
beats.

The fifth stanza shifts to the human experience so subtly that
it is hardly noticeable:

To the bottle in the ditch, to the scoop
in the oats, to the air in the lung
let evening come.

The shift from the inanimate objects — bottle, ditch, scoop, oats —
to the air in the lung nearly passes the reader by. With such placement in the series, however, humanity takes its position in the natural rhythm of the farm and establishes the pattern for the last

tercet. Evening will come, as it is accustomed to doing. Let it come, then, for Kenyon has established a perfect peace and a natural rhythm that invites its acceptance. While in earlier works that shadowland between light and darkness is often strung tight with anxiety and fear, now she speaks words of calm confidence: "Don't/ be afraid." As she has accepted the coming of evening (which is inevitable and unavoidable), so too she fully accepts the one overt claim, the one declarative sentence in the entire poem: "God does not leave us/comfortless, so let evening come." This comfort is also inevitable, so (therefore) let evening come. This final sentence provides the benediction upon the supplications that precede it.

In addition to the tone and melodic pace of the poem, other patterns contribute to the nearly immediate pleasure many readers take in it. If we consider the principles of word choice and linguistic tabulation explored in Chapter Three, we discover several revealing traits. Excluding the title, the poem contains 124 words. Of them, 17 are Middle English (13.7%), nearly all of which borrow from Old English. There are a total of 107 Old English words (86.3%). In terms of diction, then, the poem is heavily slanted toward the "low" or plain style. Indeed, although the poem does not use rhyming couplets, in many ways it resembles the English plainsong. Eleven of the eighteen lines have eight syllables (six more have nine syllables), and some match the tetrameter of plainsong. Thus Kenyon uses diction that creates a sense of unusual immediacy and intimacy with an audience.

So too does the imagery, which functions in a parallel pattern with the language. The vivid pictorial units are all drawn from things immediately observable on the farm. With the exception of the heavenly bodies that mark evening (setting sun, moon, stars), the objects of the poem are earth-rooted, elemental. We observe the heavenly bodies only from an earthly perspective, not from any abstracted elevation. Such portraits root the reader in a familiar world. Even longtime urban dwellers easily recognize the domesticity of the rural farm and its life lived by clear diurnal patterns.

In both language and imagery, then, Kenyon has created a poetic world that homes her readers. One does not have to stretch or make radical mental leaps to participate in it. Rather, one relaxes into an inviting place that perfectly matches the supplicatory and benedictory patterns of the poem.

THE FINAL POEM in the volume, "With the Dog at Sunrise," completes the cycle of searching and finding. Here the searching is specified:

> Searching for God is the first thing and the last,
> but in between such trouble, and such pain.

If *Let Evening Come* could be said to have a theme, it is encapsulated in those two lines. The searching is ongoing, but it seldom provides a stay against the confusion and disorder of this life. Indeed, in Kenyon's final volume, *Constance,* it sometimes seems that disorder has ripped her life apart altogether, that the title itself is little more than an ironic joke in a time when all things shift and slide.

CHAPTER EIGHT

Constance

Staying the Course

Albeit her briefest volume, *Constance* shows Kenyon at the peak of
her power. Its centerpiece, of course, is "Having it Out with Melancholy," but the singular power of that poem should in no way de-
tract from the cohesive artistry of the whole. It is little wonder that
this volume made a deep impact upon readers and reviewers alike.

Even David Barber, who heretofore had been a less-than-en-
thusiastic reviewer of Kenyon's work, stepped back in admiration of
the complexities of tone and tension in this volume. Writing for *Poetry,* Barber observed that Kenyon's religious and "colloquial surfaces" harbor moral issues more effectively than would a more
grandiose style: "In her hands the home truth becomes both more
pertinent and more inscrutable than readers weaned on urbane
indeterminacies might otherwise have supposed." In this review
Barber was more attuned to the tensions Kenyon sustains in her poems — that pattern discussed in this text as suspension between alternatives. Barber put it like this: "The inscrutable side of Kenyon's
poems lies in their welled-up irresolutions rather than anything re-
motely resembling willful obscurity. Their calm decorum harbors
thorny qualms."[1] Writing for *Library Journal,* Barbara Hoffert similarly applauded the tension between the carefully crafted lines and
the often terrifying subject matter.

1. Barber, Review of *Constance,* by Jane Kenyon, *Poetry* 164 (June 1994): 161.

The tension is not without reason, for in *Constance* Kenyon lays bare her battle against illness and her struggle for some degree of constancy in a tumultuous world. In a review/essay for *Poetry*, Paul Breslin observed, "From this second volume [*The Boat of Quiet Hours*] on, Kenyon's work begins to map a phenomenology of depression, a subject she writes about more eloquently than anyone I can think of since Sylvia Plath. Of course, the outcome, biographically and poetically, was vastly different." Extending his comparison to Plath, Breslin argues, "Plath has the greater intensity, sublimity, power to conjure terror; Kenyon has greater subtlety, surer moral and poetic judgment, and a capacity for emotional generosity that eluded Plath almost completely. There is very little self-pity in Kenyon's writing, and she can portray the grief of others as memorably as her own."[2] One of the central discoveries one makes in *Constance* is that Kenyon universalizes her particular war with depression into a mosaic of tragedies that besets anyone, anywhere, anytime. One never feels shut out of what is an essentially private experience; rather, through her artistry, Kenyon vividly captures our own experiences of grief and tragedy.

Discussing the poem "Having it Out with Melancholy" with Kenyon, Bill Moyers observed, "I believe that your poems help people to deal with depression." Kenyon responded, "That is my hope, because if this is just personal, then I've been wasting my time. The unrelenting quality of depression really makes its impression on people. It's this thing that will not let you go, that comes when it wants and goes when it wants. You're like a chipmunk in the eagle's talons. There's nothing you can do. Well, that's not strictly true. There is something you can do if you have mood disorders. There are medications that help people."[3] Medications, however, moderate the symptoms rather than cure the illness. They "help people," as Kenyon says, yet there is always the illness itself — opening like

2. Breslin, Review of *Otherwise: New and Selected Poems,* by Jane Kenyon, *Poetry* 170 (July 1997): 231.

3. Kenyon, *A Hundred White Daffodils* (Saint Paul, Minn.: Graywolf Press, 1999), pp. 158-59.

a dark, unknown chasm in the psyche — to contend with. Indeed, several of the poems in *Constance* are poems of contention — attempts to locate, specify, name, and thereby know the psychological monster. One looks for the vulnerable point in the monster's armor, hoping to plunge in the sword — only to discover that the monster is one's own self.

Constance is actually made up of three kinds of poems. The first two types make up most of the poems in the first three sections of the volume. In the first type, Kenyon confronts the series of deaths and illnesses of others that occurred during the period of composition. It is as if by searching for answers in the suffering of others, she might locate some solace for her own. The second type are those poems where she does in fact confront her own malady. The third type, often overlooked because of the drama of the first two kinds of poems, appear at the close of the volume, primarily in the fourth and final section, where Kenyon returns to those crystalline portraits of earlier volumes. Here the voice is more public than private, the vision more outward than inward.

ALTHOUGH autobiographical poems appear in all of Kenyon's volumes, especially when illnesses and deaths in the family led her to reflect on her youth, the most sustained treatment of such a memory appears in "The Stroller," the second poem in *Constance*. One of Kenyon's longer poems, "The Stroller" is carefully arranged around the centering point of a day in 1991. It is then, while Kenyon is helping her mother move out of the old family house, that Kenyon comes upon a drawing her father had done of her stroller, "precisely to scale,/just as I remember it." The drawing came from a period when her father was studying architecture, and she discovers it among detailed renditions of cornices and gargoyles. A shaft of love breaks through the mathematical precision of the architectural renderings. Along with the drawing of the stroller, Kenyon discovers a self-portrait of her father, and it suddenly evokes his image vividly.

Part one of the poem, "1949," is a beautifully descriptive portrait of the stroller itself, then with the toddler riding in it. Part two,

"1991," tells of Kenyon's discovery of the renderings of the stroller and her father. Part three, "1951," provides a detailed portrait of her father, so intricate that the reader can easily visualize him at age forty-seven, "a musician/who took other jobs to get by." The poignant center of the poem occurs in the second stanza:

> When he came home from his day-job
> at the bookstore, I untied his shoes.
> I waited all day to untie them,
> wanting no other happiness. I was four.
> He never went to town without a suit
> and tie, a linen handkerchief
> in his pocket, and his shoes
> were good leather, the laces themselves
> leather. I loved the rich pungency
> of his brown, well-shined, warm shoes.

The intimacy of the connection here — the little girl kneeling at her father's feet to untie his shoes — is nearly spiritual. Most striking, though, is her waiting all day for that moment. It is a grace bestowed upon her.

Part four of the poem, "1959," focuses in a similar way on Kenyon's mother. As Pauline began to take in sewing, word of her expertise began to circulate among the wealthier eschelon of Ann Arbor society. Kenyon watched from her upstairs bedroom window as the Thunderbirds and Cadillacs turned into their drive.

Part five, "1991," jars us back to the present in a sharp, decisive way. It is always this way with cleaning a house for a move. So much must be left behind:

> Disturbed but full of purpose, we push
> Father's indifferent drawings into the trash.

The "indifferent drawings," however, are those mechanical ones of architectural details. Mother keeps the self-portrait; Kenyon keeps the rendering of the stroller. These are not indifferent; they hold a life:

> Looking at it
> is like looking into a mirror
> and seeing your own eyes and someone else's
> eyes as well, strange to you
> but benign, curious, come
> to interrogate your wounds, the progress
> of your beating heart.

The lyric intensity of this closing stanza shapes a wistful self-inquisition. The portrait of the stroller captures all those things held dear — the precious innocence of the past, her father's gaze upon her. But it also holds the time that has passed since those halcyon days when "from the stroller I surveyed/my new domain like a dowager queen." Bliss and woe intermingle here, but they find a natural rhythm, not the clangor of anguish. The poem as a whole is a carefully modulated understanding of life's necessary passages.

Several other poems find their moorings in biographical materials. In "The Argument" we meet Grandmother again, this time at Uncle Hazen's funeral. Once again her dogmatism utterly bewilders young Jane's mind. Meaning to comfort her, Grandmother murmurs a verse: "All things work together for the good for those who love God" (Rom. 8:28). But after the funeral the young girl cries, "No! NO! How is it good to be dead?" Once again we stand at that razor's edge between the turning of life's natural passages and the mystery of where the story leads, searching with Kenyon for the great goodness.[4]

Those poems that confront the illness and death of others of-

4. Other illnesses of loved ones enter here. "Litter" takes place at Hall's mother's house, where the EMTs treated her for congestive heart failure before taking her to the hospital. Kenyon finds herself surrounded by the litter of medical detritus they left behind. "Chrysanthemums" relates the tense events surrounding Hall's surgery for colon cancer in 1989.

ten shade into melancholy — unavoidable, one assumes, at a time when Kenyon's own illness was pronounced. Consequently, we see her familiar pattern of tension between light and dark, the suspension of unknowing. Accentuated in *Let Evening Come,* the poetic pattern continues here. It is, in fact, encapsulated in the epigraph from Psalm 139, which expresses the larger theme for the entire volume. These verses in particular seem pertinent:

> If I say, Surely the darkness shall cover me;
>   even the night shall be light about me.

> Yea, the darkness hideth not from thee;
>   but the night shineth as the day:
>   the darkness and the light are both alike to thee.
>   (vv. 11-12, KJV)

In her interview with Bill Moyers, Kenyon elaborated on her use of the psalm: "I use a long portion of the 139th Psalm as a sort of epigraph to *Constance.* The psalmist says, darkness and light, it's all the same. It's all from God. It's all in God, through God, with God. There is no place I can go where Your love does not pursue me. The poems in this book are very dark, and many of them I can't read without weeping. I can't read many of them when I do poetry readings, but there is something in me that will not be snuffed out, even by this awful disease."[5] While the psalm celebrates the constancy of God, humanity itself is caught tumbling between light and dark.

The introductory poem to the volume, "August Rain, after Haying," immediately announces the tension. The first stanza sets the external scene: slow, steady rain soaks the arid land. The second stanza brings us inside, where "Even at noon the house is dark." As the narrator listens to the rain drip from the eaves, she observes the cleansing and renewal of the land. That renewal stands in stark contrast to the narrator's mood in the final stanza:

5. Kenyon, *A Hundred White Daffodils,* p. 166.

The grass resolves to grow again,
receiving the rain to that end,
but my disordered soul thirsts
after something it cannot name.

The baptismal imagery of the cleansed and revived earth is clear, but for the narrator there remains ambiguous longing, so indefinite that she is unable even to specify what she thirsts for.

That last stanza posed difficulties for Kenyon in the drafting and revision stages. In the first draft the stanza focused entirely upon the longing:

Everything is quiet except
my heart, which wants
blindly, painfully something
it cannot name.

In the third draft Kenyon sensed the dramatic tension she wanted. While the grass is made new, she is not:

The grass resolves to try again,
quickly receiving what falls,
but my disordered heart is longing
for something it cannot name.

Now she has captured the greater part of the tension: the grass quietly accepts what is given; she herself is uncertain of what will in fact requite her yearning. (Incidentally, the participle "is longing" is changed in a marginal notation in Hall's handwriting to "longs.") Another interesting revision occurs in the eighth draft, where "soul" replaces "heart." In the margin Kenyon also listed "mind" as an option. Throughout the drafts we can see Kenyon working toward the poignant tension between external resolution and internal yearning.

Similarly, the perfectly tight poem "Biscuit" — the fourth poem in the first section — holds a powerful tension that is not apparent on first reading. The two four-line stanzas fold tightly in upon each other, the first focusing on the dog, the second on the narrator. The lines are stripped and compact. In fact, in this poem Kenyon comes as close as she ever would to using a regular metrical pattern. The first stanza in syllabification reads 6 8 6 8; the second reads 7 6 7 7. The tightness is sustained in the imagery. In the first stanza the narrator offers the dog a biscuit "like a priest offering the host." But in the second she exclaims, "I can't bear that trusting face!" The dog gets what he expects from this priest: bread. That is the simple limit of his understanding. But the narrator is aware of — fearful of — her capacity to do harm. "I in my power," she acknowledges, "might have given him a stone," echoing Jesus' words in Matthew 7:9-12. That power is a fearful thing, turning as it will to good or evil.

In "Coats," the third poem in the third section, the collision of suffering and calm is dramatic. The first stanza reveals a man leaving the hospital. He has a woman's coat draped over one arm, and he wears ineffectual sunglasses that cannot "conceal his wet face, his bafflement." The second stanza opposes the day's unconcealed brightness to the man's dark mood: "As if in mockery the day was fair." So too, the December air is mild. Nonetheless, the man zips up his coat and ties the hood under his chin, facing "irremediable cold." Pellucid air fails to alleviate the chill of grief.

This poem evidences a poetic quality that Alice Mattison put her finger on in her essay "'Let It Grow in the Dark Like a Mushroom': Writing with Jane Kenyon." The essay itself is likely one of the most astute observations of Kenyon's progression through depressive episodes. Mattison recalls how, after Kenyon first told her the story of the man leaving the hospital, she jokingly observed, "Perhaps he was taking his wife's coat to the dry cleaners while she was in the hospital for a facelift." But that amusing picture turned into a poignant portrait of another's despair. Tellingly, Mattison goes on to say, "Jane was often depressed, and her depression did not lead her to feel sorry for herself nearly as frequently as she felt sorry for others; I sometimes found myself trying vainly to deflect

Jane's deep sympathy about a problem that I didn't mind much."[6] That deeply empathic quality, crystallized in the sharp, telling image, permits the reader access to Kenyon's own depressive grief.

BUT WHAT OF those times when the tensions turn inward, when all of one's seeing is too much like, as Saint Paul put it, looking through a glass "darkly"? Paul, who knew a thing or two about suffering himself, provides an apt metaphor for depression. The glass turns one inward upon psychological clouds. It is the nature of the illness not to be able to see beyond; the horror of the illness is to be trapped within that seeing. Such dark seeing is the essence of the centerpiece of this volume, "Having it Out with Melancholy."

In her interview with Bill Moyers, Kenyon talked candidly about her illness, stressing the fact that she experienced long stretches of the depressive episodes rather than the manic ones: "Depression is something I've suffered from all my life. I'm manic-depressive, actually, and I was not properly diagnosed until I was thirty-eight years old. In my case it's more like a unipolar depression. Manic-depression usually involves both poles of feeling. That is, when you're happy you're too happy, when you're sad you get too sad. Mine behaves almost like a serious depression only and I rarely become manic."[7] When this depression, or "melancholy," rolled over her, it was like a flattening of all being — body, mood, and mind. That is precisely the action of depression: it drains one of emotional sustenance and squeezes out joy. In a letter dated 9 August 1989 to Alice Mattison, Kenyon wrote, "To give you an idea how my mind works when I'm down: When the paper toweling runs low on the roll it makes me sad! Everything makes me sad. Birdsong makes me sad. Late summer flowers make me sad, phlox and asters."[8] In such a state, the invariable response in the depres-

6. Mattison, "'Let It Grow in the Dark Like a Mushroom': Working with Jane Kenyon," *Michigan Quarterly Review* (Winter 2000): 122.

7. Kenyon, *A Hundred White Daffodils*, p. 153.

8. Kenyon, quoted in Mattison, "'Let It Grow in the Dark Like a Mushroom,'" p. 137.

sive's brain is this: I am of no worth; What I do has no worth; Therefore, life is worthless. In such a state the temptation to end one's life can be simply overwhelming. The brain is very ill here; the neurotransmitters are all scrambled and making no rational sense whatsoever. Still, Kenyon battled on. In addition to taking medications to salve those wounded brain cells, Kenyon testified to another force that kept her from the brink: "My belief in God, such as it is, especially the idea that a believer is part of the body of Christ, has kept me from harming myself. When I really didn't want to be conscious, didn't want to be aware, was in so much pain that I didn't want to be awake or aware, I've thought to myself, 'If you injure yourself you're injuring the body of Christ, and Christ has been injured enough.'"[9]

Although Kenyon was most keenly aware of the depressive pole of her illness, she had to contend with the manic pole as well. To get a balanced picture of what she was struggling with, we should understand several key characteristics of the disorder.

It is not at all unusual for the bipolar individual to be keenly aware of the depressive side of the illness but less aware of the manic side, since during periods of mania the individual loses awareness of actions and the consequences of those actions. Clearly Kenyon never reached the psychotic stage of either depression or mania, where one is totally out of touch with reality. Instead, her mania was manifested in a less severe form known as hypomania, nonetheless devastating for all that.

In bipolar depression, hypomania is generally manifested in two ways. In one pattern, feelings of extreme giddiness, overwhelming energy, and great impulsiveness prevail. The person is capable of long periods of unstinting labor, is enormously productive, and can get by on little sleep. At the same time, however, the impulsiveness makes it hard to focus on a single task for any sustained period. Instead, the mind often races from one task to another. All too often that racing mind leads to rash actions — typi-

9. Kenyon, *A Hundred White Daffodils*, p. 161.

cally through heightened sexual expression, expenditure of large amounts of money (usually through credit cards), and such. Generally, the sense of grandiosity and superiority evoked by the mood suspends sound judgment. The concrete problem is that the sufferer has little awareness of this; in fact, many individuals simply cannot accurately remember what they've done in a manic state.

The second pattern of hypomania is also marked by racing thoughts and feelings of grandiosity and superiority, but the symptomology is different. In this pattern the individual becomes short-tempered and irritable with people and situations. He or she gets frustrated with things that don't go the expected way. Sometimes this frustration builds until the individual breaks into uncontrollable anger or rages. Or the individual handles the rage by internalizing it and distancing himself or herself from others, creating a cloud of silence against the intrusion of others.

Further complicating the disorder is the fact that the manic and depressive phases are not neatly compartmentalized or sustained for predictable periods of time. It is the nature of the illness to swing from the high to the low and back again. The roller-coaster effect creates psychological whiplash.

While Kenyon's manic phases were infrequent, they were nonetheless devastating. In an early draft of "Melancholy" entitled "The Approaching Spoon," Kenyon wrote,

Was it bananas
turned me against the world?
[No, it was the faulty reuptake of norepinephrine
    in my brain.]
Did I turn my head away
from the approaching spoon
You couldn't tell
How could you [we] know
you had a manic-depressive
who'd have about six manic
days in her whole life. . . .

189

When Kenyon gives the figure of six, however, this should in no way be construed as a literal count. No doubt she had many manic episodes of which she herself was not aware. It does suggest, however, that the major pattern of her life was the depressive one.

Kenyon was quite correct when she said she suffered from depression all of her life; it was, as she observed, part of her genetic coding. The illness was not diagnosed in her youth, but an astute eye has no difficulty discerning the mood shifts early on. While at the University of Michigan, she consulted a university doctor about the malady. He prescribed a medication that only seemed to deepen her depression. During the first two years of her marriage to Hall, Kenyon underwent psychoanalytical therapy, but therapy at this time didn't recognize the genetic roots of the illness. It focused not on a cure but rather on cognitive methods of interpreting and thus dealing with feelings.

In an essay entitled "Ghost in the House," Hall recalls that the nadir of Kenyon's illness was precipitated by the emotional turmoil of her father's death. She became the principal caregiver for him as cancer slowly wasted his body; it demanded her attention day and night. Hall remembers Kenyon's collapse in detail:

> In 1982, six months after the death, we drank a beer one night in the small town of Bristol. As we drove back, Jane sank under a torment and torrent of wild crying. At home she curled on the sofa in the fetal position and wept for three days. I wanted to hold and comfort her, as I had earlier done when she was low, but now I could not touch her. If I touched her she would want to scream.
>
> She spoke little, in gasps, but she told me that she was not angry at me, that she loved me, that her despair had nothing to do with me. It was heartbreaking not to touch her, not to be able to give comfort. Doubtless my anxious presence across the room was another burden. I understood and believed that I was not responsible for her melancholia. In later returns of her sickness, she continued to worry that I would misinterpret her feel-

ings. She persuaded two doctors to tell me that her depression was caused by the chemistry of her brain, that it was endogenous and unrelated to our life together.[10]

For treatment they first consulted with their internist, who diagnosed the illness as clinical depression and started Kenyon on a tricyclic antidepressant. Further consultations followed with Dr. Charles Solow, the head of psychiatry at Dartmouth-Hitchcock Hospital.

Following a pharmaceutical regimen for bipolar disorder is always like walking a chemical tightrope. Each medicine has its own side effects, some thoroughly debilitating. Some antidepressants can actually trigger the manic phase of the illness, requiring the use of mood stabilizers. When several drugs are used in combination, the side effects of one can exacerbate those of another. The frequent temptation for the patient is to stop taking the medicines altogether, often with the thought that anything would be better than this chemical nightmare. But invariably it is not better. Kenyon wanted more than anything to survive without medication, and in 1992 tried, as Hall put it, "going naked." The result was predictable and precipitous as she plunged once more into melancholy. That, in fact, became the immediate context for writing the poem.

But she was not done having it out with melancholy. Hall has vivid memories of her continuing struggle:

Its misery lurked at the edges of her daily life, and sometimes sprang from the shadows. I remember Jane on the bathroom floor banging her head against the toilet and pipes. Another time she arrived trembling after driving back from Concord: she had fought all the way the impulse or desire to drive off the road into a boulder or a stone wall. And I remember a terrible Christmas Day, when I gave her as usual too many presents, each of which depressed her further. Someone who is stupid,

10. This quotation is from a draft of a forthcoming essay, "Ghost in the House," given to the author and used with Hall's permission.

bad, ugly, fat, and hateful does not deserve presents; gifts mock her. After this bout lapsed, the presents I had given her always retained the tint of misery.[11]

In such a severe state of depression, thoughts of suicide hover over one like an omnipresent cloud. But Kenyon had too much sheer passion for life to succumb. She held on to her quest for the great goodness even in the most forlorn wreckage. The very fact that she was *able* to write this poem is testimony to her battling spirit.

"Melancholy" should not be understood as a poem of capitulation. On the one hand, it is a poem of ruthless analysis, but on the other it is a faithful opening of self so that others may see themselves in it. The poem follows a dialectic of two intense patterns of conflict: the constrictive pattern that melancholy imposes, forcing one inward, and the outward vision of the poet, trying to find patterns of meaning in a skewed world. It is the poem of a fighter, one *having it out* with melancholy like a back-alley brawler. The first time Kenyon read the poem aloud was at the Frost Place in Franconia. She had to pause as she read to fight back tears. So too did the audience. After the reading they lined up to talk with her, to share experiences and feelings. Always it seemed that way. Psychiatrist Peter Kramer recollects a chance hearing of a reading by Hall and Kenyon in November 1993. He describes Kenyon that day:

> Alternating readings with him [Hall] was a woman many years his junior. Her face was warm but strained, and she had done nothing to camouflage a shock of white hair that hinted at troubles seen. She appeared to be utterly self-aware, appealing in the manner of someone who has dealt with pain and manages now to meet the world straight on. She gave, as part of a friendly stage manner, an impression of daunting honesty — a woman who has little truck with small talk or false manners. And yet certain of her poems concerned the small pleasures of life.

11. Hall, "Ghost in the House," unpublished essay.

That straightforward honesty marks every word of "Having it Out with Melancholy." In Kramer's estimation, "Kenyon does not elegize melancholy, she bears witness to a scourge, as survivors bear witness to political and moral outrages. The poem is both art and a public act on behalf of fellow sufferers."[12]

FROM THE epigraph on — which originally read, "Already madness had covered half of my soul with its wing," from Anna Akhmatova — the drafts of the poem, as one might expect, underwent numerous and intense changes. In its earliest form the work consisted of a single eleven-stanza poem under the title "The Obscure Relation." Although this draft is not recognizable in the final form, Kenyon had decided to use the technique of an apostrophe to melancholy. In these early drafts one interesting stanza appears that shaped the bitter third stanza of Part One in the final form:

> You taught me to look without gratitude
> on the works of God, [—] without [/] gratitude,
> then, on myself, [/] since I am a child of God.[13]

Compare that structure to the far more charged one in the final version:

> You taught me to exist without gratitude.
> You ruined my manners toward God:
> "We're here simply to wait for death;
> the pleasures of earth are overrated."

In "Jane Kenyon's 'Manners Toward God,'" Paul Breslin finds a theme here that marks the poem with a quality of grace. Breslin points out that while the modern age has lost both a sense of God and a sense of manners, Kenyon clings to each. Other poets who

12. Kramer, "Unequivocal Eye," *The Psychiatric Times* 12 (April 1994): 4.
13. Kenyon Archives, Box 12, Folder 3.

struggle with depression in confessional poetry tend to react with a sense of outrage and betrayal. Thus, Breslin observes, "There is something disarming and almost quaint about Kenyon's regret for her lost 'manners toward God.' The 'Suggestion from a Friend' in Section Three, that belief in God might cure depression, is never altogether dismissed."[14] That tone, although surely impinged upon by moments of anger and dismay, prevails throughout the many drafts of the poem.

Perhaps the keenest decision Kenyon made in the early drafts of the poem, all of which were reduced to Part One of the final form, was how much attention to give to melancholy and how much to herself. Some of the images at this early stage become quite violent:

> You fatten yourself on my small
> courage. When I wake
> in the night I hear you gnawing
> at the pediments.

Such sharp, twisting imagery is a hallmark of such confessional poets as Sylvia Plath and Anne Sexton. In her effort to exercise poetic dominion over the illness, however, Kenyon kept crafting the drama of the conflict as opposed to highlighting her feelings during it.

At this point, approximately eight drafts into the poem, the work now titled as "Having it Out with Melancholy" had been tightened to a single thirty-line poem. Kenyon had tried dozens of variations. The margins of earlier drafts hold revisions for words, lines, and entire stanzas. Now Kenyon retyped the poem into one tight unit. The first stanza, with minor variations, here appears as it would in the final form. The third stanza would become the basis for the expanded Part Five of the final poem. But she still couldn't

14. Breslin, "Jane Kenyon's 'Manners toward God,'" in *Bright, Unequivocal Eye: Poems, Papers, and Remembrances from the First Jane Kenyon Conference*, ed. Bert Hornback (New York: Peter Lang Press, 2000), p. 49.

seem to find a finish. She kept the image of melancholy gnawing on the pediments, then added the following lines:

> You can crush a whole family like a nut.
>
> Go laminate someone else
> with your hatred of the world.
> You and I are finished, companion
> of years and days, so familiar
> I thought you were my friend.
> You're a living blunder; I can't
> imagine how you came to be.

Despite the addition, the poem seems to hang open-ended. In fact, Kenyon was still struggling, still having it out with melancholy.

For three more drafts Kenyon worked with heavy revisions, typing out new lines, images, and phrasings. Then a totally new poem appeared under the title "The Approaching Spoon" with this epigraph:

> Wait to give solids until the
> baby can sit up and open his
> mouth for the approaching spoon.

These lines, with their image of advice for feeding an infant, opened several extensions for dealing with the advice of others in "Having it Out with Melancholy." A second draft of "The Approaching Spoon" follows. Kenyon's textual revisions are included here to indicate final form. The final stanza appears handwritten at the bottom of the page under the title "One Night."

The Approaching Spoon

> *Wait to give solids until the baby*
> *can sit up and open his mouth*
> *for the approaching spoon . . .*

195

Was it bananas
that turned me against the world?
No, it was the faulty reuptake
of norepinephrine in the brain

I've had six manic days
in my whole life. Five of them
I spent writing a libretto,
and on the sixth
I bought an Electrolux vacuum cleaner!

The rest has been desolation
and faking it well enough
[to pass] as a living person

I only appeared to be ~~living~~ present
among blocks, and cotton shirts
with snaps; among schoolbooks,
red lunchboxes, report cards
in ugly brown slipcases. I really
lived among the shades, whose earthly
time is finished. Charron ~~takes them~~ [ferries us]
across the River Styx, rowing
with a spoon. when its [sic] babies
he brings in his boat, he can fit in
quite a few.

Friendly Advice

If you really believed in God
you couldn't be so depressed.

One Night

I went to bed as soon
after dinner as seemed decent

and adult (by which I mean
I waited for the sun to go down)
in order to [I needed] to be unconscious to
get out of my sore, sick soul.
The dog came into the room,
lay down with a sigh on the floor
next to the bed: it was the sound
of his breathing that saved my life.
He just breathed in and out, in
and out, and did not suffer
in any way I know about.

The two-line section "Friendly Advice" also had multiple variations,
listed here in order with strikcovers:

If you really believed in God,
~~you couldn't have such a despairing~~
~~attitude.~~
[you wouldn't be so depressed.]
~~If you really believed~~
~~in God, your pancreas would~~
~~produce enough insulin.~~

Your bones aren't really all broken!
Take off that body cast and ~~change~~ get
~~your tune!~~ with the program!

The variations here point out the absurdities of the advice. The depressive cannot suddenly cease being depressed any more than the diabetic can stop being diabetic, or the person in the body cast can get up. All three are states of being that one learns to live with.

By this point, multiple sections of the poem are clearly emerging. Kenyon has moved from a short, intense poem concentrating on being born with melancholy to a longer, wrenching poem expressing the lifetime experience of struggling with it.

Now that Kenyon had the idea of a long poem in multiple sections, she began working with it and refining it. The next draft has four sections: "Having it Out with Melancholy," "The Approaching Spoon," "Friendly Advice" (which became "Suggestion from a Friend"), and "Back" (which became a separate poem published under that title). One can readily see the relationship of "Back" to the poem of which it was originally a part. In addition to "Back," one other complete poem, "The Secret," emerged in the drafting. The opening lines mark the confession:

> I have a secret, a second life:
> I'm a bigamist. Melancholy is
> my first and lifelong companion.

Although Kenyon put "The Secret" through six complete drafts, she abandoned it rather quickly as part of "Melancholy." One can only speculate about the reasons, but several seem obvious. For one thing, the poem is overtly confessional, talking about herself in the experience of depression without modulating imagery. It thereby violated her own sense of the essential nature of the poetic work. In addition, the poem itself is repetitive of what already appeared in drafts of the larger poem. Nothing essentially new appears to warrant inclusion in the sequence. Finally, Kenyon must also have realized that the work was simply not up to her standards of diction, line pacing, and other technical criteria. As the selection process for *Otherwise* reveals, she was not shy about setting aside work that she felt didn't live up to her standards.

Through the many subsequent drafts, "Melancholy" took shape as a longer whole while Kenyon did her usual revision work of tightening lines, changing words, and adjusting the multiple parts. She changed the order of some parts in the sequence. But in particular she returned to the principles of concision and the clear, natural image that had always guided her writing. For example, compare this late draft of Part Seven, "Pardon," with the finished poem:

Being awake is an affliction . . .
A piece of raw meat
wears my clothes, speaks
in my voice, dispatches obligations
haltingly or not at all.
It is tired of trying, this
piece of meat — very, very [tired]
~~tired~~ of trying to be stouthearted,
like other people.

There is more telling here; in the final form the image carries all
the work and energy of the stanza.

THE FINAL POEM with its nine sections should not be read as a lin-
ear chronology of depression (although Part One does retain the
apostrophe to depression). Rather, it recollects a life interrupted by
the terror and the tenuous efforts to escape the jaws of what
Winston Churchill called "the black dog" of melancholy. It is more
a topography of depression, a place where one dwells. Thus we read
the poem as a series of conflicting tensions, none of which can be
truly resolved, even though the song of the wood thrush in early
morning grants momentary reprieve.

In Part One, "From the Nursery," Kenyon describes depression as lying in wait for her from the moment she was born. At that
moment, she says, "I was already yours — the anti-urge,/the muti-
lator of souls." From the start, Kenyon depicts depression as a force
that ravages and mutilates the inward life.

How to fight against it? Part Two, "Bottles," gives a rapid, stac-
cato-style listing of eleven drugs in the pharmaceutical arsenal. The
listing has a curiously equanimous effect, as if she were browsing a
grocery shelf. She doesn't comment on the efficacy of the drugs
used against the enemy but on whether or not they have a smell.
Nevertheless, the medication will prove to have salvific effects. In
his essay "Unequivocal Eye," Peter Kramer observes, "Medication is
more than a series of exotic names. It is characterized (perhaps

along with a seasonal change) as the instrument of pardon from a hell imposed by an incomprehensible god."[15]

Part Three, "Suggestion from a Friend," recalls rudely ineffective advice. But these words aren't merely ineffective; they are deleterious, nurturing the power of the malignant darkness. Such a comment hurts profoundly — in two ways. First, it represents the rank ignorance of the general public toward mental illness, particularly at the time Kenyon was writing. Common belief had it that one "caught" depression because one had done something wrong, almost as if one deserved it. Then this thought follows: If that's the case, and if it's just a mood, why then, just snap out of it. But one can't, no more than one can "snap out of" cancer, or diabetes, or a heart attack. That is one side of the cruelty of this stanza, the shortest in the larger poem. The other side speaks to the overwhelming sense of distance from God that characterizes depression itself. It is not difficult for the depressive to accept this distance as fact; after all, characteristic of the illness are feelings of low self-esteem, worthlessness, and abandonment. The "suggestion" from a friend mocks the traits endemic to the illness itself.

Part Four, "Often," opposes the suggestion. It states quite simply but effectively the way Kenyon tries to cope — by seeking the sweet release of sleep. The "dark" of that sleep is vividly counterpointed by Part Five, "Once There Was Light." Here Kenyon celebrates the experience she once had of seeing herself as "a speck of light in the great/river of light that undulates through time." The imagery is carefully wrought. She has never felt a part of the flow, but momentarily she was a speck in it. The allusion here may itself be to an episode of mania. Kenyon follows the statement with her familiar floating figure. At that moment she was "floating with the whole/human family." The use of enjambment works the lines double-time. She was part of the whole, not fragmented and disconsolate as in prior sections. And she was part of the whole human family, feeling at one with "normal" society. The experience was

---

15. Kramer, "Unequivocal Eye," p. 4.

momentary, however — this point where she "no longer hated having to exist." It was abruptly shattered by the sudden return of melancholy, captured here in the rapacious image of the crow pulling her out of "the glowing stream."

Part Six, "In and Out," would be a fascinating poem even apart from the greater drama here. Part Five ended with the headlong plunge back into melancholy. Now she has withdrawn, but the dog seeks her out. The poem as it stands consists of two tercets, the first capturing the dog's seeking of her, the second capturing his effect upon her. The first stanza is simply a physical description of the dog's act. This tercet could occur in any poem, at any place. Precisely because of the studied, calm objectivity of the narrator in the first tercet, the second hits with a shocking twist:

> Sometimes the sound of his breathing
> saves my life — in and out, in
> and out; a pause, a long sigh. . . .

Essentially, the dog breathes for her. As such the act suggests the breath of the Holy Spirit and an act of grace. But the breathing does become more ragged. Seldom does Kenyon use regular patterns of meter or even of syllabification, but notice the diminution in syllable count through this poem: 9 8 9, 8 7 7. Notice, too, that the second tercet is left open-ended, like the sigh it mentions.

In the process of drafting Part Six, Kenyon made a very significant change by cutting the poem from three tercets to two in late drafts. The third tercet, in which the narrator speaks to the situation, puts a slightly different slant on the poem:

> He wants to be near me — finds me
> in the house wherever I am — although
> I do not want to be near myself.

In the final version, the less overt tension between the tercets leads to a less definable sense of anguish.

Part Seven, "Pardon," sharply juxtaposes the pain of depression and the welcome relief from it. The opening lines of the first stanza are excruciating: "A piece of burned meat/wears my clothes. . . ." But in the second stanza, as the narrator begins experimenting with MAOIs, she experiences a sudden reprieve. The "pardon" is tenuous, for MAOIs are perhaps the most dangerous class of antidepressants, with severe dietary restrictions and potentially life-threatening side effects. Nonetheless, they prove effective:

> I come back to marriage and friends,
> to pink fringed hollyhocks; come back
> to my desk, books, and chair.

It is notable that all early drafts of the poem have the phrase "to my gardens," here particularized to the hollyhocks, with the possessive removed. But the possessive "my" is forcibly used for the objects in her study.

Part Eight, "Credo," captures what she can — and dares to — believe "only in this moment/of well-being." In the first stanza she makes it clear that the pardon of the prior section is not so much a wiping clean of the slate as a momentary reprieve, a holding in abeyance of the "anti-urge" that has been with her since the nursery of Part One. She knows that the melancholy will return: "Unholy ghost,/you are certain to come again." The second stanza pictures the way it will return, personifying melancholy as "coarse, mean"; it will simply show up, unannounced, and put its feet up on the coffee table, ready to insinuate its way back into her life. The third stanza recognizes the inevitability of that return, and her inability to prevent it. The closing line from Psalm 139:18, "When I awake, I am still with thee," is used here not as comfort but as the mocking jest of the unholy ghost.

As with other sections, Kenyon made extensive revisions to "Credo," particularly by tightening the poem from an extended personal narrative of her feelings to an objective rendition. Among the stanzas omitted, for example, were these:

I believe in your power
to make me unfit for love
or friendship at any moment,
for as long as you please;

in your power to blast the smallest
pleasure, in your power to make me
curse awakening, to curse the sperm
and egg that drew together to make me.

The plan to center on the image of the unholy ghost came relatively late, but it gave Kenyon a precise way of refocusing upon melancholy itself.

Part Nine, "Wood Thrush," stands beautifully against the pain of the larger poem and gives it a thematic wholeness. Indeed, without this section, the poem itself would be diminished, an expression of nearly unrelieved suffering. Furthermore, it would fail to capture the spirit of the poet herself. Here the constrictive imagery that has prevailed in the larger work suddenly opens outward. The section appeared almost serendipitously as a fragment among the later drafts:

Wood Thrush

I wake with the June light,
waiting greedily for the first
note of the wood thrush. Easeful air
presses through the screen with the wild,
complex song of the bird.
I am drunk with ordinary contentment . . .

The association with Keats's "Ode to a Nightingale" is immediately apparent. Compare lines 51-52 of Keats's poem:

Darkling I listen; and, for many a time
I have been half in love with easeful Death.

For Keats, of course, the bird is also metonymy for the poetic song; therefore, he claims, "Thou wast not born for death, immortal Bird!" In the final version of her poem, Kenyon seems to heighten the Keatsian allusion by having the narrator waken at four in the morning ("darkling"), greedy for the song of the thrush.

In the poem itself Kenyon gathers together all the fine tones of her poetic technique into a mellifluous whole. The poem incarnates the narrator's sense of wholeness. In the first line she admits that she is high on Nardil, yes, but is quick to add, "and June light." This is nature's annealment. Lines 2-4 play on the consonance of *w* (*wake, waiting, wood thrush*) in eager expectation. The words themselves are singled out in order of the narrator's experience: she wakes, she waits, and she waits for the wood thrush. Smoothly and elegantly we are led through the lines as well as the events they describe. The peacefulness of her waiting is highlighted by the melodious sounds in "Easeful air/presses through the screen." The full, long *e* rhyme of *easeful* and *screen* is modulated by the short *e* in the internal rhyme of *presses*. Vowel sounds also work playfully through the poem as a whole. For example, in lines 2, 7, and 11 the first-person "I" appears. But in the last line of the poem, the perfectly rhyming "bright, unequivocal eye" belongs to the thrush, thereby drawing the two together in the poet's love.

The crucial statement that Kenyon makes at this concluding point in "Melancholy," however, is that as she listens to the bird's song, "I am overcome/by ordinary contentment." The moment of joy is unadulterated by pain: "What hurt me so terribly/all my life until this moment?" Healing comes through the beneficent spirit of nature — the constant solace in Kenyon's life. It is to this moment that the poem as a whole leads. Passing through the flood of depression, she arrives safely at a moment of sheer love: "How I love the small, swiftly/beating heart of the bird/singing in the great maples;/its bright, unequivocal eye."

Overshadowed somewhat by these poems of high personal drama are several poems in which Kenyon writes directly to the audience in what may be called the "public voice" of the poet, or what she once described as the "priestly function" of the poet. One such poem is "Sleepers in Jaipur," written after Hall and Kenyon's first trip to India in 1991. The title plays off the title of Whitman's poem "The Sleepers," but here the sleepers live in constricted poverty. Even their lovemaking is constricted:

> The man and woman
> want to love wildly, uproariously;
> instead, they are quiet and efficient
> in the dark.

And their lovemaking begets only one more sleeper to flail in the impoverished dark.

Perhaps the most successful of these poems is the haunting "Gettysburg: July 1, 1863." In 1991 Hall and Kenyon visited Gettysburg — Hall to fulfill a speaking engagement at a nearby college, Kenyon to savor the history and landscape. At the time of their visit, the cease-fire ending the Gulf War was in its fifth day. The two events collide in a journal Kenyon typed on the trip. America's mood was, as she wrote, "triumphant," albeit over a war that she personally abhorred. In that context she and Hall took a tour of the Gettysburg battlefield, another field of devastation, with the events moderated by the clear narrative of a guide. The two histories fold in on each other.

Kenyon remembers reading about the Gulf War carnage in the previous day's *Boston Globe*, which ran the infamous photograph of the six-lane highway called the "turkey shoot." Here in Gettysburg she walks up Culp's Hill, where, for ten hours, Union and Confederate soldiers waged war. It is placid here now, with beef cattle grazing in a fenced-off field. Then, she writes, "I come to a place called Spangler's Spring, where the Confederate and Union soldiers stood off, by turns, to let the other side drink and fill their canteens. Why is this heartbreaking?" Kenyon continues a comparison between the primitive brutality of the war in 1863 and the same, unchanging brutality in 1991.

But how does one incarnate all that brutality, all that misdirected passion, and all that carnage in a poem? Not by trying to encompass the whole but by showing one individual soldier. Thus in the opening stanza Kenyon focuses on "The young man, hardly more/than a boy. . . ." Concentrating on his "target," he has just fired a shot. He is not angry; he's only trying to do his job. In the second stanza the reader is jolted by the accuracy of his aim at the target, another young man across enemy lines: "The bullet passed through/his upper chest, below the collar bone." He staggers out of the pasture into a grove of trees, pressing hard on the wound to try to stanch the bleeding. Then,

> He lay on the earth
> smelling the leaves and mosses,
> musty and damp and cool
> after the blaze of open afternoon.

The earth is good, and its smell brings back memories of his boyhood. He is suddenly keen to details: a cowbird calling from a fence, bullets nicking into the woods, a groan he hears that he thinks comes from another wounded soldier — "But it was his own voice he heard."

Moving from objectivity to subjectivity, from a narrative ordering of events as they happened to an interior narration of how things felt when they happened, Kenyon probes the psychological complexity of the war experience. Understanding that, one can only be amused by a remark Alice Mattison recalled having heard about the poem: "On the publication of 'Gettysburg: July 1, 1863,' about the intimate thoughts of a dying Civil War soldier, someone wrote asking Jane whether she'd arrived at the poem through channeling. 'What did you answer?' I said. We were walking in New Haven. 'I said I used my imagination,' said Jane firmly."[16] She uses that imagination powerfully here: "He became dry, dry, and

16. Mattison, "'Let It Grow in the Dark Like a Mushroom,'" p. 128.

thought/of Christ, who said, *I thirst.*" Slowly, through the final two stanzas, his awareness of life itself dissipates. All his senses shut down, until, finally,

> A streak of sun climbed the rough
> trunk of a tree, but he did not
> see it with his open eye.

Like Stephen Crane in *The Red Badge of Courage,* Kenyon achieves a quiet, controlled statement through the experience of a single dying soldier that nonetheless captures the full terror and awful finality of war.

THE THREE POEMS collected at the end of the volume — "Pharaoh," "Otherwise," and "Notes from the Other Side" — form a deliberate triptych of suffering and faith, joy and consolation. Kenyon wrote "Pharaoh" in 1992, after Hall returned home following his second major surgery, this time to remove a tumor from his liver, a metastasis of his earlier colon cancer. The surgery required the removal of the entire right half of his liver. The image of him lying in bed at night, his feet propping up the covers that were drawn up over him, suggested to Kenyon the sarcophagus of a pharaoh. It is a dangerous poem, touching fully upon the throb of another's pain, grieving for the diminution of a loved one's energy and strength, and recognizing the possible realities of the sarcophagus metaphor:

> The things you might need in the next
> life surrounded you — your comb and glasses,
> water, a book and a pen.

In spite of the understandings the poem brings — or maybe because of them — Kenyon saw the poem as one of consolation, as she explained in her interview with Bill Moyers: "It's odd but true that there really is consolation from sad poems, and it's hard to know how that happens. There's the pleasure of the thing itself, the pleasure of the poem, and somehow it works against the sadness."[17]

Kenyon wrote "Otherwise" after Hall's first surgery. It was a time convoluted by grief, suffering, and uncertainty. In the mid-1980s Kenyon had had a cancerous salivary gland removed from her neck. Her father had died of cancer just a few years earlier. And now her husband had had his first surgery. In the face of potential and actual illness and pain, the poem attempts an affirmation and celebrates the joy of the moment. With all the affirmations of things done ("the work I love") through the course of the day, there is always the understanding that "it might have been otherwise." The precariousness of one's life emerges as the underlying pattern of the poem. It might have been otherwise — precisely because life so often is. That understanding, in and of itself, grants the day, with all its routine activities, its preciousness.

From the pain and uncertainty of her husband's illness to the serene acceptance of doing "the work I love" even with the understanding that it might have been otherwise, Kenyon plunges into the farthest extent of "Otherwise" in "Notes from the Other Side," another poem likely occasioned by the possibility of Hall's death following his surgery. (He was given a 30 percent chance of living for five years.) The poem is unique in her canon. Nowhere else does she permit her imagination to transcend the things of this earth and attempt to grasp the life to come. She comes closest to doing so in the uncollected poem "What It's Like." Here the narrator is riding in the back of a truck and watching the world pass behind her. "This must be what life is like," she concludes, "at the moment of leaving it." One might sense a plangent echo of Emily Dickinson's "Because I could not stop for Death." While Dickinson often pushed her imagination to heaven's gate, however, Kenyon's vision roved this life, searching out its beauty and glory, confronting its trial and pain. Because of this very fact, "Notes from the Other Side" almost takes on the quality of an epitaph as the poet divests herself of worldly troubles.

17. Kenyon, *A Hundred White Daffodils*, p. 168.

The fascinating pattern of the poem lies in its twofold divestment. The separation from pain is most pronounced: "I divested myself of despair/and fear when I came here." On the other side there is "of course/no illness." But interestingly, Kenyon is also separated from the mundane annoyances of life: "no bad books, no plastic,/no insurance premiums." Even though her imagination soars to life beyond this realm, she is ever the keen realist. That realism itself gives the poem its thematic punch. The heart of it all is her discovery of the reality of God: "God, as promised, proves/to be mercy clothed in light."

Thus the realism of the poem is ultimately an expression of faith. In fact, in his essay "Trust in *Otherwise*" Lionel Basney argues that faith is "the characteristic religious quality of Kenyon's lyrics."[18] Faith is a matter of trust, but trust is also an assertion of one's own being. Faith isn't passive; it is active, even aggressive. In *The Orphean Passages* Walter Wangerin defines faith as "a relationship with the living God — enacted in this world, this world of the furious swirl, in which all things flow."[19] In much the same way, Basney elaborates his sense of Kenyon's religious sensibility as a combination of faith and trust active in this world:

> Faith may be the evidence of things not seen but lyrics deal in seen things and in the question of whether we can trust our understanding of them. As Kenyon's poems juxtapose Scripture, quite specific dramatizations of suffering and doubt, and records of the quotidian world, they enact not the question of faith — "What do you believe?" — but the question of trust, "What do you rely on?" Trust, I think, is the religious attitude these poems are enacting.[20]

18. Basney, "Trust in *Otherwise*," in *Bright, Unequivocal Eye,* p. 103.

19. Wangerin, *The Orphean Passages* (San Francisco: Harper & Row, 1986), p. 11.

20. Basney, "Trust in *Otherwise*," p. 103.

In its rich play on the several levels of reality and the grasp of the imagination, "Notes from the Other Side" stands as one of Kenyon's foremost achievements. She began the poem with the discovery of that spiritual reality. The first note for the poem appears handwritten across a 4 × 5 card containing the last two lines of the poem. In the lower left corner the context for the lines appears in a brief note: "I left behind that amalgam. . . ." In the first typed drafts she began with these lines: "That amalgam of boredom and despair/by which I lived. . . ." One entire stanza appears that would soon be deleted:

> Here there are no dull parties,
> no long conversations at dinner
> with strangers in whom one pretends
> to be interested.

Here too, the final stanza is worded differently:

> As for God we have [at last] what was promised —
> Forgiveness clothed in light.

Clearly the lines have an off-the-cuff tone. God's forgiveness — mercy in its final form — is tacked on as an afterthought to the divestments listed in the main body of the poem. The tensions between the two realities — this earth and God's grace — fail to materialize.

Several drafts later, Kenyon began approximating the poetic structure of the poem, moving toward the tight, two-line stanzas:

Notes from the Other Side

At last I divested myself of that boredom
And despair by which I lived.

Here there are no bad books, no [/] plastic,
No insurance premiums, and, of course,
No illness.

No more catching one's own eye
In the mirror, or tilting one's head
To make the roll of fat under the chin
Vanish . . .

Contrition does not exist. Nor is there
Gnashing of teeth. No widow howls
As the first clod of earth
Strikes the casket.

The poor we no longer have with us.

Our calm hearts strike only the half
Hours and the hours.
    And God, as promised,
Proves to be mercy clothed in light.

Now the essential poem was set, needing only the refinement of line and diction that Kenyon concentrated on as she worked toward the final draft. Simply in terms of artistic craft, she was also searching after the great goodness, that incarnation in poetic form of keenly felt and expressed belief.

SOME HAVE CALLED *Constance* Kenyon's dark volume. She herself admitted as much. Yet both the title and the epigraph from Psalm 139 point us not toward the unending dark but toward the expectation of light and mercy celebrated in "Notes from the Other Side." That expectation is the constant of the volume, the thing that endures beyond the suffering, the thing by which one steers a course through the suffering. The illustration for the cover of the volume, the painting by Albert Ryder of a boat pulling toward shore against dark water, is an apt metaphor for the text. Once again we ride the little boat, pulling for a shore where the great goodness dwells.

CHAPTER NINE

Otherwise

Old and New Poems

In November 1994, Fiona McCrae, who had replaced Scott Walker as editor of Graywolf Press, proposed the collection of Kenyon's poems that would become *Otherwise*. Her letter arrived about ten months after leukemia had begun its virulent course through Kenyon's body. Kenyon had been diagnosed with the disease in January 1994, and standard chemotherapy hadn't helped. Kenyon now faced a bone-marrow transplant as the only option for extending her life. The transplant was performed at the Fred C. Hutchinson Cancer Center in Seattle, Washington, on November 18. After Kenyon was discharged from the hospital on December 20, she was taken to an apartment in Seattle where Hall was staying. There he undertook her care, programming pumps to infuse medicine into her system and the like.

Properly understood, the bone-marrow transplant is not a surgical procedure. First, with doses of cytotoxin and total body irradiation, every bit of a patient's bone marrow is destroyed. Then a small portion of new marrow from a donor is infused. After the transplant, one hopes to have new blood cells appear, which show that the new marrow is beginning to take over and grow. At the same time, one hopes to find no leukemic blood cells whatsoever, since they are a sign that the transplant has failed. In Kenyon's case, the early blood counts gave grounds for optimism, but even after she and Hall returned to Eagle Pond Farm in late February, the days were tenuous with concern.

Well before they came back, Hall had already photocopied selections from Kenyon's previous collections and assembled copies of new poems from her study. The selection process for *Otherwise* was something that Kenyon planned to undertake during her recovery. In early March, however, Kenyon developed problems with her gallbladder and had to have it removed, a setback that again drained her energy. It was during this time that she dictated "The Sick Wife," a poem that neither Kenyon nor Hall considered finished. Nonetheless, Kenyon agreed to include it in *Otherwise.*

Then the catastrophic news came: on April 11, 1995, blood tests revealed that Kenyon's leukemia had returned, and that there was really nothing further to be done. At this point, Kenyon had not been able to do any actual compilation of the volume — but now she went at it with all she had. In his afterword to *Otherwise,* Hall details the frenetic hours they spent trying to complete the manuscript during the eleven scant days before she died. Hall immediately faxed the unpublished new poems to Alice Quinn at the *New Yorker,* and on the day before Kenyon's death, Quinn faxed back that the magazine had bought five of them. Of the remaining poems, two went to *Harvard Magazine;* one went to the *Atlantic;* and the rest were sent to *Poetry.* All of these magazines had strongly supported her work in the past, and did so now. After Kenyon died, Hall consulted with her close writing partners, Joyce Peseroff and Alice Mattison, in order to make final decisions on the very few changes Kenyon had made on several poems.

Kenyon left uncollected several poems that were published in literary magazines. "What It's Like" appeared in *Ploughshares* in 1979.[1] Of the uncollected poems, this one is most typical of Kenyon's artistry, providing a concrete scene with the sudden vivid insight emanating from it. The first stanza shows her riding in the

---

1. Kenyon, "What It's Like," *Ploughshares* 5, no. 2 (1979): 58.

back of a pickup, leaning against the cab. She notes the specific, familiar things receding and observes,

> Whatever I saw
> I had already passed. . . .
> (This must be what life is like
> at the moment of leaving it.)

Kenyon published "Indolence in Early Winter" in *New Letters* in 1980.[2] Here her use of metaphor and language work as nicely as in any of her poems. She receives a long letter that details recent divorces and remarriages. Her response is acerbic: "Forgive me if I doze off in my chair." It is cold in the house as the snow comes and the stove burns low, and there is a strong implicit comparison to the letter and the failed marriages. This is a forceful poem. Particularly striking is the narrator's consistent tone — slightly arch and disapproving, but also tinged with a bit of lament. And there is a sarcasm here that we don't often find in Kenyon's work. "At the IGA: Franklin, New Hampshire," published in *The Ontario Review* in 1989,[3] captures the rural qualities of a small New England town. Here at the IGA folks gather; their histories converge.

Also omitted from *Otherwise* were a number of poems collected in earlier volumes. Several poems were omitted from *The Boat of Quiet Hours:* "The Painters," "Teacher," "Whirligigs," "April Walk," "No Steps," "Siesta: Barbados," and "Killing the Plants." Among these, "Killing the Plants" is an intriguing poem. Here the narrator is caught between repotting a few ailing plants or tossing them on the compost heap. Tugged by their "example of persistence," she gives them "a grudging dash of water," taking a sort of middle road before she must make a definitive choice.

Similarly, there were a substantial number of omissions from

---

2. Kenyon, "Indolence in Early Winter," *New Letters* 47, no. 1 (Fall 1980): 23.

3. Kenyon, "At the IGA: Franklin, New Hampshire," *Ontario Review*, no. 31 (Fall/Winter 1989): 87.

Let Evening Come, several of them quite interesting. In "After Working Long on One Thing" we find a fascinating metaphorical connection between a hummingbird's erratic but sustained search for nectar among the hollyhocks and the poet's writing. "Where," she queries, "shall I turn/this light and tired mind?" "Leaving Barbados" is a longer descriptive poem, replaying a trip to Barbados like a detailed mental photograph. "Waiting" has its own peculiarities. Sitting in a station wagon with their golden retriever, three little boys wait for their mother to come out of the grocery store. Kenyon figures that they are visiting New Hampshire for the summer, and imagines the routine they will settle into in their cottage. But she is struck by the waiting itself, for "I too am waiting, though if you asked/what for, I wouldn't know what to say." The tone is mixed, part bewilderment and part acceptance of her lot. "Three Crows" evokes a vivid picture of Turgenev, who was in love with Pauline Viardot for forty years. Unlike the three crows flying off together, Turgenev was alone. In the final stanza he admits, "'I lived . . . all my life/on the edge of another's nest.'" Three additional poems were also omitted from the collection: "Cultural Exchange," a recollection of the trip Hall and Kenyon made to China; "At the Dime Store," a recounting of an encounter with a handyman years after he did work on the farmhouse; and "Spring Snow," a poem that captures Kenyon's restlessness with late-season snow and her eagerness for the bloom of spring. The primary reason for their omission, one would guess, is that the three tend to duplicate scenes and thoughts in other poems.

The omissions from *Constance* also include several intriguing poems. In "Climb," the narrator and a friend climb Mount Kearsarge. Arriving at the top, they spot a hawk soaring below them on "muscular shoulders." "Fear of Death Awakens Me" expresses that fear in two dark metaphors: watching a cloud-shadow passing over a ravine and "swimming unexpectedly into cold water/in a spring-fed pond." One imagines the depths of the spirit and the chill of death. Metaphor works similarly in "The Secret," where a ring in the shape of a honeybee seems frozen in search of answers to an eternal mystery. "A Portion of History" provides one of those snap-shot-clear portraits of daily New England life in which Kenyon delighted.

Perhaps the one truly regrettable omission from *Constance* is "Windfalls," a poem that reveals Kenyon's sense of playfulness in nature. The poem is carefully controlled in form. The first of the three five-line stanzas describes the wind, after a snowstorm, tossing the heavily laden branches of oaks and pines. It is as if a second storm hits when the snow swirls off the branches. The narrator appears in the middle stanza here — an unusual tactic for Kenyon. If she does use it, she brackets the narrator's reflections with natural images (see "Three Songs at the End of Summer"). Here the narrator stops in the blowing snow, puts out her arms, and looks upward. She reflects, "It is good/to be here, and not here. . . ." She is "not here" like the spirited rapture of the wind. But in the third stanza we find that she is bodily very much here, like the nearby deer, whose "fresh cloven prints" under the apple tree reveal their presence. Although she can't see the deer, they are rooted to the earth, just as she is. "Windfalls" is a rich, affirmative poem, full of the kind of delight that reminds one of Robert Frost's poem "Birches": "Earth's the right place for love, after all."

Of all the earlier volumes, *From Room to Room* had the highest number of omissions. Eleven of the original fifty-one poems and the six Akhmatova translations were omitted. This is not altogether surprising. The poems in this volume focused on Kenyon's move to New Hampshire, and they vary in effectiveness: like photographs in a scrapbook, some simply tell the story better than others. Then too, by the time Kenyon was preparing *Otherwise,* she had outgrown the artistry of a number of these poems. For example, the succinct and witty "The Shirt" was always an audience favorite at her readings, but it was probably not necessary to include other poems of this sort, such as "The First Eight Days of the Beard," "The Socks," and "At a Motel near O'Hare Airport."

Other poems, however, share links with later poems, and one wishes they were included. "The Box of Beads," for example, is an exquisite work wherein Kenyon tries to construct a memory of her maternal grandmother by examining the broken strings of beads she inherited. This poem is essential to that pattern of Kenyon's poetry wherein she confronts and interacts with her youth. In the same way, "Starting Therapy" is essential to her later poems dealing with depression. The tensions in this poem spin finely, hovering between wit and fear. The first stanza sets the pattern with its opening lines: "The psychiatrist moves toward me,/a child's sweater in his hands." The narrator recognizes it as her old white cardigan. As the psychiatrist begins to help her put it on, the reader senses the eerie associations building. Then Kenyon slams the point home: "He puts it on me backwards./This thing is a straightjacket!" The stanza ends with an ironic twist: "Anybody in his right mind can see/this sweater doesn't fit." Panic arises in this stanza, with just enough deft poetic control to deflect it and hold it in momentary abeyance. The responsive imagery in the second stanza of the poem is perfectly controlled:

> Thinking someone is at the door
> I open it to find a small brain
> hovering over the porch.

It simply hovers there, neither entering nor leaving, so the narrator slams the screen door on it. One realizes with the narrator, however, that the screen door is permeable. This poem is one of those small, highly polished jewels in Kenyon's canon — the imagery perfectly suited, the tensions between past and present keen, and the sense of psychological dissociation pronounced.

In addition to the poems omitted from her four published volumes, Kenyon also omitted her earlier, unpublished poems. According to Hall, Kenyon felt these simply did not compare with her mature work. Some fifty-seven individual poems and four varied collections of them exist in the Kenyon archives. Several of these poems are set apart by the designation "Early Poems," including one of her rare forays into metered verse, "Tetrameter Ode." Another grouping of poems was collected in a folder called "Automatic."[4] These are largely fragments and topical poems.

THE NEW POEMS collected in *Otherwise* soar over several topics in the full, free range of Kenyon's artistry. To be sure, there is nothing here with the dramatic power of "Having it Out with Melancholy" or the unnerving power of the triptych that concludes *Constance,* but each work is touched with the grace of precision and beauty. They range from the oddly wonderful poem "Happiness," in which happiness inspirits not only people but also natural objects, to poems about the decline and death of Hall's mother, to poems about Hall's recovery from surgery, to reminiscences about the trips the two took together. Although the range varies widely, a surprising note of whimsy threads through a number of them, even at times a humorous sense of delight over the discoveries the poems unfold.

In "Dutch Interiors," for example, Kenyon begins with a rare pun:

> Christ has been done to death
> in the cold reaches of northern Europe
> a thousand thousand times.

Immediately we enter with her into the world of countless art museums, wondering how many different ways the crucifixion might be rendered. After a time, the renderings seem much the same. There, of course, lies the ironic point of the crucifixion also: it is ongoing, according to theologians — always new and re-enacted at the moment of grace.

But this is the world of art. In yet another museum, next to one more depiction of the crucifixion scene, there hangs an odd counterpart:

4. In his bibliography included in *A Hundred White Daffodils,* Jack Kelleher provides a complete list of the poems collected in *Otherwise,* as well as a book-by-book listing of the omissions. See pp. 213-15 in *A Hundred White Daffodils* (Saint Paul, Minn.: Graywolf Press, 1999).

Suddenly bread
and cheese appear on a plate
beside a gleaming pewter beaker of beer.

Kenyon's response to the shift is telling:

Now tell me that the Holy Ghost
does not reside in the play of light
on cutlery!

The Holy Spirit is found in common things and everyday moments, not only in the crucifixion. Life is infused with the Spirit's play of light. So emphatic is Kenyon in the discovery that she employs the exclamation mark, a piece of punctuation that rarely appears in her poetry.

"Mosaic of the Nativity: Serbia, Winter 1993" also broaches a theological issue, albeit in an altogether more serious tone. With three stanzas, the poem follows a threefold pattern. God appears in the first two lines of the first stanza, personified by the poet's imagination: "On the domed ceiling God/is thinking." He looks down upon his people passing below. Though made for joy and blessed by God, they mingle in confused argument. The colon at the end of the first stanza signals what God overhears in the second stanza. The poem shifts to the people passing under the dome, unaware of who looks down upon them. The people accept Cain's sign: they do evil and accept it as their lot. The third stanza returns to God's response. His joy has been mired in the muck of evil. Still, he "thinks Mary into being." She unfolds from God's thought — "curls in a brown pod" suspended from the golden dome — and inside her, also like a brown pod, "Christ, cloaked in blood,/lodges and begins to grow." God's response to what he sees is grace.

Kenyon's social commentary also appears in these late poems, particularly in the three "Man" poems. "Man Eating" portrays a man focused intently upon eating yogurt; he is fully engaged in this small, present moment, unmindful of any of the larger implications of life. "Man Waking" ironically portrays a man living in perpetual darkness. In response to the light filling his bedroom, "his body curled/like a grub suddenly exposed." He is filthy ("The smell of his skin and hair/offended him"), unconcerned about his responsibilities, and seeking "utter darkness." When he pulls the covers over his head, he is dismayed that he can still see his hand so clearly. In his essay "Our Lady of Sorrows," Gregory Orr observes,

> To me this is a poem of pure thanatos, of isolation, of retreat into depression and despair. The man doesn't even want to see his hand, an object that connects him to the world. But the amazing thing about a poem that comes of the depths, out of the abyss, is this: it tells us that the human spirit still exists even at these depths; that it can give shape and form, articulate expression, to its condition, and this gives us hope.[5]

This ability to bring hope, Orr argues, marks Kenyon's poetry with a transformational quality that separates her from those poets content with only depicting a photographic reality. The third poem in the trilogy, "Man Sleeping," recalls a homeless man Kenyon saw sleeping outside the Sackler Museum in Washington. He lay belly down over his belongings, as if prostrating himself, "like Abel, broken, at his brother's feet." Suddenly questions of guilt and redemption implicitly arise in the poem. Who was Cain here? Who destroyed Abel?

Several poems in this collection draw on the death of Hall's mother. The sequence is initiated with "The Call." The phone rings in the very early morning, summoning Hall to the nursing home "to see his mother, it may be,/for the last time." "In the Nursing Home" portrays Hall's mother in the narrowing confines of her last days. The initial image in the first stanza depicts her "like a horse

---

5. Orr, "Our Lady of Sorrows," in *Bright, Unequivocal Eye: Poems, Papers, and Remembrances from the First Jane Kenyon Conference*, ed. Bert Hornback (New York: Peter Lang Press, 2000), p. 36.

grazing," a lovely and natural figure of a creature at ease. The bucolic, peaceful scene seems positive in its suggestion. But, as with
Robert Frost's use of the simile in "The Silken Tent," the initial image intensifies dramatically, and the likening of woman to horse
takes a different tone. While the horse grazes peacefully on a hillside pasture, the negative metaphor arises in the fences that keep
closing in upon that peacefulness.

The second stanza evokes the weariness of the horse. Once
she ran "wide loops" around the pasture. No longer now, as the
fence of aging constricts her. She has "stopped even the tight circles." At a standstill, she drops her head to graze where "grass/is
dust, and the creekbed's dry." At this point the image is fully constricted. Nothing sustains the enfeebled figure. Thus the last two-
line stanza comes as a supplication:

> Master, come with your light
> halter. Come and bring her in.

The extended image here responds beautifully to the diminishment
of the first two stanzas. The enjambment at "light" responds to the
lines in the first stanza where someone comes "every night" to pull
the fences in. The "light halter" responds to the weary end of life described in stanza two, when it is time to be "brought in."

In this series, "How Like the Sound" describes one of the
times when Kenyon and Hall visited his mother in Hamden. She
had had another one of her attacks and had been permanently hospitalized. The poem captures the realization of encroaching death.
The first lines of the opening quatrain rupture with emotion: "How
like the sound of laughing weeping/is." The second quatrain pictures Hall in his mother's chair, his face contorted by grief: "Not
since childhood/had you wept this way, head back, throat/open like
a hound." In the final quatrain, sorrow gives way to practical considerations. Hall adds a note to the list he is making — *"call realtor"*
— and hides his "red face" behind the newspaper.

These poems of personal sorrow evoke Kenyon's memory of

reading to her own father as he lay dying. "Reading Aloud to My Father" situates us at her father's deathbed. Haphazardly picking up a book to read, she starts with lines from Nabokov:

> The cradle rocks above an abyss . . .
> and common sense tells us that our existence
> is but a brief crack of light
> between two eternities of darkness.

Bleak, disturbing words. Is that all there is — this existential rocking above nothingness? Are there no better alternatives than this? In the days that follow, Kenyon can't put the lines out of her mind. "I think," she says, "Nabokov had it wrong. This is the abyss." Here's the issue: Is life the tenuous existence that only points to, or shadows forth, the solidity of eternal reality? It's what Plato wanted to believe. It's what C. S. Lewis called in many books the "longing for heaven" or the "surprise by joy" — that sense that what we long for in this life is fully realized only in eternal life. In *Mere Christianity* Lewis put it like this: "Most people, if they had really learned to look into their own hearts, would know that they do want, and want acutely, something that cannot be had in this world."[6] In "Reading Aloud" Kenyon says the longing explains why "the dying so often reach/for something only they can apprehend." Here too, in summary, is the longing out of the abyss for the eternal reality — the longing of Plato's creatures moving about the cave, the longing that Kenyon herself felt for much of her life.

This brings us, fittingly, to the last poem Kenyon ever wrote. She did not put this one through her normal process of multiple drafts. She never shared it with her workshop group. There wasn't time. By the second week of March 1995, it seemed that she was re-

---

6. Lewis, *Mere Christianity* (New York: Simon & Schuster, 1996), p. 120. In the chapter entitled "Hope" in *Mere Christianity,* Lewis expands his discussion of this longing, which he calls *sehnsucht:* "Probably earthly pleasures were never meant to satisfy it, but only to arouse it, to suggest the real thing" (p. 121).

covering well from gallbladder surgery, and Hall felt able to leave her for several hours to go to a basketball game with his son. He tells the story like this: "Our friend Mary Jane Ogmundson stayed with her, and Jane dictated a draft of 'The Sick Wife.' Typed, it lay on a reading table beside her chair. On several occasions she dictated a revision, and a new draft replaced the old. She would have made more changes if she had lived."[7]

The striking thing about "The Sick Wife" is that it is a poem without self-pity. As in her earliest verse, Kenyon recognizes the fact and uses the descriptive image or picture to embody the emotions attendant upon the fact. In the first stanza the setting is clear. She rides with her husband to buy groceries but is too weak to go with him into the store. Her strength is failing: "she had learned what it's like/not to be able to button a button." In the second stanza, she watches from inside the car as others pursue their daily routines. It is midday, so only mothers with small children and retired folks step across the parking lot. "How easily they moved," she says, "with such freedom." In the last stanza we suddenly realize that she is not simply in a car but that the parked car itself has been a metaphor for her sick state. The realization is powerful and disturbing, for the car windows are also the poet's eyes — the "bright, unequivocal eye" — alert to all nature and all circumstances. As the car windows begin to "steam up" with the condensation of her breath, so her eyes fill with tears — expressing the full understanding of her diminished physical state. The cars around her, also metaphors of other people's lives, pull away so briskly "that it made her sick at heart." Kenyon's final poem: a powerful engagement of reality to the last.

7. From the afterword in *Otherwise* (Saint Paul, Minn.: Graywolf Press, 1996), p. 220.

CHAPTER TEN

Without

It is difficult to conclude a study of Jane Kenyon's poetry with a formulaic, critical summary. Although one could indeed expand upon the craft of her verse — the intense lyric, the startling image, the exact word, the skilled line pacing — all such are devices to incarnate the life of the poem. That life consists of relationships, particularly with nature, with God, with herself and her past, and with society. Nearly all of these relationships, however, were grounded in that most fundamental of human relationships, marriage — her twenty-three-year marriage to Donald Hall.[1] It shaped the contours of both her poetic life and her personal life. To find the summary wholeness, we need also to look through Donald Hall's eyes, particularly his recording of that relationship in *Without*.

JANE KENYON was diagnosed with leukemia on January 31, 1994. Shortly before that, she and Hall had completed a joint reading at Bennington College, and Kenyon seemed to be fighting flu-like symptoms on the way home. Hall flew on to Charleston for a reading and a lecture. When he called Kenyon, he learned that she had suffered a nosebleed so severe that she had had to go to the hospital

---

1. Hall and Kenyon celebrated their twenty-third wedding anniversary during the eleven-day period of her dying.

to have it treated. Kenyon described it as "humongous." Blood work ensued. She received the diagnosis during the winter season, when the days gave small promise to the "amorist of light." She fought the disease for fifteen months. In "Life after Jane," Hall recalls the spiraling devastation of the side effects from her treatment:

> For more than a year, she endured spasms of chemotherapy, a pneumonia that leukemics get, shingles, delirium, loss of re-mission and its brief restoration, total body irradiation, a bone-marrow transplant, and "graft versus host" disease of the stom-ach. Side effects included neuropathies in hands and feet, mouth agony from the radiation, loss of mentation, a brief psy-chotic episode, loss of control in her fingers, fatigue, bone pain and constant nausea.
>
> During all this time I remained at her side, and most days I worked on poems.[2]

All the desperate efforts of medical science were brought to bear upon the insidious invader: chemotherapy, irradiation treatments, and finally the bone-marrow transplant that raised so much hope but ultimately failed. Throughout the ordeal, Hall was at Kenyon's bedside; in the last days they prepared final selections for *Otherwise* and worked on her obituary and memorial service. But also, in his own unstoppable effort to deal emotionally with his wife's dy-ing, Hall wrote: "While she was dying, I continued to sit at her bed-side trying to write. Mostly I wrote about what happened inside me."[3]

The writing was more than an interior excavation of emotional states, however. It was a way for Hall to write his way out of what Robert Frost called "desert places." In fact, Hall himself used that term in an interview for *Southern Humanities Review* in 1988:

2. Hall, "Life After Jane: An Essay," *Northeast: The Hartford Courant Sunday Magazine*, 27 August 1995, p. 8.
   3. Hall, "Life After Jane," p. 8.

There are deserts everywhere. The life I have contrived for myself is the happiest life I can imagine living. I love what I do. I am happily married. But no one who has looked hard at human nature, be he poet, psychiatrist, or philosopher, has been able to deny the desert. No one has found the pathway that leads into the paradise where we can feed on wild fruit in permanent bliss. Paradise ended when Adam and Eve got chased out of there.

I believe in being as happy as I can. I don't believe in seeking unhappiness. (In parts of my life I don't think I could have said that.) Still, there will be times of depression and despair. Things come from the outside that are miserable, that you aren't responsible for, but you will feel grief and loss nonetheless. There will be things that happen inside, and mistakes you will make with the best intentions.[4]

This sense of the desert places was never far from either Kenyon or Hall. Their recognition of the "Happy Place," to play on the title of one of Hall's volumes, made them all the more fit to face the other. Neither of them, in Hall's words, was a denier; both were proclaimers.

Without is a proclamation — a personal lamentation shaped by superb artistic talent. In an interview with Michael Scharf for *Publishers Weekly* after the publication of the book, Hall described the intensity of the volume. Surely, he recognized, it would be taken "as a companion to the grief of others." Indeed, good art, great art, does precisely that: it embodies the lives and emotions of others. Hall himself commented on how important it is for the poet to transform intensely personal experience into a work of art that speaks to others: "Art is what gets [us] from here to there. I may have failed in what I attempted to do, but a poem is not a poem unless it is a work of art. It may begin with a scream of pain, but you

4. Hall, in an interview with Dave Barney, "Happy Men in Desert Places," *Southern Humanities Review* 22, no. 3 (1988): 236-37.

make that into a work of art or you have utterly failed."[5] Most certainly *Without* is a scream of pain made into art.

How does Hall achieve this? Many readers of Hall's works are stunned by the fact that he puts his poems through literally hundreds of drafts. All that proves is that he works very hard indeed at his craft. In fact, it says very little about the poetic task, except as a measure of process, of turning the scream of pain into art. As Hall pointed out in *Goatfoot Milktongue Twinbird*, he seeks to marry the two ancient and traditionally opposed ways of seeing the poetic task. One is *vates*, or the idea that the poet is divinely inspired and utters words he himself scarcely understands. It is the idea of poet as prophet, essentially helpless in the thrall of the muse. In an interview with George Meyers Jr. for *Ploughshares*, Hall discussed the mysterious origins of a poem, how a "paraphraseable content" plays in his mind in search of a form. Differentiating this from the muse-like idea of the *vates* dictation, Hall added,

> Parts of the mind are always asleep, always dreaming; many sorts of mental activity continue, without alert awareness or with infrequent awareness. I observe things come into my brain, whole, and sometimes understand that they are made of parts that have combined somehow and somewhere. Sometimes I feel as if I can encourage a benign receptivity that stimulates combinations. Often when I look later at language that has come "as if dictated" I can identify bits and pieces — sources in experience, in things overheard, in ruminations, in reading.[6]

In Hall's experience, *vates* is a way of holding oneself open to life, alert to the moment and the ideas it brings.

5. Hall, "Donald Hall: Elegies from Eagle Pond," an interview with Michael Scharf, *Publishers Weekly*, 23 March 1998, p. 73.

6. Hall, *Goatfoot Milktongue Twinbird: Interviews, Essays, and Notes on Poetry, 1970-76* (Ann Arbor: University of Michigan Press, 1978), p. 72.

Hall refers to this as "the vatic voice,"[7] and describes it this way: "Two characteristics that distinguish the vatic voice from normal discourse are that it is always original, and that we feel passive to it. We are surprised by it, and we may very well, having uttered its words, not know what we mean."[8] The poet cannot control this voice; he only learns to listen to it.

The other traditional concept is *poiein,* the idea of the poet as craftsman (the Greek word means *maker),* working the poem into shape. The *vates* is controlled, directed, and given artistic expression by the *poiein.* Like the sculptor with his chisel, the poet exercises the gift, the talent, and the labor of the craft.

How do *vates* and *poiein* work in the context of *Without?* The *vates* takes the shape of a Job-like, biblical lamentation. It gives voice to a universal sense of loss, that which touches the inconsolable infant at his mother's absence or that which hurtles through the mind of the bereaved. In these poems, as in the book of Job, grief wells up and is cast out like a surging wave against no certain recipient. These are poems of prostration, offering bewildered emotions from the bent knees of reason's failure. The parallel with Job doesn't end with lamentation, however. Job sought answers, insisting — even in the face of his friends' dogmatism or skepticism — upon a reason for his affliction. So too, Hall searches the clinical facts of his grief — the loss of Kenyon to leukemia — by the studied imposition of craft, or *poiein.* Accordingly, the poems in *Without* have a controlled dramatic range, moving from a clinical statement of the facts of the case to an outpouring of grief over the personal meaning of those facts.

Order is further imposed by overall structure. *Without* is structured essentially according to the triad of Kenyon's illness, her death, and the year of grief following her death. The structure pro-

---

7. Hall first used this term in an address he gave in November 1968 to the Conference on Creativity of the National Council of Teachers of English. The address is included in *Goatfoot Milktongue Twinbird,* pp. 1-5.

8. Hall, *Goatfoot Milktongue Twinbird,* p. 3.

vides the reader with a wholeness of event, both physical and psychological. And just as life and death clash throughout this progression, the unnerving tension one experiences is compounded by Hall's use of both common and arcane speech, familiar figures and grotesques, passionate desire and passionate grief. Dualities and tensions are ever-present as Hall leads us down the dangerous path.

The opening poem, "Her Long Illness," is continued at intervals and seemingly gives us the first objective portrait: the counterpart, perhaps, to Kenyon's poem "The Sick Wife." But the objectivity strains and nearly collapses with the last lines of the first fragment. It snowed one morning when Jane was in the hospital, and her eyes caught the wonder of the dark sky full of white flakes.[9] With the IV pump, which she calls "Igor," pushed along, she and Hall walk "as far/as the outside door/so that she could smell the snowy air."[10] Here's the scene that breaks one's heart — the vitality of the patient longing for the out-of-doors when it is closed off to her because of her illness.

From the varied cadence of "Her Long Illness," Hall moves to the carefully cadenced and reflective poem "'A Beard for a Blue Pantry.'" The nostalgia is triggered by a letter from Jane's friend Alice Mattison, telling of a dream she had in which Hall wrote a poem by the title of this one. For Hall, the mention of "beard" first triggers a recollection of a trip to California that he and Jane made in the early years of their marriage. On the return flight, Jane drafted her poem "The First Eight Days of the Beard," collected in *From Room to Room*. The title evokes other associations that Hall renders poetically in situations not altogether based on fact. He describes shaving off his beard while a cat named Bluebeard sat atop the breadbox in the pantry, bird-watching out the window. And then he says,

9. At this point in the discussion it seems natural to move from "Kenyon" to "Jane," since Hall uses his wife's first name throughout *Without*.

10. Hall, *Without* (Boston: Houghton Mifflin, 1998), p. 1. All further references to the poems will be made parenthetically in the text.

Jane made bread so honest
it once went blue in the pantry

overnight in a heat wave. (2)

In fact, they never did have a cat named Bluebeard. Kenyon never
had a loaf go blue. All invention. But when he goes on to reminisce
about the fluid rhythms of their life together, about how, each
morning, they went to their separate rooms to work, he is telling
the painful truth. And indeed, the truth dwells in the color blue,
which infiltrates the poem to the last image, where Jane's once-
abundant hair "is gone now, like Bluebeard/who sickened and
dwindled away" (3). The nostalgia narrows, squeezing through blue
panes into the present.

With the third and fourth fragments, the reader becomes
aware of the structural technique Hall employs throughout the first
section. He renders all the fragments of "Her Long Illness" in the
third person, as if in an effort to objectify the illness. The alternat-
ing poems he writes in the first person, now fully involved emotionally and poetically in the event. He makes no attempt to distance
himself narratively, but writes from within the experience. The har-
monized narration provides the effect of a delicate balance of emotion, even of *vates* and *poiein*. Two selves attempt to work their way
toward a unified understanding. The third-person narrator is confined to immediate events in the present of Jane's illness. But the
"I-teller" is the nostalgic narrator, recollecting things past. This
teller provides many details of the couple's life together, as well as
the two poems in memory of their mothers: "Song for Lucy," Hall's
mother, and "Blues for Polly," Jane's mother.

As the poems evolve in the first section, they also merge in
tension to the present moment. The more nostalgic poems themselves become hurried and tense. After his mother's death, Hall
travels to Connecticut to get her house ready for sale. The poem is
marked by rushing lines and frenetic verbs:

> I hurried from room to room, cellar to attic,
> looking into a crammed storeroom, then turning
> to discover a chest with five full drawers.

The house, overflowing with memories and possessions, is having its way with him. When he is finally finished trying to save what he cherishes, he drives "four hours/north with my hands tight on the steering wheel" and collapses into bed with Jane. The next day, as he counts out pills for her, he is struck by the accumulations that mark their years of marriage. He focuses upon a small porcelain box, where a fragile porcelain couple "stretch out asleep,/like a catafalque" (10).

In time he and Jane make the long trip to Seattle for the bone-marrow transplant, this last desperate warfare in the trenches of survival. The pain of all the possibilities surges through these poems. Real people, loved ones, die in the trenches. The night before Jane entered the hospital, they slept together, "as they understood,/ maybe for the last time." He curved into her body, so that they lay together like spoons, "and the spoons clattered/with a sound like the end man's bones" (19). Then the infusion, and the hope for success. The poems here achieve familiar cadences; the narratives even out. Husband and wife return home and reach the point where they believe that her health will be restored:

> It was reasonable
> to expect that in ten or twelve months
> she would be herself. (34)

The verbs that follow all signal their hope: "She would dress and eat her breakfast./She would drive her Saab. . . ." Yet each of those verbs is compromised by the modal auxiliary "would." No true sense of the future — "she *will* drive" — prevails. The expectation is tentative at best.

The very next poem openly mocks that hope: "'It was reasonable/to expect.' So he wrote" (35). This poem works two ways in the volume. It concludes the efforts of medical science detailed in the first section; it also points toward the second section with the title "Last Days," a reference to the precious few days they will have together until Jane dies. One feels the crushing weight of reality coming. Indeed, the hematologist enters the consultation room with the frank admission "I have terrible news." The doctor weeps along with patient and husband. The bewildered narrator pleads for answers. Why now? How long? But "Jane asked only: 'Can I die at home?'" (35).

With that simple request, the first section of the volume concludes. In stark, confrontational lines, Hall has faced the enemy and fought against it. And now what to do? "Can I die at home?" He and Jane return home to Eagle Pond Farm. "He wailed/while she remained dry-eyed — silent,/trying to let go" (36).

THE ALMOST feral aggression of the first section seems to subside in the second section, which details Jane's last days. The morning after returning home, the two work together on *Otherwise*, plan her funeral, and write her obituary. The work continues the following day. Seeing his wife visibly weaken before him, Hall suggests they wait a bit to continue. Her old adamancy of spirit rises up: "'Now,' she said./'We have to finish it now'"(37). The press of time is like a vise. But after another day spent choosing poems, Jane's old wry humor arises: "'Wasn't that fun?/To work together? Wasn't that fun?'" (37). Yes, but the repetition of "Wasn't that fun?" — a phrase she used so often in her writing workshops when something pleased her immensely — now comes as a diminishing echo.

While the poems in the first section shift between first-person and third-person narratives, providing both an inside and an outside view of Jane's illness, the second section is without any shifts: the poet is now totally consumed in the last days of Jane's life. He sees himself objectively, as the "he" tending his dying wife. The details of the reality seem overwhelming and nearly unbearable: "'What clothes/should we dress you in, when we bury you?'" (38).

They talk about past adventures and travels, about everyday pleasures, about their sex life. The hours pass, marked in sharp detail
by the progression of the disease claiming her body, her life. She
feels herself slipping away:

> "Dying is simple," she said.
> "What's worst is . . . *the separation*." (42)

Friends come and go to say good-bye. When Hall gets up to put letters in the mailbox, she speaks her last words: "O.K." Throughout
this section of poems, Hall focuses intensely upon Jane's eyes,
keeping our attention there. They are the unifying figure, but also
the most vital sign of her personality. Her eyes marked her poetry
with its resplendent visual imagery. Now her eyes hold her husband
when her body is no longer able to do so:

> When she no longer spoke,
> they lay alone together, touching,
>   and she fixed on him
> her beautiful enormous brown eyes,
>   shining, unblinking,
> and passionate with love and dread. (42)

Fittingly, this section concludes with these lines:

> He watched her chest go still.
> With his thumb he closed her round brown eyes. (45)

The title poem, "Without," rips into the heart of the volume
like a howl of pain, contained only by seven-line stanzas. The key to
the poem lies in line 9: "the year endured without punctuation."
Without punctuation there is only progression, not meaning. Here
the lack of punctuation, including capitalization, is itself a metaphor for the onrush of emotions and events. They swirl together.
The prominent words are *no* and *without*:

no snowdrop or crocus rose no yellow
no red leaves of maple without october

no spring no summer no autumn no winter
no rain no peony thunder no woodthrush (46)

Into the nothingness, the clinical language of the past year intrudes like ragged shards: "acute/lymphoblastic leukemia," "pain vomit neuropathy morphine nightmare," "vincristine ara-c cytoxan vp-16." They are part of the undoing.

If the poem is stream of consciousness — and it is only partly that, because the images are so carefully arranged and unified — it is nonetheless one of the great expressions of without-ness. It is not vacuity of spirit or sensation; rather, it is overwhelming pain of the spirit and a sea of brutal sensations, none of which tie meaningfully together. Grief breaks life down; separation disrupts all presumed order. The tissues of meaning are disconnected without Jane.

"WITHOUT" is the transitional poem, the outpouring of grief that points toward the third section. Here Hall details his efforts to rebuild a life without Jane. "The Gallery" drives home the loss — literally. Hall nails a gallery of portraits to the wall behind his desk: Jane at twenty-four; Jane at forty-five, "foxy/and beautiful." "Letter with No Address" begins a sequence of poems in which the poet talks to his dead wife, sharing community news and describing the progress toward spring in her beloved gardens. Still, the pain sears:

I remember bone pain,
vomiting, delirium. I remember
pond afternoons. (50)

Against the twofold pain of memory and death, Hall establishes a bulwark of routines. But each new moment brings new memories:

235

> Your presence in this house
> is almost as enormous
> and painful as your absence.

There is one routine that is undeniable: "Three times today/I drove to your grave" (52).

After the anguish of the first section with its bombardment of medical terms, after the threnody of Jane's dying in the second section, and after the nearly inarticulate howl of "Without," the poems in this section are prosaic, nearly flat. Here too, form is meaning. Days are ticked off; the seasons change. This is reportage — the poems forming a series of letters that describe the interior wasteland in which one event is as arid as the next. "Midsummer Letter," one of the longer poems in the collection, works through a list of such events, but then gives way to the grief that never seems to part:

> I'll never read Henry James
> aloud to you again. We'll never laugh
> and grunt again as your face
> turns from apparent agony
> to repose, and you tell me
> it registered 7.2
> on the Richter scale. (58)

The pattern endures in "Letter in Autumn," where Hall begins to clean out some of Jane's things, trying to impose order. He is able to clean out her car — but no more:

> I cannot discard
> your jeans or lotions or T-shirts.
> I cannot disturb your tumbles
> of scarves and floppy hats.
> Lost unfinished things remain
> on your desk, in your purse
> or Shaker basket. . . . (61)

In "Letter at Christmas," time itself seems warped by emotions. Hall draws an analogy from the wooden clock that Jane had given him their first Christmas together. For six weeks the watchmaker had it for repairs:

> Now it speeds
> sixty-five minutes to the hour, as if
> it wants to be done with the day. (63)

So too Hall tries to speed the day, seeking the salve of time. The poem itself is an amalgam of times: "For three hours we played"; "Most years we woke up by six"; "This year. . . ." But the note that threads through it all is this:

> I want never to joke or argue
> or chatter again. I want never
> to think or feel. (63)

The assertive *never* lies like a dark counterpoint to the Christmases past that he remembers celebrating with Jane. "This first Advent alone" finds him "sick with longing."

The Christmas season inevitably evokes the spiritual patterns of the year that had marked the harmony of their lives together. Religious moments have marked previous poems, including the brief poem in the first section that describes Jane's receiving communion at home: "grace was evident/but not the comfort of mercy or reprieve./The embodied figure/on the cross still twisted under the sun" (17). Christ's work is not finished here; it appears incomplete and powerless to effect the miracle of healing. In "Letter at Christmas" Hall recalls Jane's opening the "daily window" of her Advent calendar, her annual reading of the Gospels, and her expectation that "The Child would be born again" (64). This year the expectation withers. Instead, the cat, Ada, delivers a dead mouse, and Hall disposes of it:

> I toss the dead mouse outside
> on Christmas afternoon
> and wash my hands at the sink. . . . (67)

Here is the ironic offering, the empty gift — the carcass of a mouse.

The following poems continue to tick off the days and seasons of the year. As Hall put it in "Without": "hours days weeks months weeks days hours." The lines echo in "Midwinter Letter":

> I lean forward from emptiness
> eager for more emptiness:
> the next thing! the next thing! (74)

The next times and things pass in a blur, now punctuated by memories that sneak up and surprise him at every turn. Time passes like the stream that flows down Mount Ragged, interrupted and riffled by rocks in the throat of the stream. Gradually, however, the land itself begins to work a miracle of restoration. This was Jane's nature, and it seems to contain her memory, if not her presence. In "Letter at Christmas" Hall finds himself feeding the birds at Jane's feeders, and notes, "I stand trembling with joy/to watch them" (66). He adds, "Feeding your birds/consoles me now" (67). In "Letter in the New Year" he walks Gus as Jane used to do:

> I puff as Gussie
> and I walk over packed snow
> at zero, my heart quick
> with joy in the visible world. (69)

During these days, when the agony of grief presses against the fragility of routines, when momentary joy knocks on the heart, then ducks back into the shrubbery, Gus is the constant companion. Like nature itself — and the use Hall makes of it to steady the year following Jane's death — Gus is restorative. His demands are minor; his companionship is invaluable. In "Letter after a Year" Hall reports,

> Every day Gus and I
> take a walk in the graveyard.
> I'm the one who doesn't
> piss on your stone.

All these contrarieties, the emotional tensions, come together in the final poem, "Weeds and Peonies." The title itself is metaphoric for the volume. Jane's neat gardens of beloved peonies are now flecked with weeds. They grow together. The poem itself plays off against Kenyon's poem titled "Peonies at Dusk," collected in *Constance*. There the white radiance of the peonies burn with light in the growing dusk, flowers so huge "They're staggered/by their own luxuriance." Kenyon is drawn to their lavishness:

> In the darkening June evening
> I draw a blossom near, and bending close
> search it as a woman searches
> a loved one's face.

Like the earlier act of filling Jane's birdfeeders, Hall's act of walking among the peonies, "white as snow squalls," leads him to search out his loved one's face. He imagines Jane with Gus, going for a hike up the mountain. Now the realization comes full, like the peonies: "but you will not reappear, tired and satisfied,/and grief's repeated particles suffuse the air" (81). The peonies hold her memory, if not her presence. Hence the last lines:

> Your peonies lean their vast heads westward
> as if they might topple. Some topple.

Works Cited

Akhmatova, Anna. *Anna Akhmatova: Selected Poems*. Trans. Richard McKane. London: Oxford University Press, 1969.

———. *The Complete Poems of Anna Akhmatova*. Trans. Judith Hemschemeyer. 2 vols. Somerville, Mass.: Zephyr Press, 1990.

———. *My Half Century: Selected Prose*. Ed. Ronald Meyer. Ann Arbor: Ardis Press, 1992.

———. *Poems of Akhmatova*. Trans. Stanley Kunitz with Max Hayward. Boston: Little, Brown, 1973.

Baker, David. Review of *Let Evening Come*, by Jane Kenyon. *Poetry* 158 (June 1991): 161-64.

Barber, David. Review of *Constance*, by Jane Kenyon. *Poetry* 164 (June 1994): 161-65.

Barrett, William. *Irrational Man*. Garden City, N.Y.: Doubleday, 1962.

Borroff, Marie. *Language and the Poet: Verbal Artistry in Frost, Stevens, and Moore*. Chicago: University of Chicago Press, 1979.

Breslin, Paul. Review of *Otherwise: New and Selected Poems*, by Jane Kenyon. *Poetry* 170 (July 1997): 226-40.

Corn, Alfred. Review of *Let Evening Come*, by Jane Kenyon. *The New York Times Book Review*, 24 March 1991, p. 26.

Crick, Francis. *Of Molecules and Men*. Seattle: University of Washington Press, 1966.

Driver, Sam N. *Anna Akhmatova*. New York: Twayne, 1972.

Eliot, T. S. *Collected Poems: 1909-1962*. New York: Harcourt, Brace & World, 1970.

Farrowe, Anne. "Into Light All Things Must Fall." *The Hartford Courant,* 27 August 1995, p. 9.

Frost, Robert. *Selected Letters of Robert Frost.* Ed. Lawrence Thompson. New York: Holt, Rinehart & Winston, 1964.

Goldstein, Laurence. "Remembering Jane Kenyon." *Xylem* 12 (Winter 1996): 54-64.

Gregerson, Linda. Review of *The Boat of Quiet Hours,* by Jane Kenyon, *Poetry* 151 (February 1988): 421-23.

Haight, Amanda. *Anna Akhmatova: A Poetic Pilgrimage.* New York: Oxford University Press, 1976.

Hall, Donald. "Donald Hall: Elegies from Eagle Pond." Interview with Michael Scharf. *Publishers Weekly,* 23 March 1998, pp. 72-73.

————. *Goatfoot Milktongue Twinbird: Interviews, Essays, and Notes on Poetry, 1970-76.* Ann Arbor: University of Michigan Press, 1978.

————. "Happy Men in Desert Places: An Interview with Donald Hall" by Dave Barney. *Southern Humanities Review* 22, no. 3 (1988): 225-37.

————. *Here at Eagle Pond.* New York: Ticknor & Fields, 1990.

————. "An Interview with Donald Hall" by David Hamilton. *The Iowa Review* 15, no. 1 (Winter 1985): 1-17.

————. "An Interview with Donald Hall about *The One Day*" by George Meyers Jr. *Ploughshares* 17 (1991): 71-75.

————. "Life After Jane: An Essay." *Northeast: The Hartford Courant Sunday Magazine,* 27 August 1995, pp. 6-8.

————. *Life Work.* Boston: Beacon Press, 1993.

————. "Ox Cart Man." Interview with Jay Woodruff. In *A Piece of Work: Five Writers Discuss Their Revisions,* ed. Jay Woodruff, pp. 229-73. Iowa City: University of Iowa Press, 1993.

————. *Poetry and Ambition: Essays, 1982-88.* Ann Arbor: University of Michigan Press, 1988.

————. *Seasons at Eagle Pond.* New York: Ticknor & Fields, 1987.

————. *Without.* Boston: Houghton Mifflin, 1998.

Hornback, Bert, ed. *Bright, Unequivocal Eye: Poems, Papers, and Remembrances from the First Jane Kenyon Conference.* New York: Peter Lang Press, 2000.

Jamison, Kay Redfield. *An Unquiet Mind: A Memoir of Moods and Madness.* New York: Alfred A. Knopf, 1996.

Katrovas, Richard. "History and the Transpersonal Talent." *New England Review* 7 (Spring 1989): 340-50.

Kenyon, Jane. *A Hundred White Daffodils*. Saint Paul, Minn.: Graywolf Press, 1999.

———. "Interview with Jane Kenyon" by Bill Moyers. In *The Language of Life: A Festival of Poets*, ed. James Haba, pp. 218-38. New York: Doubleday, 1995.

———. *Otherwise*. Saint Paul, Minn.: Graywolf Press, 1996.

———. *Twenty Poems of Anna Akhmatova*. With Vera Sandomirsky Dunham. Saint Paul, Minn.: Nineties Press and Ally Press, 1985.

Kramer, Peter. "Unequivocal Eye." *The Psychiatric Times* 12 (April 1994): 4.

Leider, Emily. "Emily Akhmatova: A Clear and Elegant Howl." *San Francisco Review of Books*, September 1977, pp. 26-28.

Lewis, C. S. *Mere Christianity*. New York: Simon & Schuster (Touchstone Edition), 1996.

Mattison, Alice. "'Let It Grow in the Dark Like a Mushroom': Writing with Jane Kenyon." *Michigan Quarterly Review* (Winter 2000): 121-37.

McKee, Louis. Review of *Let Evening Come*, by Jane Kenyon. *Library Journal*, 15 May 1990, p. 80.

Muske, Carol. Review of *The Boat of Quiet Hours*, by Jane Kenyon. *The New York Times Book Review*, 21 June 1987, p. 13.

Norris, Kathleen. "Exploring the Poetry of Doubt and Daring." *Books and Religion* 17 (1990): 30-32.

Polivanov, Konstantin, ed. *Anna Akhmatova and Her Circle*. Trans. Patricia Beriozkina. Fayetteville: University of Arkansas Press, 1994.

Styron, William. *Darkness Visible*. New York: Random House, 1990.

Unterecker, John. "Shape-Changing in Contemporary Poetry." *Michigan Quarterly Review* 27 (1988): 487-502.

Wangerin, Walter Jr. *The Orphean Passages*. San Francisco: Harper & Row, 1986.

Index